The Land between the Two Rivers

The Land between the Two Rivers

Early Israelite Identities in Central Transjordan

THOMAS D. PETTER

Winona Lake, Indiana
Eisenbrauns
2014

www.eisenbrauns.com

Library of Congress Cataloging-in-Publication Data

Petter, Thomas D. (Thomas David), 1963– author.

The land between the two rivers : early Israelite identities in central
    Transjordan / Thomas D. Petter.
            pages cm
        Includes bibliographical references and indexes.
        ISBN 978-1-57506-291-4 (hardback : alk. paper)
        1. Jordan—Antiquities.   2. Iron age—Jordan.
    3. Ethnoarchaeology—Jordan.   4. Ethnicity—Jordan.   5. Jews—
    History—1200–953 B.C.   6. Bible. Old Testament—Antiquities.
    I. Title.
        DS153.3.P49   2014
        933′.502—dc23
                                                        2013048123

Contents

Maps 1–6 vii
Preface and Introduction xiii
Abbreviations xix

CHAPTER ONE
Central Transjordan as "Tribal Frontier" 1

CHAPTER TWO
Theories of Tribal Ethnicities 16

CHAPTER THREE
Contested Histories of Northern Moab 35

CHAPTER FOUR
Localized Identities 56

CHAPTER FIVE
The Mādabā Plateau Region during the Early Iron I 75

CHAPTER SIX
Prospects for Historical Dynamics 99

APPENDIX A
Gazeteer of Iron I Sites in Central and
Northern Transjordan 104

APPENDIX B
The Collared Pithos as a Chronological Marker 118

Bibliography 122
Indexes 148
    Index of Authors   148
    Index of Scripture   152

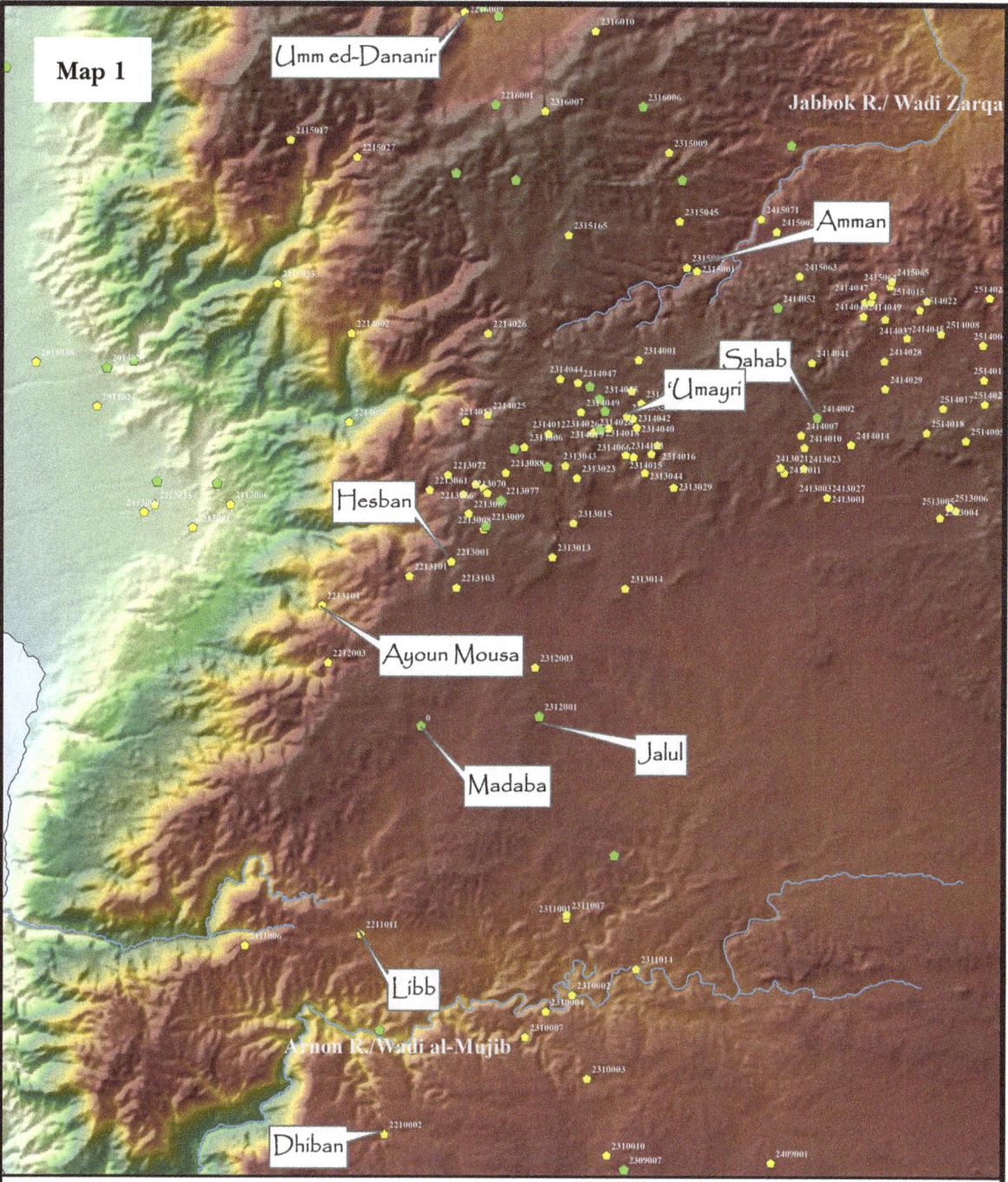

Map 1

Umm ed-Dananir

Jabbok R./ Wadi Zarqa

Amman

Sahab

'Umayri

Hesban

Ayoun Mousa

Jalul

Madaba

Libb

Arnon R./Wadi al-Mujib

Dhiban

Topography derived from SRTM data,
courtesy of NASA.
Site locations from JADIS Database.

Iron I Central Transjordan

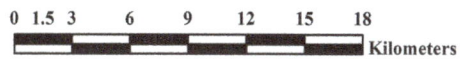

Legend

Iron I

Elevation

High : 3833

Low : -470

N
W   E
S

0 1.5 3   6   9   12   15   18
Kilometers

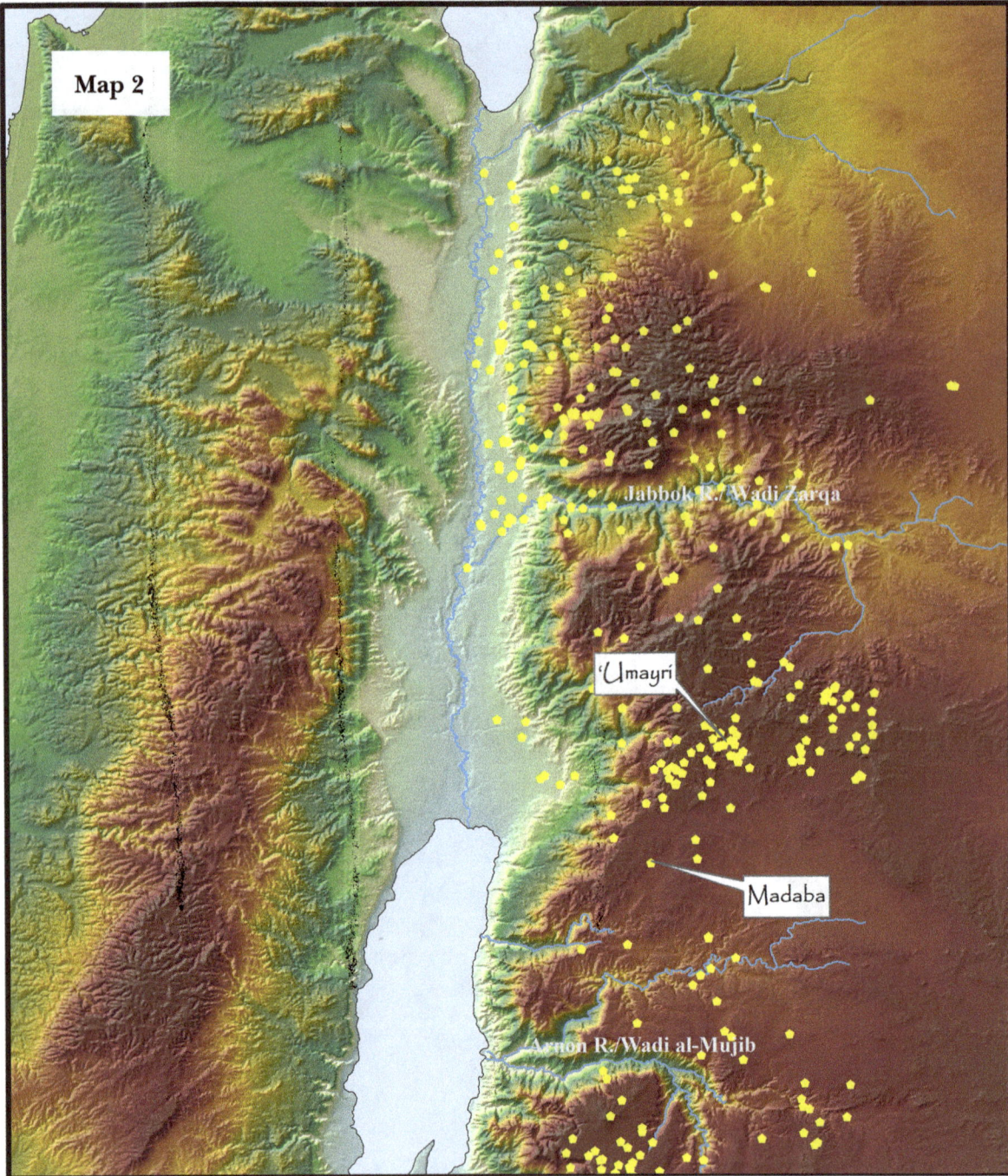

Map 2

Jabbok R./Wadi Zarqa

'Umayri

Madaba

Arnon R./Wadi al-Mujib

Legend
Iron I
Elevation
High : 3833
Low : -470

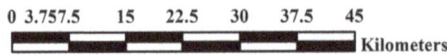

Iron I Central &
NorthernTransjordan

Topography derived from SRTM data,
courtesy of NASA.
Site locations from JADIS Database.

0 3.75 7.5 15 22.5 30 37.5 45
Kilometers

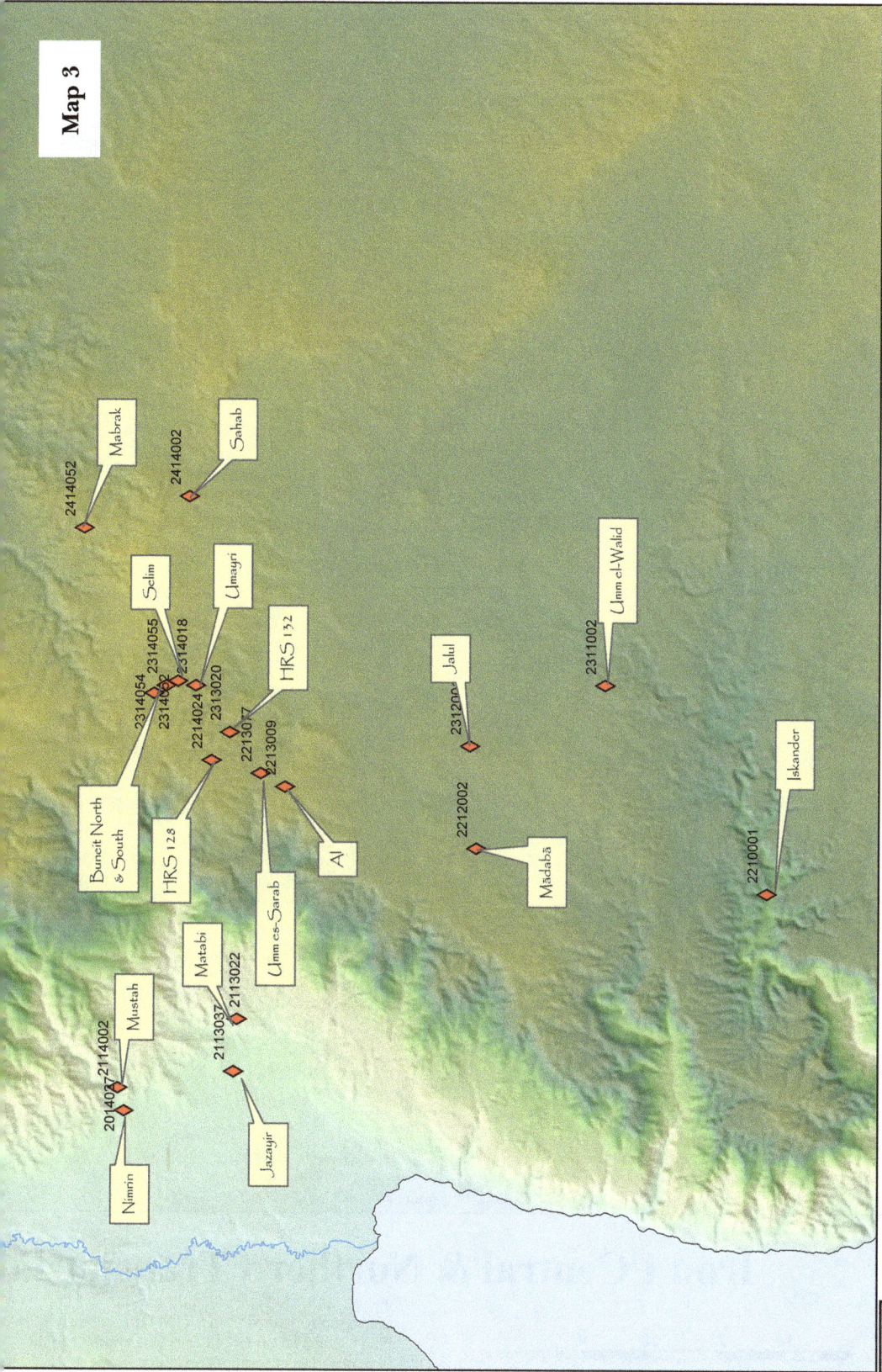

Map 3

Late Bronze Age
Madaba Plains Region

Topography derived from SRTM Data, courtesy of NASA.
Site locations from JADIS Database, courtesy of the
Jordanian Department of Antiquities.

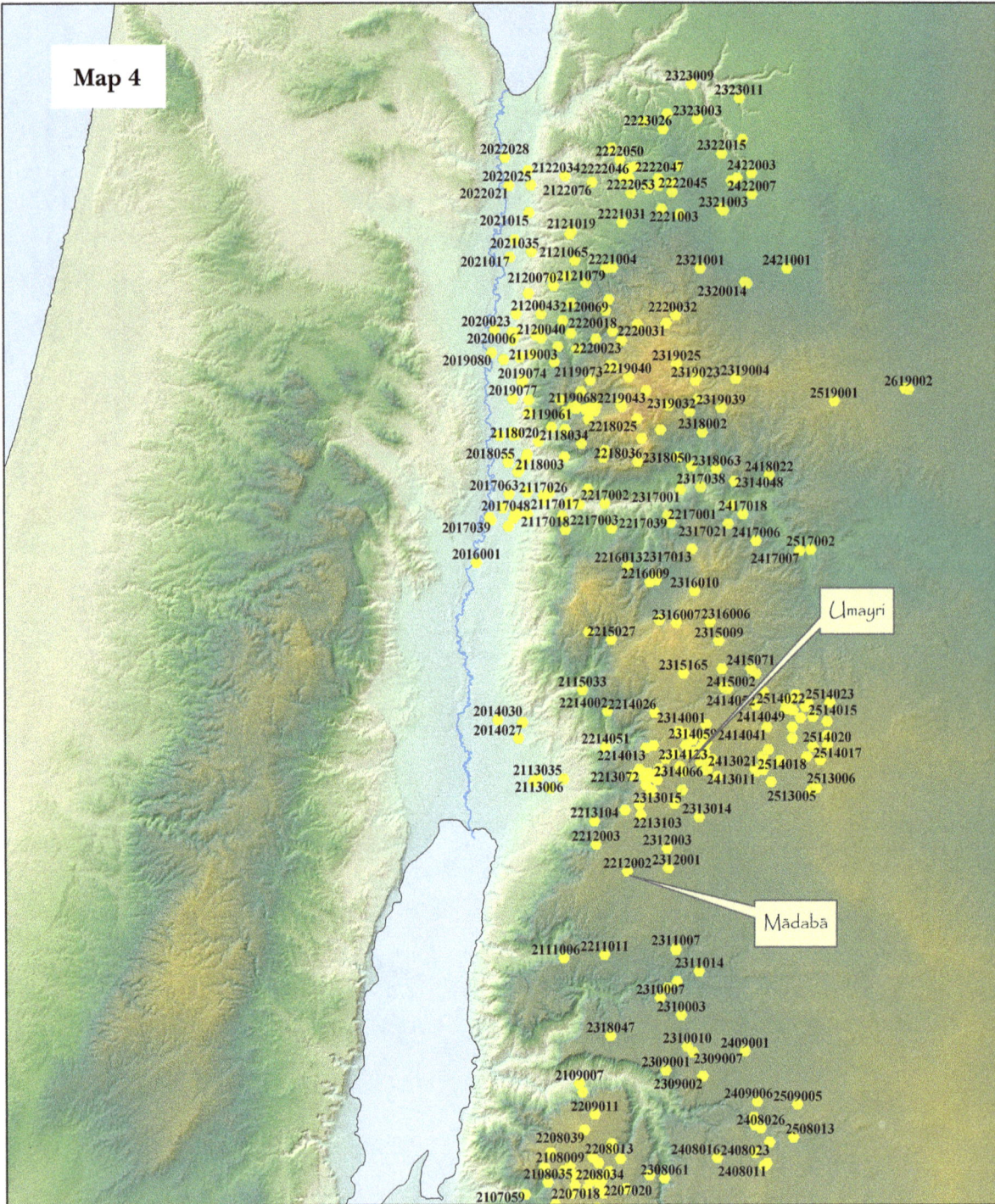

Map 4

Iron I Central & Northern Transjordan

Umayri

Mādabā

Legend
Iron I
Jordan River

Elevation
High : 3079m
Low : -422m

0   10   20   30   40
Kilometers

Topography derived from SRTM Data, courtesy of NA?
Site locations from JADIS Database, courtesy of the
Jordanian Department of Antiquities.

2323009
2323011
2323003
2223026
2322015
2022028 2222050 2422003
2022025 21220342222046 2222047 2422007
2022021 2122076 2222053 2222045 2321003
2021015 2121019 2221031 2221003
2021035
2021017 2121065 2221004 2321001 2421001
21200702121079
2120043 2120069 2220032 2320014
2020023 2120040 2220018 2220031
2020006 2220023
2019080 2119003 2319025
2019074 21190732219040 23190232319004 2619002
2019077 2319032 2319039 2519001
21190682219043
2119061 2318002
21180202118034 2218025
2018055 2218036 2318063 2418022
2118003 23180502318063 2314048
20170632117026 2317038
2017048 2117017 2217002 2317001 2417018
2117018 2217003 2217039 2217001
2017039 2317021 2417006 2517002
2016001 2317021
22160132317013 2417007
2216009 2316010
23160072316006
2218027 2315009
2315165 2415071
2115033 2415002
2114002 2214026 24140 22514022 2514023
2014030 2314001 2414049 2514015
2014027 2214051 23140592414041 2514020
2214013 2314123 2413021 2514017
2113035 2213072 2314066 2413011 2514018 2513006
2113006 2313015 2513005
2213104 2313014
2213103
2212003 2312003
2212002 2312001

2111006 2211011 2311007
2311014
2310007
2310003
2318047
2310010 2409001
2309001 2309007
2109007 2309002
2209011 2409006 2509005
2208039 2408026 2508013
2108009 2208013 24080162408023
2108035 2208034 2308061 2408011
2107059 2207018 2207020

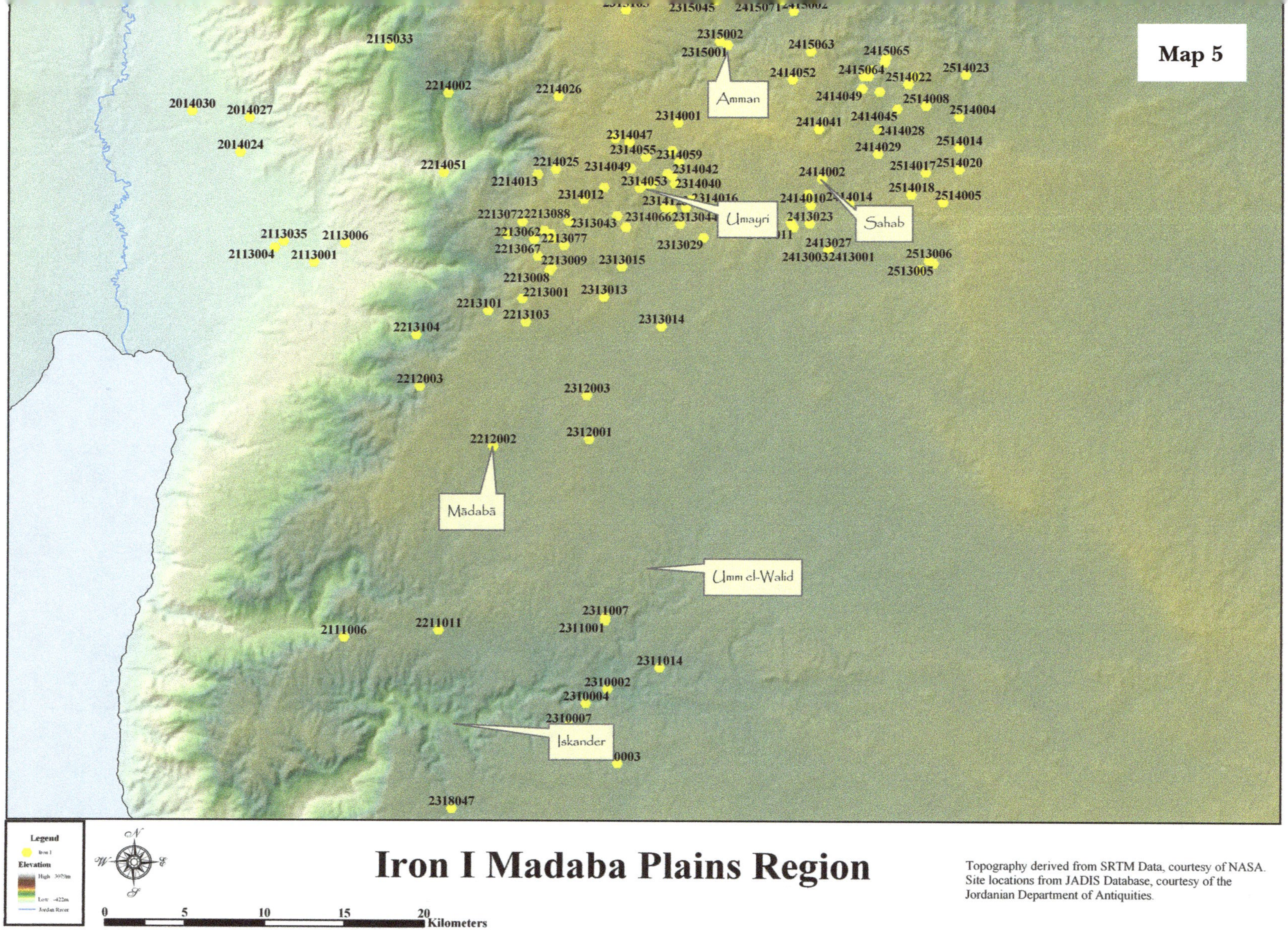

Map 5

Topography derived from SRTM Data, courtesy of NASA.
Site locations from JADIS Database, courtesy of the
Jordanian Department of Antiquities.

Iron I Madaba Plains Region

2514023
2514004
2515033
2415065
2415064 2415022 2514008
2415063 2414045 2414028 2514014
2515045 2415002 2415001 2414052 2414049 2414041 2414029 2514017 2514020
2415001 2414001 2414002 2414102 2514018 2514005
Amman 2414047 2414014 Sahab 2513006
2214026 2314001 2314059 2414042 2414002 2413023 2513005
2214002 2314055 2314040 2414053 2314016 2413001
2214013 2314049 2314012 2314043 Umayri 2414102 2413001
2214051 2314025 2313088 2313072 2313029 2413003
2215033 2314053 2313077 2313015 2313006
2213072 2313062 2313067 2313009 2313013
2113006 2213008 2213001 2313014
2113035 2113001 2213301 2213103
2113004 2213104 2312003 2312001
2014030 2014027 2212003 2312002 Madaba
2014024 2212002 Umm el-Walid
2211011 2311007 2311014
2311001 2310002
2211006 2310004 Iskander
2310007 0003
2318047

Legend
Iron I
Elevation
High 1075m
Low 425m
Jordan Rivers

0   5   10   15   20
Kilometers

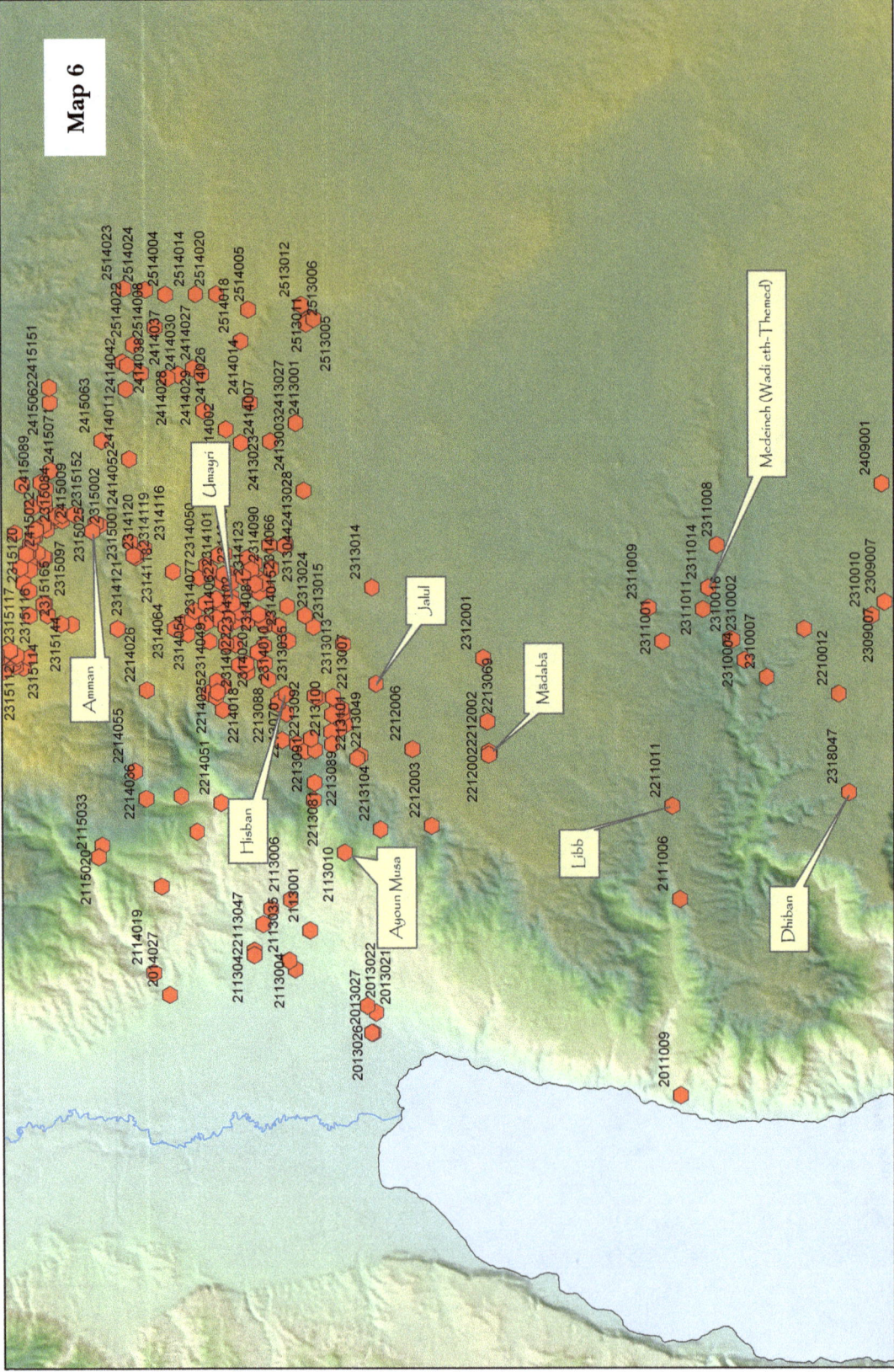

Map 6

Iron II Madaba Plains Region

Topography derived from SRTM Data, courtesy of NASA.
Site locations from JADIS Database, courtesy of the
Jordanian Department of Antiquities.

Legend
Iron II
Elevation

0   5   10   15   20

Preface and Introduction

Preface

This book had its genesis in one of my early graduate courses at the University of Toronto's Department of Near and Middle Eastern Civilizations. The essay I wrote on the Late Bronze / Iron I transition in Transjordan, perhaps not unlike the patterns of abatement and intensification that are described in the following pages, morphed into a dissertation and now into a monograph. The original thesis hinged partly on the projection that early Iron I levels would eventually be uncovered at Tall Mādabā within the modern city of the Hashemite Kingdom of Jordan. As it turns out, only two years after the dissertation's defense, the Tall Mādabā Archaeological Project, directed by Deborah Foran, did find Late Bronze / Iron I levels on the western acropolis. Mādabā, usually visited for its famous mosaics and Byzantine churches, could now officially take a front seat among the cities connected to early biblical and Moabite history. Recent renewed interests in Israel's origins in Transjordan have also added to the sense that now might be an opportune time to begin a new process of integration.

Given the plethora of well-documented opinions regarding the fundamental question of Israel's origins, it also seems appropriate to acknowledge the present synthesis's inherent limitations. Although historical conclusions are drawn, the proposed model of ethnic identity in early Iron I Transjordan cannot pretend to substitute for a comprehensive history of the region along with a full analysis of textual and archaeological data. Nevertheless, the study may serve as a baseline to readers who are not familiar with current discussions on the settlement history of the region east of the Jordan in general and ethnic identities in particular.

It is with gratitude that I acknowledge the many people who helped me in the research and writing of the initial dissertation. For their financial support, I recognize the University of Toronto (University of Toronto Fellowships; Thesis Completion Grant), the Province of Ontario (Ontario Graduate Scholarship), the Tell Mādabā Archaeological Project, and the American Schools of Oriental Research (Travel Grant).

I am particularly thankful to my dissertation committee, Profs. Timothy P. Harrison (supervisor), the late Brian Peckham, and J. Glen Taylor. Tim Harrison gave me the initial impetus to pursue this dissertation topic and provided judicious guidance throughout the process. Brian Peckham's congenial and crucial input was always à propos, as were Glen Taylor's expertise and encouragement. I also recognize the input of Profs. E. J. Revell, J. S. Holladay, Jr., and the late T. C. Young, Jr., who almost persuaded me to write on an*other* early Iron Age region (western Iran).

For the preparation of this book, I acknowledge my research assistants who over the years have contributed toward the completion of this project: Chris Anderson, Eric Welsh, Philip Bollinger, Andrew Walton, Ryan Junkin, and Adam Smith. I am grateful to the Board of Trustees at Gordon-Conwell Theological Seminary for granting me a half sabbatical, which enabled me to complete this project. Heartfelt thanks also go to Stephen Batiuk for generating the maps and the corresponding gazetteer and to Debra Foran and Stanley Klassen for allowing me to use their latest research on the excavations at Tall Mādabā. I particularly appreciated Tim Harrison's keen editorial eye and suggestions for the monograph version of the work. Finally, I am deeply grateful to Jim Eisenbraun for accepting this book for publication.

On a personal note, I acknowledge family and friends who have supported and encouraged me over the years, particularly my wife, Dr. Donna Petter, my son Marcus, and my *compagnons d'armes* in all four corners of the world. This volume is dedicated to my friend Ron Smith.

Introduction

The past few years have witnessed exciting developments in the study of the early Iron I period in central Jordan (the region bounded by the Wadi Zarqa / biblical Jabbok in the north and the Wadi Mujib / biblical Arnon in the south; see map 1). Until recently, knowledge was limited primarily to tomb materials typologically linked to assemblages from sites in the hill country of western Palestine. With ongoing excavations at several sites in Transjordan, we are now beginning to see substantial settlements that will shape (and re-shape) our understanding of the region during the early Iron Age as well as the Late Bronze / Iron I transition. Until more-specific relative and absolute chronologies are produced for the area (Strange 2001; see chap, 5 below), the approximate dates 1200 to 1000 B.C. for the Iron I remain the accepted general chronological framework. In terms of settlement patterns, the LB II is well represented in central Transjordan and is followed by a period of intensification during the Iron I. The increase in settlements has been noted particularly on the dry, eastern margins of the highlands. Site distributions point to a clustering in the south-central highlands (south and north of the Wadi Mujib/Arnon River) and on the eastern margins of the Mādabā Plateau. The main settlement type in the Iron I was the fortified agropastoral village situated near or on a perennial water source. Sites were fortified with a case-mate wall and in one case a large tower (Khirbet al-Mudayna al-ʿAliya [Rout-ledge 2000a; 2004]; Khirbet Lehun [Homès Fredericq 2000; Swinnen 2009]). Domestic dwellings, usually of the "four-room" type, were distributed along the wall, sometimes with their broad room attached directly to the casemate construction. In some cases, this resulted in an open central area that was probably used as an animal pen. The material assemblage is typical of the highland culture of the southern Levant, mostly composed of cooking pots, collared pithoi, and kraters. Tomb assemblages, which also include flasks, pyxides, bowls, and kraters, confirm the relatively homogeneous nature of the assemblage.

It is difficult to overstate the influence of L. Marfoe's social frontier model (Marfoe 1979) on the theoretical foundations of many discussions on the history of early Israel in the southern Levant. Distilled in its simplest form, the model claims that, in the Late Bronze–Iron I ferment, subsistence strategies by tribal groups adapted to varying and changing circumstances. Against a backdrop of long-term cyclical processes, these shifting social conditions set the foundations for an understanding of the nation-states of the Iron II. Marfoe's dynamic social model assumes that multiple lines of evidence should be used to reach historically and socially relevant conclusions. Texts and material culture, often informed by ethnohistorical and ethnoarchaeological perspectives are weaved together in sometimes compelling arguments, as in Stager's classic study of the Israelite family (Stager 1985; see Levy 2010). However, the application of these frontier dynamics to questions of ethnicity yields variegated outcomes. While the debate continues about which (if any) texts should be admitted as evidence in historical-archaeological reconstructions, several important studies in the recent past have reaffirmed the culture-historical assumption of covariance between ethnicity and material culture. In other words, it is claimed (again), material cultural traits of the Iron I (famously, the four-room house and the collar-rimmed store-jar) do indeed signal Israelite ethnicity.

Similar winds have blown across the theoretical landscape of the study of the early Iron Age in Transjordan. The prevailing historical reconstruction for the Late Bronze–Iron I ties the process to the Mādabā Plateau Region (MPR). Based on comparative ceramic analysis with sites in the highlands of Palestine, the MPR is considered to have witnessed the earliest presence of this new highland culture in the southern Levant. In its classic form, the synthesis links the fortified settlement of Tall al-ʿUmayri, situated at the northern edge of the MPR, to the tribe of Reuben (Cross 1988; 1998; Herr 1999). Then, according to this view, it is on the basis of the primacy of the Reubenite tribal group and an east-to-west migration that Israel and Yahwism emerged in the highlands of Cisjordan. While a more recent interpretation of the model has backed away from singling out Reuben (Herr and Clark 2009), the culture-historical mechanisms that account for the settlement process essentially remain in place.

Taking into consideration the social dynamics inherent in a frontier tribal area, in this book I examine ethnic identity during the early Iron I phase in the central highlands of Jordan. As a contested tribal zone, this region witnessed a dynamic process of shifting ethnic identities during the transitional period that ushered the Iron Age. Thus the homogeneous picture suggested by the material-cultural evidence makes the identification of distinct ethnic groups in the MPR difficult to sustain. To single out an individual group (the Reubenites, or any other specific tribe) as the apparent sole catalyst of Yahwism is equally problematic to reconcile with Hebrew sources that, on the one hand, view Reuben in an essentially negative light, and on the other, acknowledge the precarious status of the territories of Transjordan ("Gilead" and "Machir") claimed by Israelites tribes. Instead, it appears more constructive to suggest that the early Iron I in Transjordan should be viewed within a general material-cultural sphere that is autochthonous to the region. This does not mean, however, that in terms of their origins, the main tribal groups in the MPR had no kinship ties with a larger-Israel group. To this effect, the available literary evidence seems to point to a plurality of tribes with Gad/ Gilead, Reuben, and Moab appearing as part of the regional diversity.

Although the material culture tells little about the identity of the Iron I inhabitants, it does provide a framework of interpretation for the nature of the settlement process. The clear presence of substantial fortifications already during the Late Bronze / Iron I period at key sites ('Umayri and Mādabā), along with the documented contested nature of the region should give us pause in proposing models of settlements that do not factor in *conflict* as one of the principal mechanisms. The Merneptah Stele, the Mesha Stele, and the Israelite texts all allude to interactions that can hardly be viewed as "peaceful" or "symbiotic." This sort of framework fits well with current research on tribal societies in which identities are forged in contradistinction to other groups (expressed through tribal loyalty). However, in keeping with frontier dynamics, the textual data also point to another reality—namely, the Canaanization of Israelite culture during the period of the Judges. Thus, even if a case could be made for a "pristine" Israelite material culture, the "perfect storm" of Canaanization and conflict dynamics on the frontier essentially cancels out those material-cultural traits during the early Iron Age in central Transjordan.

In chap. 1, I review the influence of the social tribal frontier model in light of the current models of highland settlement in both Palestine and Transjordan. Chapter 2 outlines a framework of ethnic identity defined on a continuum of *both* primordial (that is, bloodlines and other seemingly passive factors) *and* instrumental (active social processes) attributes rather than as mutually exclusive terms. While covariance (the so-called one-to-one relationship between material culture and ethnic identity) may be a signal for the presence of discrete socioethnic groups in some contexts (for example, the Philistines on the coastal plain of Israel), it may not carry the same clear signal in other ecological settings. This is especially true in genuinely tribal social frontier zones, such as the highlands of central Transjordan. Chapter 3 presents textual evidence that supports the concept of northern Moab as a historically contested frontier zone. In chap. 4, I review documentary evidence that points to a dynamic view of ethnic identity in Israelite texts. The data suggest that the primary marker of ethnic identity is religious loyalty (that is, Yahwism for Israelite tribal groups). Equally present is the concept of Canaanization, whereby the early Israelite tribes abandoned their ancestral/ essential Yahwistic roots for Canaanite identities. The reverse phenomenon also obtains in that members of other ethnic groups also could shift their identities to adopt the Israelite identity. In the context of Transjordan, the situation is complicated by the perception of the region as standing at the periphery. Furthermore, with respect to one tribal group's preeminence, apparently no single tribe could claim this status among Israelite tribal groups in Transjordan. Thus, Reuben's primogeniture in biblical genealogies does not necessarily mean that this particular group functioned as the main tribal head in early Israel. Instead—in keeping with the abatement and intensification patterns documented in the region throughout its history—tribal groups' identities shifted in similar patterns. Thus, it is no surprise to find the variagated groups described in the documentary sources weaving in and out of the narrative history of the region. Both Israelite and Moabite tribal histories stand as witness to this process. Chapter 5 turns to the age-old question of ethnicity in the material record. With emerging data from Tall Mādabā, our picture of the early Iron Age continues to confirm the notion of a relatively homogeneous regional assemblage. Any case for covariance in the MPR, therefore, seems difficult to sustain in light of the current data. Consequently, no migration patterns (e.g., east to west) can be confirmed archaeologically. Similarly, the available evidence regarding religious behavior reflects very little that might be distinctive of a particular pan-tribal ethnic group.

If the voice of material culture may appear somewhat muted with respect to the Iron I population's ethnic identity, textual data, as interpreted in this book, may speak with a clearer voice. I take the evidence to suggest that both Hebrew and Moabite tribal memories documented the presence of groups with primordial ties to the Israel-group in central Transjordan in periods preceding the rise of their respective monarchies (Iron II). However, written sources (particularly from the book of Judges) also document the circumstantial nature of these groups' ethnic awareness during the Iron I. As an early "diaspora" across the Jordan River, the Transjordanian tribes' commitment to the "mainland" was variable at best (see Judges 5). Thus, strictly primordial conceptions of ethnic identity in Transjordan (which the Reubenite primacy assumes) should give way to an approach that factors in Canaanization as a way to explain ethnic processes in the areas during the Iron I. This *longue durée* process of tribal emergence and dissolution actually reflects a typical pattern in marginal zones, where tribal groups amalgamate and separate depending on the varying sociohistorical forces that are inherently at play in frontier regions.

Abbreviations

General

ABH	Archaic Biblical Hebrew
BH	Biblical Hebrew
chap(s).	chapter(s)
cm	centimeter(s)
D	Deuteronomist writer/source
DH	Deuteronomistic History
E	Elohist writer/source
EB	Early Bronze Age
fig(s).	figure(s)
FP	field phase
ha	hectare
J	Jahwist writer/source
LB	Late Bronze Age
LXX	Septuagint
m	meter(s)
MB	Middle Bronze Age
MI	Mesha Inscription
MPR	Mādabā Plateau Region
MT	Masoretic Text
NRSV	New Revised Standard Version
P	Priestly writer/source
pl(s).	plate(s)
RSV	Revised Standard Version
SBH	Standard Biblical Hebrew
v(v).	verse(s)
vol(s).	volume(s)

Reference Works

AASOR	Annual of the American Schools of Oriental Research
AB	Anchor Bible
ABD	*Anchor Bible Dictionary*
ABRL	Anchor Bible Reference Library
ADAJ	*Annual of the Department of Antiquities of Jordan*
AJA	*American Journal of Archaeology*
AnOr	Analecta Orientalia
AOS	American Oriental Series
ARA	*Annual Review of Anthropology*
AUSS	*Andrews University Seminary Studies*
BA	*Biblical Archaeologist*
BAR	*Biblical Archaeology Review*

BASOR	*Bulletin of the American Schools of Oriental Research*
BBRSup	Bulletin for Biblical Research Supplement Series
Bib	*Biblica*
BZ	*Biblische Zeitschrift*
BZAW	Beihefte zur Zeitschrift für die alttestamentliche Wissenschaft
Cah. Sci. Hum.	*Cahier des Sciences Humaines*
CBQ	*Catholic Biblical Quarterly*
CBR	*Currents in Biblical Research*
COS	*The Context of Scripture*
ErIsr	*Eretz-Israel*
HSM	Harvard Semitic Monographs
HTR	*Harvard Theological Review*
IEJ	*Israel Exploration Journal*
JAA	*Journal of Anthropological Archaeology*
JADIS	Jordan Antiquities and Database Information System
JAR	*Journal of Archaeological Research*
JAEI	*Journal of Ancient Egyptian Interconnections*
JBL	*Journal of Biblical Literature*
JCSSH	*Journal of Comparative Studies in Society and History*
JESHO	*Journal of the Economic and Social History of the Orient*
JNES	*Journal of Near Eastern Studies*
JSOT	*Journal for the Study of the Old Testament*
JSOTSup	Journal for the Study of the Old Testament Supplement Series
JSSEA	*Journal of the Society for the Study of Egyptian Antiquities*
KTU	*Die Keilalphabetischen Texte aus Ugarit*
MPP	*Madaba Plains Project*
	MPP 1 = Battenfield and Herr 1989
	MPP 2 = Battenfield and Herr 1991
	MPP 3 = Clark 1997
	MPP 4 = ʿ*Umayri* 4 = Herr 2000a
	MPP 5 = ʿ*Umayri* 5 = Herr 2002b
NEA	*Near Eastern Archaeologist*
NEAEHL	*New Encyclopedia of Archaeological Excavations in the Holy Land*
OEANE	*Oxford Encyclopedia of Archaeology in the Near East*
OJA	*Oxford Journal of Archaeology*
Or	*Orientalia*
PEFA	*Palestine Exploration Fund Annual*
PEQ	*Palestine Exploration Quarterly*
RB	*Revue Biblique*
RBL	*Review of Biblical Literature*
SBLDS	Society of Biblical Literature Dissertation Series
SBLMS	Society of Biblical Literature Monograph Series
SHAJ	*Studies in the History and Archaeology of Jordan*
TA	*Tel Aviv*
TynBul	*Tyndale Bulletin*
VT	*Vetus Testamentum*
ZAH	*Zeitschrift für Althebräistik*
ZAW	*Zeitschrift für die alttestamentliche Wissenschaft*
ZDPV	*Zeitschrift des deutschen Palästina-Vereins*

CHAPTER ONE

Central Transjordan as "Tribal Frontier"

As one of the crucial transitions in the settlement history of the southern Levant, the Late Bronze–Iron I period has been the subject of considerable attention (see Levy and Holl 2002: 86–90). A significant theoretical underpinning in this current discussion is found in O. Lattimore's model of shifting frontier (Lattimore 1962). This concept, initially used to describe the Chinese frontier beyond the Great Wall, has been adapted to the southern Levantine context. The shifting social frontier model presupposes a high degree of social, economic, and ultimately, political fluidity. A survey of the current literature, however, reveals that this fluid social model is applied only selectively to the data. Discussions about social organization readily emphasize the social fluidity inherent to the cultures of the central highland region, but this shifting frontier setting is unevenly applied to questions of group identities. In this chapter, I plot these discussions and propose to view the region, especially Transjordan, as a genuinely tribal social frontier. This "ecotone" thus will have a great deal of impact on our study, including our perception of ethnicities.

Defining the "Shifting Social Frontier"

The notion of *frontier* forms the underlying assumption of many discussions dealing with the processes of sociohistorical changes in the southern Levant (Stager 1985a; see below). Thus it is important to trace the origins of the concept and its incorporation into current syntheses of early Israelite settlement in Cisjordan and Transjordan. O. Lattimore first explored the concept of frontier in his classic study of the outer limits of Imperial China (that is, the land beyond the Great Wall). The geographical regions of the Chinese frontier included the forests, steppes, and fields of Manchuria, the oases and deserts of central Asia, and the highlands of Tibet, but the *locus classicus* of the frontier was the Mongolian steppe (Lattimore 1962: 53). The frontier was not only a fixed geographical border (marked in time by the Great Wall) but an environmental boundary between arable lands and the steppes and a *social* boundary between agriculturalists and pastoral nomads. The Great Wall should not be considered a rigid political border but a fluid demarcation of differing environments. To understand "frontier" history, therefore, requires a deep awareness of environmental factors. Societies adapt and evolve in order to develop and control their environments. More specifically, Lattimore linked the shifting nature of the frontier to the notion of a marginal zone situated between the steppe, which was outside the minimum-rainfall isohyet, and the well-irrigated regions. These marginal belts acquired a strategic significance as they influenced both the agriculturists of the arable zone and the pastoralists of the steppe zone. Though pastoral nomadism was deemed inferior to agriculture, this mixed culture came under the influence of both but was never mastered by either (Lattimore 1962: 25, 423, 468).

In his study of Mesopotamian social history, R. Adams (1974) adopted Lattimore's concept of a fluid social frontier, arguing that the oscillating relationships between core and periphery in the region—where periodic waves of tribal invaders unified the region following periods of fragmentation—closely paralleled Lattimore's description of the Chinese frontier. These waves spanned several millennia and included Akkadians during the later Early Dynastic Period, Amorites after Ur III, Kassites during the later phases of the Old Babylonian Period, Arameans in the 1st millennium B.C., and the Arab conquest. In addition, the textual references to the building of border fortifications (the "wall against the Martu" during the Ur III period) provide another parallel between China and Mesopotamia, with respect to agriculturists in the heartlands and nomadic pastoralists on the peripheries (Adams 1974: 2). However, Adams was not as concerned with geography as with the concept of a shifting frontier within a socioeconomic framework—specifically, the need to view pastoralism and agriculture on a continuum. Agricultural producers, pressed by the demands of political centralization (taxation), maximization, and the environmental uncertainties of irrigation agriculture in the Mesopotamian floodplain (salinization and siltation among other factors), sought an adaptive lifestyle, including pastoralism in times of scarcity (Adams 1974: 3).

This uncertainty (Adams's "omnipresent threat of subsistence failure") also played a crucial role in the production and maintenance of a stratified society. It led him to view urbanism in Mesopotamia as an ecologically adaptive phenomenon. The role of agricultural uncertainty in the arid Mesopotamian climate produced a differentiated outcome involving both ecological circumstances and variable human response. What is important to emphasize, however, is that for Adams the concept of a shifting frontier affected social relationships as well (Adams 1974: 10–11).

L. Marfoe, one of Adams's students at the University of Chicago, applied the concept of a shifting frontier to settlement patterns in the Baqʿa Valley and the highlands of the Lebanon Mountain range (Marfoe 1979). He viewed the Baqʿa Valley as "a dynamic system of free-floating, shifting alignments of political poles and their adherents" (1979: 14). The people of the marginal zone between the frontier highlands and the valley consisted of a highly mobile population, "shifting in subsistence strategies, shifting in loyalties, and shifting through highly permeable sociocultural boundaries" (1979: 14–15). Like Adams, Marfoe argued that we should abandon static models that dichotomize categories such as the *desert* and the *sown* (1979: 10–117). Marfoe made the case that the shifting frontier was a highly adaptable concept, yielding useful descriptive dividends particularly during periods of transition. Though Marfoe's locus was Lebanon, he made a number of observations at the end of his study concerning the southern Levant that have laid the foundation for the adaptation of this concept in analyses of the Late Bronze–Iron I transition in Palestine and Transjordan. In particular, he highlighted the need to move away from static models of territorially well-defined cultural groups. Cultural change should not be viewed as a uniform and consistent process. Instead, Marfoe advocated an approach that views transitional phases as "shifts in balance between dynamic social systems" (Marfoe 1979: 34–35). As a result, to plot social transformation and state formation processes, one should also pay attention to small tribal social units, which a priori includes individuals (Marfoe 1979: 27, 34–35; see Routledge 2004: 91).

The Social Frontier Model Applied
to the Highlands of Palestine

Foundational Studies

Marfoe's imprint on L. Stager's influential "Archaeology of the Family in Ancient Israel" is clear (Stager 1985a; see also Stager 1998: 149–50). Similarly to the Baqʿa Valley in Lebanon, Stager defined the Palestinian highlands as a frontier, which he viewed as both obstacle and refuge, in which free land could be found (Stager 1985a: 5). In contrast to Marfoe, however, Stager also incorporated Lattimore's notion of the closing frontier, a process that for Lattimore was linked to population pressure and technological change (Lattimore 1962: chap. 1). Stager argued for a similar process in Iron Age Israel. The frontier opened to settlement in the Iron I concurrent with a process of deforestation (in the Baqʿa, deforestation occurred later in time) but also in conjunction with the appearance of technologies involving terracing, cisterns, and Iron Implements. As highland communities moved from a "segmentary lineage" system in the Iron I to a "segmentary state system" in the Iron II (Stager 1985a: 24), the frontier began to close through a process called lineage capture, in which social networks expanded through patrilineal marriage. According to Stager, the process corresponded with the consolidation of Iron I settlement in the hill country. The Iron II social structure and the development of the Israelite segmentary state should be understood in the light of this patrimonial continuum. The house-of-the-father tribal social concept remained but also included kingship and, ultimately, the divine realm (King and Stager 2001; Schloen 2001). As a process of state formation, this can be conceptualized as a tribal kingdom during the Iron II (Master 2001).

W. Dever published his own influential research on the EB IV transition within a year of Marfoe's study. While Dever did not specifically deal with the Lattimore/Adams concept of a shifting frontier, his "dimorphic society" (see Rowton 1974) in which sedentarism and nomadism are in a symbiotic relationship clearly resonates with it (Dever 1980; 1995). Likewise, working with similar assumptions, in one of his early and oft-quoted discussions of the Late Bronze–Iron I transition, Dever made a point of characterizing the region away from "unicausal" models (i.e., the Albright-Wright-Yadin conquest model; Dever 1992: 104, 106) toward a flexible approach that allows for more variegated processes to explain the "collapse" of the Late Bronze Age. In this early iteration, he leaned heavily on systems theory, and embraced the peaceful infiltration and peasant revolt models as more viable explanations (1992: 103).

Subsequent applications of the frontier model include S. Bunimowitz's study of the Late Bronze from a *longue durée* perspective. Bunimowitz focused on sociopolitical causes, particularly the Egyptian influence in Canaan. During the 18th Dynasty, Egypt brought considerable changes to the sociopolitical structure of the region. According to Bunimowitz (1995: 327), the frontier "came down" from the highlands into the lowlands, inner valleys, and coastal region. Then, during the Late Bronze–Iron I transition, the situation was reversed, the frontier retreated, and nonsedentary groups reoccupied the lowlands and the highlands (1995: 328).

In summary, what these studies all share is a deliberate hermeneutic away from rigid and chronologically narrow political-historical pronouncements toward socioeconomic trends based on long-term processes.[1] As a result, they advocate flexibility in understanding the complex issues surrounding the "catastrophe" (cf. Drews 1995) that brought the Late Bronze Age society to an end, ushering in the Iron Age, and state formation in Iron II.

The Social Frontier Model Applied in Current Theories of Settlement

In keeping with these earlier social frontier conceptualizations, current discussions concerning early Iron I settlement have fitted into two general categories: (1) the sedentarization of pastoral nomadic groups (Finkelstein 1994; 1995; Finkelstein and Silberman 2001; Levy and Holl 2002; Rainey 2007; Rainey and Notley 2006; Faust 2006), or (2) the ruralization of various populations, including urban populations (Dever 2003: 129–51; 1992; Killebrew 2005; Stager 1998; 1985a). A third approach, emphasizing nationalism, questions the validity of placing the emergence of Israel prior to the Iron II. According to this view, Israel as a distinct ethnic group is thought to emerge during the late Iron II or during the Persian Period (see Mullen 1997).[2] As important as the question of ethnic identity is during the Iron II, Postexilic, and Hellenistic Periods, the topic of post-Iron I ethnicity falls outside the scope of this study (see Dever 2003).

---

1. L. Marfoe, evoking F. Braudel's now well-worn phrase *la longue durée*, characterized it as "historical undercurrents" measured in "millennia" rather than decades (Marfoe 1979: 3).

2. It must be noted that discussions of nationalism in ancient Israel do not necessarily reflect a minimalist approach (see Grosby 2002: 45).

The two prevailing approaches of sedentarization and ruralization attempt to account for the well-documented increase of sites in the highlands of Cisjordan during the Iron I. To explain this population explosion (from 88 sites in the Late Bronze to 678 in the course of the Iron I; see Stager 1998: 135; Rainey 2007: 46), the traditional conquest scenario in which outsiders (that is, the Israelites) came into the region to occupy it by force (see Albright 1939) is set aside in favor of people movements that are either indigenous (usually associated with the ruralization approach) or coming from the outside (usually connected with the sedentarization model).[3] Whether one's model emphasizes indigenous or nonnative populations, no one seems to deny the possibility that some outside elements also settled the highlands, either from adjacent ecological zones (Transjordan; see Rainey and Notley 2006: 112) or even from Egypt (Dever 2003: 182; Levy and Holl 2002: 83; Holladay 2001; Killebrew 2005; see Herr 1983: 29–30).[4] Another point of apparent agreement concerns the relationship between the Iron I and Iron II populations. Since there is no clear evidence of massive population growth over the course of the Iron Age in Cisjordan (from 678 sites in Iron I to 852 in Iron II [Stager 1998: 135]), it is reasonable to assume a degree of connectedness between these first settlers and the Iron II Israelite polity, which indicates that the latter group found its origins in the former.

In keeping with A. Alt's Peaceful Infiltration model, I. Finkelstein has explained this demographic shift on both archaeological and ethnohistorical data grounds (Finkelstein 1994; 1988). Synthesizing records from 19th-century A.D. bedouin subsistence patterns and his excavations of a small Iron I farmstead at ʿIzbet Sartah, Finkelstein concludes that the most plausible way to account for this demographic transformation is to chart a sedentarization movement by pastoral nomads into the highlands (Finkelstein 1988; see Alt 1968). These nomads, who lived in symbiotic economic relationship with the urban settlements during the Late Bronze, were forced to adapt in the wake of the socioeconomic collapse of the Late Bronze city-states. The shift in subsistence strategies resulted in the abandonment of the nomadic and pastoral lifestyle and an adoption of a sedentary agro-pastoral economy (Finkelstein 1994: 153–62). Although now skeptical of this idea, Finkelstein also used the survey data to argue for a settlement increase that moved chronologically from east to west (1994: 160).

---

3. In the classic biblical-archaeological methodology of the 20th century, the correlating of destruction phases in the Late Bronze with the coming of the Israelites into the land is a quest that has been abandoned by many historians (Mazar 1990b: 329–34; Stager 1998: 32–33; Dever 1992: 103). It is important to note that some do continue to maintain adapted versions of the conquest approach within either a LB IIB setting (Kitchen 2003; Hoffmeier 1997), or less commonly within a LB I context (Hoerth 1998).

4. J. S. Holladay particularly highlights Hittite long-distance trade. However, in the case of the Late Bronze Amman airport structure, which L. Herr argues should probably be connected to Hittite funerary practices, Holladay suggests Egyptian origins instead (Holladay 2001: 167–73).

Probably the best known piece of evidence presented in favor of this sedentarization model comes from the ʿIzbet Sartah *hazer* settlement, whose semi-circular shape, Finkelstein argued, resembles a Bedouin encampment (1996: 205). In addition he viewed the Iron I settlement increase as part of a cyclical pattern that began already during the EB I and MB II (1994: 155). This long-term process was considered typical of a marginal zone where people shifted from nomadism to sedentarism according to the varying circumstances (Finkelstein and Mazar 2007: 75–76). Since the settlement increase during the Iron I has been duplicated previously, Finkelstein, I.Finkelstein concludes that the particular Iron I material culture cannot be taken to reflect ethnic identities, but instead must be seen as the result of a highland population motivated by functional priorities (1994: 169; see chap. Two). As a tribute to the enduring influence of the sedentarization model (see Levy and Holl 2002), A. Faust, in his recent monograph on Israelite ethnic identity, essentially follows Finkelstein in plotting this sedentarization process. In marked contrast, however, Faust still favors a cultural as opposed to strictly functional- interpretation of the material culture (2006: 14; see chap. Two).

L. Stager and W. Dever highlight the problems related to some elements of this hypothesis (Stager 1998; Dever 2001, 2003). The east to west movement in light of survey data may be hard to discern in light of the available ceramic evidence (Stager 1998: 135; Dever 2003: 178; see chap. Five).[5] The famed ʿIzbet Sartah Stratum III structure lacks sufficient horizontal exposure to estimate whether its shape was oval or not (Dever 2003: 162). The significant proportion of cattle bones in Stratum III also creates some doubt as to the pastoral-nomadic subsistence strategy of these new settlers (ibid.). Stager concludes that house shape and configuration were probably dictated by ecological considerations and do not speak to the settlers' alleged nomadic background (Stager 1985a: 17; see Dever 2003: 164).

In spite of disagreements with Finkelstein's interpretation of the ʿIzbet Sartah materials, the notion of pastoral-nomadic tribal groups resorting to more sedentary patterns of subsistence in times of transition retains a powerful explanatory appeal for many (see Rainey 2007). In this respect, the ruralization model (Stager 1998; 1985a) adopts a similar premise, namely the settlement *de novo* in the highlands of small agro-pastoralist farmsteads. In this interpretation, Giloh represents the type-site of this settlement pattern (see Mazar 1980; 1981; 1990b). Continuity in material culture (particularly cooking-pot morphology) from the Late Bronze to Iron I is noted, but real changes also occur in the material assemblage. Technology (such as terracing and cisterns), domestic architecture, and storage vessels are highlighted to illustrate the differences between the Late Bronze culture and this new emerging highland culture (Stager 1985a; Dever 1992).

Whereas Stager includes pastoral-nomadic groups who shifted subsistence strategies (from nomadic grazing to agriculture) to account for the settling of

---

5. A fact which Finkelstein himself now concedes (Finkelstein 2011).

the highlands (Stager 1985a; see Rainey 2007), Dever has argued that urban populations were largely responsible for the move to the highland frontier following the collapse of the Late Bronze city-states. Dever thus adapts the Gottwald Peasant Revolt model (Dever 2003: 182–89; Gottwald 1985) and reconstructs the context as class warfare struggle between Late Bronze city states elites and their oppressed non-elite populations. Unlike the original Peasant model, however, he does not single out disgruntled urbanites, and also includes *shasu*-like pastoral nomads (see Weippert 1971), *ʿapiru*-like roamers (see Mendenhall 1962), and foreign refugees. This eclectic background, what Killebrew names "the mixed multitude" nature of the settlers (Killebrew 2005: 13),[6] leads Dever to conclude that a heterogeneous, but still mostly autochthonous population, occupied the highland during the Iron I (Dever 2003: 181–82).

To summarize, the emphasis on frontier has been particularly popular in explaining transitional periods in ancient Palestine. The shifting frontier is defined geographically as the highlands, but in keeping with the original Lattimore model, also as a socioeconomic or sociopolitical concept. For all the public debates between the urban-based or desert-based migrations, these approaches share remarkable similarities: Both end up voicing a similar narrative of population eclectism (with the "Shasu" designation taking somewhat pride of place in designating the "outsiders"). More significantly, both views are deeply committed to the frontier notion of adapted strategies of the settlers. The bulk of the disagreements lie in whether the specific identities of the inhabitants can be recognized in their material culture (see chap. Two). Regarding the rural vs. urban debate, it is important to remember that Marfoe envisioned a model where there was enough fluidity to account for variageted approaches to relocation. Hence nomads might have settled concurrently with urbanites who took to the countryside. Also, while there seems to be some assumptions of military confrontations (Stager 1985a: 25–26), the processes envisioned are essentially symbiotic and processual, clearly invoking Alt's "Peaceful Infiltration" model. Even the rare studies that advocate a decidedly migratory approach to Israelite settlement (e.g., Levy and Holl 2002), carefully avoid the charge of a return to the old political-historical conquest framework.

The Social Frontier Model applied to the Highlands of Jordan

The ecology of the highlands of Jordan, when compared with the highlands of Cisjordan, cautions us from drawing parallels too closely (Routledge 2004: 90–93). In ancient Israel, the more clearly separated ecological regions

---

6. Killebrew proposes that this "mixed multitude" resembles the one described in Exodus 12:38. In contrast to the Exodus account, however, the setting of the rebellion is in Canaan (in keeping with her indigenous model) under Egyptian domination rather than in Egypt (Killebrew 2005: 152).

of the lowlands (the coastal plains and the northern valleys) and the hill country only approximate the Jordan valley region ("lowlands") and the central
highlands along the escarpment from the Kerak Plateau to Irbid.[7] The marginal zones beyond the 200 mm isohyet (minimum rainfall for dry farming)
are situated in the eastern portions of the plateau, and along the Dead Sea escarpment. Thus, the Transjordanian region may qualify as a better candidate
for a genuine shifting frontier zone (see Rainey 2007: 47).

Foundational Studies

Studies that have conceived the Transjordanian highlands as a frontier
have come from the Early Bronze Age (Palumbo 1991, 2001; Harrison 1997),
the Iron I (McGovern 1987) and the Iron II (Routledge 1996; 2004). Palumbo
has described the Early Bronze–Middle Bronze transition as a process of adaptations to shifting physical as well as political conditions (see also D. Esse's
"adaptive strategies" [1991]). Closely following Marfoe (1979), he views variations as "shifts along a spectrum of available economic strategies and sociocultural roles" (Palumbo 2001: 237). Palumbo stresses the resilience of life in
the region. T. Harrison's study is particularly important in its documenting
of shifting patterns of settlement in the Mādabā region during the EB II–
III (1995; 1997). During times of intensification, settlements spread eastward
into the marginal zones bordering the desert. During times of abatement
(EB IV), settlements clustered in ecologically optimal zones along the spine of
the so-called King's highway and along the wadi systems that descend toward
the Jordan valley. This points to a return to a crucial dimension of the original
Shifting Frontier model, namely, the ability of populations to switch from pastoralism to agriculturalism, or vice-versa. In keeping with Marfoe's long-term
outcomes, Harrison' study provides us with a valuable foundation to examine
settlement patterns in the region during subsequent periods.

In this regard, P. McGovern's application of the frontier model to the Late
Bronze–Iron I transition in Jordan (1987) appeared to hold significant appeal, since it is situated in the region north of the MPR. From the perspective
of the Baqʿa Valley and the site of Khirbet Umm ad-Dananir in the central
highlands south of the Wadi Zarqa, McGovern connects his reconstruction to
a Late Bronze city-state socioeconomic collapse (see Dever 1992). This shift
is attributed both to the geographical isolation of the Jordanian highlands,
and to environmental changes such as a decline in precipitation (see Strange
2001: 293–94). As a result, the Late Bronze city-state system was not able to
survive. Urban populations, unable to work within these centers shifted their
subsistence strategies by moving to small outlying communities. Technological changes coincide closely with the identification of an emerging Iron I culture (cf. Stager 1985a). The increased importance of Iron Industry and new
pottery types (coil-building technology) are "the visible symbols of the new

---

7. For good surveys of the ecology of ancient Jordan, see Macumber (2001), Mac-
Donald (2000), and Harrison (1997).

order" (McGovern 1987: 268). What McGovern projected was a movement from the city to the countryside in Late Bronze–Iron I, and then back to cities in the late Iron II. Perhaps due to its heavy reliance on systems theory (for a measured critique of systems theory, see Schloen 2001), and overdependence on the Late Bronze city-state model of Cisjordan (Routledge 2004: 91–92), McGovern's synthesis has failed to gain a widespread influence on subsequent scholarship.

M. Weippert, building upon the pioneering historical geography of his mentor M. Noth (1944), adapted the sedentarization model to the Transjordanian context (see Weippert 1979; 1971). Weippert proposed that Late Bronze *Shasu* semi-nomads in Cisjordan and Transjordan gradually and peacefully turned to agriculture due to population pressure, while leaving open the possibility that outside groups also moved into the region. This peaceful settlement led to the emergence of polities later known as Israel (in Cisjordan), Ammon, Moab, and Edom (Weippert 1979: 33–34). In a later analysis, reflecting a more minimalist perspective, Weippert casts serious doubt on the reliability of biblical sources for historical reconstruction, particularly the period preceding the United Monarchy. For instance, according to him, Numbers 21, a text that is crucial for biblically-based reconstructions of the Israelite settlement in Transjordan, offers little or no insight into Israel's prehistory (Weippert 1997: 22). Nevertheless, the model itself of "peaceful infiltration," and the preeminent role attributed to the Shasu, has proved to be remarkably resilient in Transjordan, as derivatives of Alt's model has for Israel.

While the Noth-Weippert model represents an early attempt that was inclusive of Transjordan (for the conquest framework attached to Transjordan, see Glueck 1939: 243–51; Van Zyl 1960),[8] F. M. Cross's "Reubenite Hypothesis" sets the foundation for current discussions concerning the settlement process east of the Jordan River. Writing on the emergence of Yahwism, Cross registers his own change of opinion with respect to the location of Mount Sinai, relocating it from the Sinai Peninsula (Jebel Musa) to east of the Gulf of Aqabah, in southern Edom / northern Midian (Cross 1988: 59). However, the substance of Cross's article concerns his proposal for the tribe of Reuben's preeminence during the earliest phase of the Israelite settlement in Transjordan. In his synthesis, Cross weaves together evidence from what he considers archaic poetry in the Hebrew Bible, narrative texts (principally Judges, Samuel, and Deuteronomy), and the Mesha Inscription. Cross assumes Reuben's role from the genealogical data of Gen 49:3 and Deut 33:6, which point to Reuben as the "firstborn of Jacob." Later, in Iron II, the tribe of Reuben disappears from references in the biblical text (see 1 Samuel 11 and 2 Sam 24:5). Reuben's initial preeminence is further emphasized by the presence of an

---

8. Glueck outlines the classical migration/conquest of settlement in Transjordan. Van Zyl's *Moabites* (1960) represents one of the earliest attempts to write a formal history of central Transjordan. He too favors the traditional trajectory of migratory incursion of outside tribes (the Israelites) into the region at some point during the Late Bronze.

alleged Reubenite shrine in "the valley opposite Beth-peor"[9] (Deut 3:29; 4:46; 34:6; Josh 13:20).[10] According to Cross, the Mesha Inscription (lines 14–18; ca. 850 B.C.[11]) and what he considers to be P (Priestly texts) accounts in Num 25:6–17 and P's editorial comments in Joshua 22 attest to this early shrine. The primacy of Reuben receives further support from what is typically called the "Epic" strand of textual traditions (see chap. Three). Cross connects Mosaic legal traditions given "beyond the Jordan, in the valley opposite Bet Peor" (Deut 4:44–46) to the tribe of Reuben. Moses' burial place in the same area is added confirmation of the elevated status of Reubenite territory.

Cross views what he identifies as the different traditions behind the controversy at Baal Peor (same locale as Beth-peor [Cross 1988: 50]) in Numbers 25 as giving further credence to his hypothesis. According to this reconstruction, which Cross assigns to the traditional-critical Priestly source, the blame is placed on the Moabites. It is an Aaronid (Phinehas) who saves the day (Num 25:7 = the pro-Aaron tradition in this scheme). In contrast, Cross's Epic version (J) follows a pro-Moses/Reuben tradition (that is, Mushite). The enemies are now the Midianites, and it is Moses who restores order (Num 25:5).

Reuben's religious importance is assigned on the basis of the traditions that link the emergence of Yahwism to southern Edom (Teman, Mount Paran, Midian, and Seir, among others; see Hab 3:3; Stager 1998: 142–49). Based on the absence of material cultural evidence in the Sinai Peninsula during the Late Bronze–Iron I transition and the presence of Late Bronze / Iron I data at Qurrayat (northern Hijaz), he links the emergence of the tribes to the area of northern Midian / southern Edom. Israel's religious identity is particularly highlighted in that Yahwism migrated, as it were, from the regions of Midian in the south to central Transjordan and then across the river into the highlands of what would become Israel proper. The tribe of Reuben is featured prominently in this migration process. Cross links his "proto-Israel" with an early, if ephemeral, Reubenite preeminence to the movements of *Shasu* on the caravan route between Egypt and Midian during the 13th and 12th centuries B.C. (Cross 1988: 60–61; see Rainey 2001; 2007). Thus Cross effectively revives the old Midianite hypothesis which linked the origins of Israel and Yahwism to Midian and to the settlement process in Transjordan (Blenkinsopp 2008).

The Primacy of ʿUmayri

The above background provides the framework within which L. Herr has set the archaeological record recovered from Tall al-ʿUmayri (Herr 1999; 1998). This fortified site, situated at the southern entrance to the Ammonite foothills, has stratified Late Bronze / Iron I levels. Evidence is drawn from a typological study of cooking pots and collared-rim store-jars, using (among

---

9. All Hebrew translations are mine unless otherwise noted.

10. Cross (1988: 55) identifies the valley as ʿAyoun Musa, but its exact location remains disputed (McDonald 2000: 209). See map 1.

11. "[A]nd Kemosh said to me, Go. Take Nebo from Israel. . . . I took from there the vessels of Yahweh." The town of Nebo is probably Kh. al-Mukhayyat (contra Cross).

others) parallels from the el Burnat/Mount Ebal site, which has been interpreted as one of the earliest Iron I highland sites on the West Bank, in the traditional territory of Manasseh (Zertal 1986–87). ʿUmayri is linked regionally
to the sites of Tall Hisban, Tall Jalul, Tall Jawa (JADIS site #23114048), and Tall
Mādabā—all located within 20 km of one another (Herr 1999: 71–72, fig. 1). In
the *Eretz-Israel* 26 (Cross Volume) essay, while Herr admitted that the inhabitants of these sites could represent other groups (e.g., Ammonites, Amorites,
or Moabites), he felt that the convergence of evidence supported the primacy of Reuben proposed by Cross. Based on its geographical location, Tall
al-ʿUmayri could in effect qualify as a Reubenite site, which would then place
the beginning of the settlement process in the 13th century B.C. Significantly,
the other related sites in the region are also included in this early Reubenite
settlement (Herr 1999: 72). According to this reconstruction, simultaneously
or perhaps slightly later, other tribal groups began to settle the highlands of
Cisjordan. The highland culture on both sides of the river may have formed
alliances that, perhaps under Reuben's lead, eventually provided the basis for
a polity named Israel (1999: 72). Although Herr has reduced the significance
of Reuben in his most recent analysis (Herr and Clark 2009), the chronologically derived east-to-west migration from Transjordan to the highlands of
Israel still forms the backbone of his case. Significantly, the chronological
migration approach has continued to hold a certain sway in historical reconstructions of the southern Levant during the Late Bronze / Iron I transition,
particularly concerning the emergence of Israel and Yahwism. In one of his
last works, A. Rainey tracked a similar east (Transjordan)-to-west (Cisjordan)
pattern of migration for the early Israelite tribes (see map 1 above; Rainey
and Notley 2006: 111–12).

Another, lesser-known viewpoint that also emphasizes the importance of
the settlement at ʿUmayri, comes from C. H. Ji. Although he takes the argument in a different geographical direction (1995; 1997b), Ji views the early
Iron I as a period of intensification, followed in late Iron I and early Iron II
by a period of abatement (contra Harrison 2009). Intensification resumed in
Iron IIB and especially in Iron IIC. ʿUmayri is a key site for his late Iron I/
early Iron II abatement phase. The pattern cannot be duplicated at Jawa, but
Ji thinks the situation is reflected in the settlement history of Jalul and Hisban,
although he cautions that the data there is fragmentary (Ji 1995: 122–23).
His analysis of survey data points to a contrasting settlement pattern in the
Irbid-Yarmuk region of northern Jordan, where there was no apparent abatement in late Iron I/early Iron II. The increase in the number of Iron I sites
in the southern regions is taken to reflect a demographic influx moving from
north to south. Thus, according to this particular view of the sedentarization
process, pastoralists of indigenous origins, perhaps from the Irbid Yarmuk
area, gradually expanded and moved southward during the LB II (Ji 1995:
131–32). Following Halpern (1983), Ji links a west-to-east trend to the movement of some early Israelite tribes. This tribal movement may have included
Machir and Reuben (Ji 1995: 134). The presence of collared-rim store-jars in

Jordan is a crucial indicator of his reconstruction. According to Ji, the tribes of Reuben and Machir/Manasseh would have brought these wares in their eastward movement. Ji does allow for the possibility of a concurrent indigenous development of the storage-jar pottery tradition on both sides of the river, but for him the tradition west of the Jordan ultimately takes precedence.

The Tribal Frontier of Central Transjordan

One of the most fruitful discussions about plotting the history of central Jordan during the Iron Age has focused on the social organization of the tribe.[12] The emphasis is quite welcome because tribal dynamics seem to provide a better integration of the social frontier and ecological realities present in Transjordan (see P. Khoury and J. Kostiner, *Tribes and State Formation in the Middle East* [1990; see van der Steen 2010: 172]). Following the work of E. van der Steen in particular, a consensus has now emerged regarding the fundamental importance of tribal categories to reconstruct past identities and historical processes in the southern Levant (van der Steen 2010; 2006; 2004; van der Steen and Smelik 2007). Van der Steen defines tribal dynamics by means of several core ideals. Notions of loyalty (based on real or manipulated kinship ties; see chap. 2 below), flexibility in economic pursuits, territorial mobility, and shifting interrelationship (alliances and conflicts) form the framework "within which society in the Southern Levant has functioned ever since the Early Bronze Age" (van der Steen 2004: 3–5; van der Steen and Smelik 2007: 150). Not even external impositions (e.g., a foreign ruler) can fully eliminate these tribal structures (van der Steen 2004: 5). Her perspective stands as an obvious challenge to more-linear evolutionary models of sociopolitical organization. In its classic form (see Service 1962), the linear evolutionary scheme follows a chronologically meaningful sequence from the egalitarian "band" to the "tribe" (with some level of differences) to the "chiefdom" (two-tiered settlement hierarchy) to the final, implicitly more-developed and stratified, society of the "state." In contrast, for van der Steen, these complex stratified societies could still be referred to as tribal; hence the designation of "tribal kingdom" in recent literature (van der Steen 2010: 172; Bienkowski 2009).

In their now-classic formulation, Ø. LaBianca and R. Younker (1995; see LaBianca 1999) spell out a processual interpretation for the highlands of central Transjordan. Based on the premise that societal institutions are structured to facilitate the procurement of food and the securing of water sources, the tribe was the social organization that evolved as a "unit of subsistence." For the agricultural area of the central plateau, it would be "land-tied" (or sedentary) tribalism. Tribes organized themselves both at the local level and at the macro

---

12. For an attempt at understanding the social organizational context of the highlands in Cisjordan during the early Iron Age, see R. D. Miller's *Chieftains of the Highland Clans* (2005). Miller's vision of Iron I Cisjordan as a hierarchical society with regional centers ("complex chiefdom") has been criticized, perhaps unfairly, as too limiting in a social landscape that probably was too diverse to be described under one narrow organizational rubric (Edelman 2006).

level in the form of "imposed supra-tribal polities" (LaBianca and Younker 1995: 403). In addition to organizing around the procurement of foodways, one of the roles of these polities (taking the example of the modern tribes of the Hashemite Kingdom of Jordan) was to mobilize the various tribes in response to external threats. In an Iron II context, therefore, the ruler of a supratribal polity should not be understood within the usual nation-state framework but within a tribal setting made up of both nomadic and sedentary polities. The Mesha Inscription, which points to Mesha as both king (*mlk*) and chief shepherd (*nqd*; see 2 Kgs 3:4), is used to support this argument. The image of "pastoral" kingship stands in contrast to the city-state notion of kingship (LaBianca and Younker 1995: 408–9).[13] This tribal configuration is then used to aid in the difficult task of assigning territories to specific tribes within the region (Ammonites, Moabites, Reubenites, and Gadites, in particular). Thus, in typical frontier language, shifting dependence on pastoralism (range-tied) and/or agriculture (land-tied) caused the borders between these tribes to fluctuate.

While the above traits seem to cross sociohistorical boundaries, a real debate has developed with respect to the particulars of a tribal identity in specific historical settings. In this regard, as B. Routledge has pointed out, LaBianca's model runs the risk of blurring historical lines. Routledge questions the notion that kin-based tribal groupings cannot be organized along territorial lines within a "state" social structure (Routledge 2000b; see 2004). Based on his reading of the Mesha Inscription (ca. 850 B.C. / Iron IIB), Routledge argues that Mesha's kingship in the 9th century B.C. may not have been established on fluid territorial "tribal" control based strictly on descent (what is called a "segmentary-lineage" model). Instead, according to him, the Mesha Inscription offers a vision of the land of Moab as a unified territory under the political control of Mesha. Thus force and consent work together in what he calls "hegemony" (see Bienkowski 2009: 10). In Routledge's exegesis of the Mesha Inscription, social segmentation (hierarchy) and political organization are deliberately and structurally brought together in the syntax of the inscription. This proposed social structure is based on B. Stein's pyramidal model of the segmentary state, in which social segmentation encompasses *both* lineage (in the case of Mesha, around Dibon, see "Mesha . . . the Dibonite," line 1) *and* territories outside his kin-based authority, the land of Moab north and south of Dibon/Karhoh[14] (Routledge 2000b: 234–43).

P. Bienkowski has questioned whether one can speak of a hierarchical social structure in a tribal-kingdom setting such as in the time of Mesha in the 9th cent. B.C. (Bienkowski 2009). In his view, to speak of a Moabite *state* and

---

13. D. Master, in his discussion of state formation in 10th-century B.C. Israel (Iron IIA), argues for shifts between sedentary and nomadic lifestyles without a great change in the relationship between the ruler and the ruled (Weber 1978: 954–56 in Master 2001: 128).

14. Probably Kir-hareseth in the Old Testament (2 Kgs 3:25; cf. van der Steen and Smelik 2007: 147).

resulting identity is anachronistic and represents a modern construct imposed on the available data (2009: 10–11). What is particularly damaging to this model, according to Bienkowski, is the alleged organizational transfer from tribal heterarchical (decentralized) ideals to hierarchical structures brought about by the new "king." To be sure, there is truth to the tribal decentralized impulse as a persistent and transcendent category, even after a tribal "strong man" emerges as king over the people (van der Steen 2010: 172). Furthermore, claims of covariance between certain pottery types and ethnic identities in the Iron II should be based on solid contextual evidence (Bienkowski 2009: 8; see chap. 2 below). However, Harrison notes that the Mesha Inscription does seem to project new territorial realities and a resulting group identity based on Mesha, the Dibonite's building programs and territorial claims over northern Moab (Harrison 2009: 30–32). Furthermore, to omit discussions of the Egyptian and biblical documentary sources (Harrison 2009: 30–32)—which, in the case of the latter, clearly attest a Moab polity and identity during the Iron II—reflects an overly skeptical view of the value of these texts for historical reconstruction. It also sets some helpful boundaries on the application of ethnohistorical realities in Late Ottoman tribal contexts (van der Steen 2010: 172). While these data are indeed valuable and I embrace them in this book, they must be used with sufficient flexibility and, ultimately, be subservient to the available ancient sources.

The tribal-state-formation debate exposes some of the problems with the processual nature of the LaBianca model when it is applied strictly to questions of state formation: territorial boundaries may not be so fluid, at least in the Iron IIB period (Harrison 2009). In other words, these tribal processes are also historically conditioned, as the Mesha Inscription (and 2 Kings 3) seems to indicate. The notion of borders and tribal kingship, particularly as it relates to the region north of the Wadi Mujib (biblical Arnon) in premonarchical settings will be discussed further when biblical and Moabite documentary sources are examined in chap. 3.

Summary

Many studies of the Late Bronze–Iron I transition period have emphasized the inherently fluid nature of the central highlands of Transjordan. This sensitivity is reflected in explanations about shifting subsistence strategies in light of the ecological realities of the region during this period. In the classic shifting-frontier model, pastoralists could become agriculturalists and vice versa, which in turn reflected long-term trends. Likewise, some discussions about social organization note the equally fluid nature of tribal societies. Thus, tribal groups within a shifting social frontier presumably presupposed considerable flexibility in both territorial and social terms. Alliances could be made (and broken) frequently. Likewise, boundaries could be altered on account of these shifting alliances.

However, when it comes to discussions of ethnicity during the Late Bronze / Iron I and early Iron I periods, substantially different approaches exist. Chapter 2 sets a theoretical framework in which to identify ethnic identities in past cultures and plots the variegated answers to the question in current discussions about the emergence of Israel in the southern Levant.

CHAPTER TWO

Theories of Tribal Ethnicities

Over 30 years ago, C. Kramer's article "Pots and Peoples" (1977) outlined some of the problems involved with linking an ethnic group to a ceramic assemblage.

The association of Habur Ware with the Hurrians was originally proposed (Mallowan 1956) on the basis of the distinct geopolitical sphere in northern Mesopotamia where the ware was attested. However, historical sources indicate that the region alternated between phases of political stability and fluidity during the floruit of Habur Ware (ca. 1900–1600 B.C.). In addition, as Kramer noted, the paucity of Hurrian linguistic data (limited mostly to personal names) and the ethnolinguistic diversity of the region where Habur Ware was attested make it extremely difficult to isolate a Hurrian presence at the sites. Relying on ethnographic data, Kramer also identified an economic interdependence between pastoralists and agriculturalists. Even the traditional ethnic designations *Arab* and *Kurd* seemed to reflect local social and political boundaries rather than cultural boundaries in the region (for a similar phenomenon, see the Hutu/Tutsi discussion on p. 19 below). Consequently, Kramer concluded that this fluid and variegated context makes it impossible to link the Habur tradition to a specific ethnic group, whether Hurrian, Assyrian, or any other. Assigning ethnicity to material culture should be based on more than one category of material culture and should include textual data, if at all possible (Kramer 1977: 94–108).

Today, her synthesis is remarkably in tune with current anthropological discussions concerning the question of ethnic boundaries in antiquity (see Derks and Roymans 2009; see also van Soldt 2005). Questions about whether ethnic identity can be identified in the archaeological record continue to elicit various answers ranging from a confident "yes" (where material culture and ethnic identity nicely coincide) to more agnostic postures (cultural and ethnic identities should not be equated; Derks and Roymans 2009: 3).

When we turn to the southern Levantine context in general and Transjordan in particular, a similar debate is reflected in recent discussions, with a tilt toward the cultural-ethnic coincidence end of the spectrum (see Dever 2009; 2007; Faust 2006; Kletter 2006; Killebrew 2005). Other factors dominating these discussions concern what constitutes admissible evidence. Are we to focus on the material-cultural data as our sole primary source? Should a carefully defined anthropological model of ethnic identity serve as a map to plot ethnic identities in the past? How much or how little should documentary data (such as biblical texts) influence our conclusions?

Within the context of Transjordan, all the above issues are important for addressing the question whether a territorially defined ethnic group (for example, Reuben) should be singled out on the basis of the available material-cultural and textual evidence. More specifically, if we acknowledge the fluid nature of a frontier zone, particularly during transitional phases, we should at least be prepared to examine the possibility that this shifting environment affected ethnic identities as well.

The Primordial-Instrumental Continuum

The abstract term *ethnicity* appeared for the first time in anthropological literature in the 1940s (Banks 1996: 4). In its broadest sense, *ethnicity* refers to the field of study that classifies peoples and relations between them. The term relates to a group's essence or to the qualities belonging to a certain group—in other words, a group's identity. Thus, the lines between ethnicity/ethnic identity (used interchangeably in the literature; Hutchinson and Smith 1996: 4; see J. C. Miller 2008) and social entities, such as a tribe, are sometimes hard to disentangle.

The historical linguistics of the term are well documented. Ethnicity and the adjectival form "ethnic" find their etymology in the Greek *ethnos.* Greek lexicons list a relatively consistent semantic range. By the 1st century A.D., the word came to refer generally to the non-Greek-speaking populations (Tonkin et al. 1989: 11–12; Lentz 1995: 305). Until recently, the most common understanding of *ethnos* evoked concepts of race and bloodlines and phenotypical features. *Webster's New International Dictionary* captures that consensus by defining *ethnic* as "relating to a community of physical and mental traits in races, or designating groups of races of mankind discriminated on the basis of common customs and characters." The primary conduit of ethnic identity is channeled through bloodlines and related to phenotypical (physical) features (see Jones 1997: 40–45).

The primordialist perspective has received its most succinct treatment in the work of C. Geertz (1963), who remains the main voice of this view of ethnic identity (see Nash 1989; Shils 1957). Geertz identified what he considers the "ineffable" components of ethnic identity (1963):

- Assumed blood ties ("untraceable but yet sociologically rich kinship")
- Phenotypical physical features (skin color, facial form, stature, hair type, etc.)
- Language
- Region
- Religion
- Custom

As Geertz elaborates, it is clear that these traits are nonnegotiable, and they are received at birth. The primordial bonds of ethnic identity provide a sense of natural affinity that are even stronger than social interaction (Geertz 1963: 110).

Beginning in the early 20th century, and then probably as an aftermath of World War II, primordial discussions of ethnicity have avoided the biologically charged language of race[1] and have used cultural categories instead (Jones 1997: 45; Tonkin et al. 1989: 114). The turning point came with F. Barth's edited volume *Ethnic Groups and Boundaries* (1969). In his groundbreaking study, Barth questioned the value of the *etic* (objective) primordial definition of ethnicity and proposed instead an *emic* (subjective) definition (Barth 1996: 75–82). Ethnicity is defined in bipolar terms, in light of the "other" (see Malkin 2001: 12–13). In contrast to primordialism, his instrumentalist approach to ethnic identity focused on self-awareness and self-definition. The disruptions caused by political and economic changes represent some of the salient mechanisms through which existing groups reconstitute themselves in pursuit of shared common interests. As a result, new ethnic identities are formed (see Bentley 1987).

The competing approaches of instrumentalism and primordialism have sparked an ongoing debate. On the one hand, Geertzian primordialism is criticized particularly for being an abstract concept, devoid of social significance (Eller and Coughlin 1993; Jones 1997: 69). The determinism of bloodlines and cultural background given at birth is rejected. On the other hand, some have questioned the instrumental reliance on socioeconomic categories. To define *ethnicity* in socioeconomic terms alone presents the risk of creating definitions that are so open-ended and subjective that ethnicity can be reduced to mere "interest groups" (Jones 1997: 75; Malkin 2001: 15–16). Subsistence strategies may help shape ethnic identities, but they need not be the only defining factor. If ethnic identity is attached to economic and political relationships alone, the cultural dimension of ethnic identity ends up playing a subservient role (Jones 1997: 77). Past and present ethnic-based conflicts around the world certainly cast a shadow on the idea that ethnicity can be viewed strictly in instrumentalist terms and be reduced to mere social "invention" (Malkin 2001: 1).

Instead, it seems that any definition of ethnicity should be set within a particular social context. Primordial traits should be subsumed to the inevitability of social processes. For some groups, religious affiliation may constitute the main characteristic of ethnicity, while for others, it will be phenotypical (physical) or linguistic features. Also, what characterizes a group in one context may be different in another. Thus, it is possible that any of these markers may be manipulated according to certain priorities or ideologies.

---

1. A trajectory made infamous by A. Rosenberg's *Der Mythus des zwanzigsten Jahrhunderts* (1930).

The Hutu-Tutsi conflict in the Great Lakes region of Central Africa presents a striking example of the fluidity of the elements that convey ethnic identity. In his reassessment, R. Lemarchand demonstrates how primordial categories have been manipulated to justify the bloodshed. In the case of the Hutu and Tutsi, the primordial categories of bloodlines, phenotypical features, language, and geographical boundaries cannot be singled out as clearly determining ethnic markers. Both groups speak the same language (Kirundi), both share the same political organization (monarchy) and, prior to their conflicts of the past 50 years (1965, 1972, 1988, 1991; Lemarchand 2003: 211), they lived peacefully with each other for centuries. Their society comprised complex hierarchies based on power, status, and privilege that "*cut across* [emphasis mine] ethnic identities" (Lemarchand 2003: 209). The semantic range of the designation *Hutu* also indicates a much more fluid situation than a primordial approach might warrant. Although *Hutu* has the expected cultural meaning in terms of ethnic identity, the term also refers to a social status as "social subordinate" (*fils social*; 2003: 213). The closest one might come to ethnic identity on the basis of a typical ethnic feature is in terms of occupations. The Tutsi are usually pastoralists whereas the Hutu are agriculturalists. However, as R. Lemarchand cautions, due to their complex economic ties, even this category cannot be cast in rigid terms (2003: 212). In fact, the primordial lines are so blurred that, in the 1930s, one observer characterized the Hutu and Tutsi as sharing a common culture (Zuure 1931: 14, in Lemarchand 2003: 216).

In spite of these shared traits, the Hutu/Tutsi conflicts have been framed in the light of primordial ethnic ideologies. Lemarchand explains this manipulation of perceived primordial ties on account of social inequality as the primary factor in ethnic identity. With the degradation of their traditional, complex sociopolitical hierarchies, the two characterizations of Hutus as "ethnic" and as economically subordinate to the Tutsi became increasingly one and the same. The socioeconomic and ethnic statuses of each group were simplified, resulting in "ethnic" warfare between the two groups (Lemarchand 2003: 217–18). Thus, in the case of the Hutu-Tutsi, although ethnic identity has been assumed to be primordial, when the situation is examined within its social context, their ethnicity takes on characteristics that are clearly instrumental—that is, shaped by socioeconomic and cultural factors.

Dynamic "Habitus"

F. Barth and M. Weber before him recognized the importance of social dynamics and linked the variables of ethnic identity to social organization and customs (Barth 1969: 10; 1994: 12; Weber 1978: 389–95). This attention to a specific social context is especially important in our case because the concern is for a *past* as opposed to a present ethnic identity. Although ethnicity in a tribal society looks significantly different from ethnicity in a state-ordered society in a modern context (as ethnographic data indicate; see Keyes 1981; Geertz 1963; Glazer and Moynihan 1970), these social considerations should also contribute toward achieving a greater understanding of the particulars of ethnicity in ancient societies. This social-contextual approach to ethnicity thus requires that an appropriate theoretical framework be in place to help recognize ethnic change.

P. Bourdieu's theory of practice towers as one of the most influential contemporary sociological models of human practice (see Grenfell 2008; Jenkins 2002; Postone et al. 1993). His work is not easy to decipher due in part to the technical language he used and, not unlike Weber, the cross-disciplinary nature of his approach (Webb et al. 2002: 1–4). His theory of practice hinged on a departure from structuralism after his fieldwork in colonial Algeria (Bourdieu 1977: 3–4). The break from conventional practice in sociology was not a total abandonment of objectivism, however, but rather, an attempt to introduce subjectivism to the discussion in social research. For Bourdieu, objectivism and subjectivism should be retained, since the empirical and the theoretical provide checks and balances for each other (Webb et al. 2002: 35). The individuality and intentionality inherent in subjectivism are balanced by objectivism's "laws, rules, and systems" (2002: 36).

Bourdieu's attempt to resolve the etic-emic conflict is manifested in his well-known theory of practice based on *habitus* (Bourdieu 1977; see Webb et al. 2002: 31–32). *Habitus* is carefully defined so that any theoretical framework applied to the field of research is in feedback with the subjective limitations of the researcher and the subjective realities encountered in the field.[2] The usefulness of the notion lies in its model of culture in which identities are shaped alternatively by self-awareness and by "passed-on" social norms—that is, by "systems of durable, transposable dispositions" (Bourdieu 1977: 72; see Jones 1997). Nevertheless, these objective structures are themselves subjected to adaptations, "collectively orchestrated without being the product of the orchestrating action of a conductor" (Bourdieu 1977: 72).

In recent years, S. Jones has introduced the concept of *habitus* to the study of ethnic identity in antiquity (Jones 1997; 1999; see Morgan 2009). Her own approach builds on the work of G. Bentley (1987), who applied Bourdieu's approach to questions of ethnicity. In an attempt to move the discussion beyond the primordial-instrumental debate (see Glazer and Moynihan 1970; Epstein 1978: 112), Bentley steered the discussion toward a balance between the unstated and inherent dimensions found in ethnic sentiments. He found in Bourdieu's *habitus* a suitable model that avoids some of the particularity and subjectivity associated with instrumentalism (Bentley 1987: 48). A greater appreciation for temporal (that is, historical, as opposed to strictly social) per-

---

2. According to Bourdieu, a cultural field may be "institutions, rules, rituals, conventions, categories, designations and appointments which constitute an objective hierarchy, and which produce and authorize certain discourse and activities" (Webb et al. 2002: xi).

spectives as well as the incorporation of both individual and corporate dimensions of ethnic identity mark this approach (Bentley 1987: 49–50).

Following Bourdieu's class-struggle approach in defining *habitus*, Bentley plotted ethnic change in the context of regimes of domination. Ethnic authority figures (for instance, elders in a tribal society) may be aware of their strategies of maintaining dependent relationships with their subjects. However, *habitus*, the unconscious element, is what allows these "structures of domination" to perpetuate themselves. In the words of Bourdieu, these structures must be "euphemized" in order to survive (Bourdieu 1977: 196 in Bentley 1987: 42). Variations in ethnicity occur when shared dispositions are disrupted through changes usually identified as political and economic. According to Bentley, these shifts can be identified either as revitalization of "existing self-conceptions and modes of domination" or as a "shift in personal identity as new modes of domination are instituted in response to changed environmental circumstances" (Bentley 1987: 45). Although his class-struggle approach to ethnic change is not persuasive (Jones 1997; Yelvington 1991) and the underlying determinism unappealing, his work remains a useful baseline for moving beyond the instrumental/primordial debate. Disruptions in the *habitus* are bound to affect ethnic identity at some level.

With this framework in place, S. Jones (1997) turned her attention to the formation of ethnic identities in the past. She built on Bourdieu's practice theory to help understand ethnic identity (Jones 1997: 87–105). As part of a contextual approach to the question, she supplied a historical overview of the study of ethnicity in archaeology and sought to integrate multiple lines of evidence. This methodology has the advantage of opening new avenues of research in this protracted debate (1997: 125–26).

Jones altered the notion of *habitus* by carefully answering the potential charge of determinism that could be leveled at Bourdieu and Bentley. The category of "passed-on" characteristics, however, was preserved. Since these traits belong to a social context, however, they would be affected by a variety of other factors as well. Jones's approach is presented with enough flexibility that it may be applicable to varied sociohistorical domains. It is up to the researcher to fill in the details of what constitutes "passed-on" features. Where Bentley oriented his definition of ethnic identity from within the group and its *habitus* (Bentley 1987: 173, cited in Jones 1997: 90), Jones shifted the trajectory and maintained instead that ethnicity is a "consciousness of difference" rather than of similarities (1997: 94). Moving on further from the typical Bourdieu approach, instead of a rigid one-to-one relationship between *habitus* and ethnicity, she considered the variables of interaction between different groups. In other words, ethnic identity may be affected by the degree of interaction with other groups. In her model, *habitus* and ethnicity are cast in terms of dynamic but not necessarily covariant relationships (Jones 1997: 97).

In reactions to her study, Jones has been chided for an apparent distaste for culture history, as though she rejects the very idea that material assemblages carry cultural values (see R. D. Miller 2004: 56; Joffe 2001: 211; Dever 2001: 116). If I understand her correctly, however, she does not question the possibility of identifying a particular assemblage that may have cultural (ethnic) implications. Rather, her issue is with the assumption by cultural-historical scholars that an assemblage must necessarily be linked to a particular ethnic identity. She does not appear to rule out the possibility that ethnicity can be recognized in the material record on the basis of typology, seriation, and stylistic variations (1997: 112–16). Drawing on ethnoarchaeology (see David and Kramer 2001; Watson 1999), she asserts that production strategies (*chaîne opératoire*, Lemonnier 1986) reveal deliberate choices made by the potter and that these choices hold valuable information concerning stylistic matters (Jones 1997: 112–16; see Gosselain 1998; David and Kramer 2001: 168–224).

However, because style (or the absence of style; see Faust 2006) itself is a highly adaptable, fluid, and active medium of communication, these stylistic variations may or may not necessarily correspond to ethnic boundaries (see David and Kramer 2001: 218–24; Jones 1997: 112–16; Stark 1998; Gosselain 1998). Fluctuations of this sort have been documented in different social and ecological environments, including New Guinea (Welsch and Terrell 1998) and northern Cameroon (MacEachern 1998). To complicate matters further, whenever stylistic variations do correspond to ethnic boundaries in a particular social context, other elements of style freely cross ethnic boundaries in the *same* social environment. In support of these variations, Jones cites I. Hodder's famed ethnographic study of the Baringo District in northern Kenya (Jones 1997: 114; see Hodder 1982).

To maneuver a way out of this cultural-functional stalemate, Jones proposed that her dynamic view of *habitus* provided a suitable basis for examining this fluid record. Ethnic markers (or, "objectified" cultural practices [Jones 1997: 128] in the material culture) should not be viewed separately from their social context, which is subject to "instrumental contingencies" (1997: 128). On the one hand, the fluidity of the shared dispositions within a particular social context makes it very difficult to establish a general rule in terms of what elements of culture might be viewed as reliable ethnic markers. These "passed-on" features of culture are eminently adaptable and undergo changes and shifts linked to specific socioeconomic and historical circumstances, especially interaction with other groups. On the other hand, ethnic identity may still be identified through the convergence of lines of evidence including the material record. The aim, therefore, should be to set the specific sociohistorical context in order to ascertain which cultural elements reflect ethnic identity and, if possible, which elements underwent transformations that were linked to ethnic change.

Jones has provided an effective starting point for discussion concerning the reconstruction of ethnic identity in past cultures. Furthermore, her dynamic approach to *habitus* is flexible enough to include many components found in a given social domain. There are some elements that remain unstated, however.

Since she appeals to a multivariate approach that presumably includes textual sources, the question of ethnolinguistics (that is, the relationship between a certain language or dialect and ethnic identity) deserves further theoretical attention (Derks and Roymans 2009: 2–4; Derks 2009). In fairness, since she was concerned with ethnicity in the material-cultural record, there are inherent limits on what can be covered. Nevertheless, this question is especially relevant with respect to past cultures that have left many textual records (e.g., ancient Israel or ancient Greece; Hutchinson and Smith 1996: 10–11). Thus a related question concerning the relationship between material culture and ethnicity applies to the relationship between language and ethnicity: to what degree did these languages communicate ethnic identity?

The answer to this question bears a striking resemblance to the material culture–ethnicity debate. The analysis of ethnicity in ethnographic data, though only in its infant stages, seems to indicate a fluid situation where no one-to-one relationship can be guaranteed. For example, in New Guinea, arguably the focus of some of the best ethnographic research available for ethnolinguistics (between 1,900 and 2,100 languages; Terrell 2001: 199), some language groups may in fact share common cultural values, trade, and social relations with others, even though they do not speak the same language at all. Along the Sepik coastline of New Guinea (700 km), for example, where over 60 languages have been documented, these linguistically discrete groups are nevertheless joined together through enduring social ties of "inherited friendship" between "people, *families* [emphasis mine], and communities" (Terrell 2001: 206; see Sillitoe 1978: 11). Likewise, ethnolinguists find it notoriously difficult to distinguish a language from a dialect, especially in the case of extensive contacts between dialects and neighboring languages (Terrell 2001: 213). One conclusion drawn from this is that the only real difference between a language and a dialect is to be found at the social level (Sebba 1997: 3, cited in Terrell 2001: 213).

In historical linguistics generally and Northwest Semitics in particular, the relationship between languages and ethnic identities reflects similar complexities (see Rainey 2007: 42). In the case of the Arameans, for example, we are only beginning to understand what constituted an "Aramean" in the first millennium B.C. (Dion 1997: 7; Von Dassow 1999: 249). Similarly, because the commonalities in the language of the Mesha Inscription and Standard Biblical Hebrew outweigh the differences (Young 1993: 33–38; Parker 2002), language alone will not be sufficient for plotting ethnic identities and boundaries between Iron II Israel and Moab.[3] The problem is exacerbated during the premonarchic period. The presence of dialects in Biblical Hebrew, especially

---

3. The same caution applies to earlier periods. Thus, Rainey's Aramean/Aramaic proposal to explain Israelite origins is ultimately not persuasive since it is based on very limited linguistic data (e.g., presence/absence of *wayyiqtol*; see Rainey 2007).

in texts long viewed as archaic[4] may be warranted on the basis of attested morphological variations (Young 1993: 126). However, to plot ethnic identities *only* on the basis of these variations seems to represent too great a leap in terms of both quantitative and qualitative data (Garr 1985; see also Rollston 2011). Nevertheless, in the case of material-cultural and ethnic covariance, one cannot discount the likelihood that, in certain contexts, a strong bond between ethnic identity and language may in fact have existed, even in frontier settings (Derks 2009).

In summary, when plotting past expressions of ethnic identity, one should ideally supply evidence drawn from stylistic patterning in the material culture and competing textual sources that expresses both self-identification and contrasting views. Relevant ethnohistorical and ethnoarchaeological data should also supplement the picture to paint a social context in which the dynamics of the particular ethnicities may be discerned. However, this convergence of data may not always be possible to find (see Kramer 1977: 95). Nevertheless, application of some of the lessons learned in the field of ethnicity studies will undoubtedly help in interpreting the evidence available for the early Israelite settlement in highland Transjordan (and Cisjordan) with greater theoretical sensitivity than has sometimes been achieved.

Problems with Current Perceptions of Iron I Ethnicity

The field of ethnic studies in the southern Levant is dominated by discussions about the emergence of ancient Israel and thus cannot be examined apart from theories of settlement (see chap. 1). Despite all the debate, the prevailing theories of sedentarization of pastoral nomads (Finkelstein 1994; 1988; Levy and Holl 2002; Herr 2000: 177; Faust 2006; Rainey 2007) and ruralization of urban populations (Dever 2003; Stager 1998; Killebrew 2005) do concur that the highland population consisted of heterogeneous groups that appeared as a result of the ferment caused by the collapse of the Late Bronze. The point of contention, of course, is the identity of these highlanders.

A survey of the literature[5] reveals that the cultural approach, in spite of its contested status in anthropological circles (see Whittaker 2009; J. C. Miller 2008), retains a certain explanatory attraction in southern Levantine archaeology. Regardless of the problems related to covariance, the relationship between certain aspects of the material culture and ethnic identity remains an appealing solution to the question of ethnic identity during the Iron I.

The Case for Covariance

Perhaps the most developed cultural perspective has come from W. Dever. Although his definition of ethnic identity appeals to F. Barth's instrumen-

---

4. See recent discussions that have questioned the notion of Archaic Biblical Hebrew (Young and Rezetko 2008: 335; Young, Rezetko, and 2008; see chap. 3).

5. For a helpful review of current scholarship, see Faust 2006: 20–29.

tal construct, his understanding of ethnic identity appears to tilt toward the primordial end of the spectrum.[6] While social processes are acknowledged (for example, social taboos; Dever 2003), in Dever's view, the material-cultural assemblage of the Iron I highlands in Israel points to an identifiable ethnic group who in turn will later become the Israelite Iron II polity: "the Israelite people" (2009: 92) or, as he initially called them, the "Proto-Israelites" (1995: 206–7).

Dever's views are well publicized (2009; 2007; 2003; 2001; 1995) and can be summed up as follows. In spite of Late Bronze continuities, the documented new assemblage in the highlands is linked to the "Israel" of the Merneptah Stele (Dever 2001: 117–18; 1995: 204; see Yurco 1997; Stager 1985b). The principal ethnic marker in his analysis is the four-room house (Dever 2003: 197). The absence of pig bones in the highlands is taken to indicate a social taboo that also reflects Israelite ethnic identity. In fact, "the presence or absence of pig bones may thus be our best archaeological indicator of the much-debated 'ethnic boundaries' and their physical extent" (Dever 2001: 113). To a lesser degree, the same principle of covariance is proposed for the collared pithoi and cooking pots (Dever 1995: 205). In addition, since Philistine material culture seems to correspond to a different ethnic group on the coastal plain, Dever argues that we have a similar ethnocultural occurrence in the highlands (Dever 2001: 115–16). Both A. Killebrew and A. Faust have essentially developed this line of argument more fully. Faust has especially answered the questions of a cultural covariance approach—namely, the presence of the four-room house layout outside Israelite territorial boundaries (see, among others, Finkelstein 1996) and its apparent antecedents with Late Bronze houses (see Holladay 1997: 106–7). Other questions relate to the documented Late Bronze–Iron I ceramic continuity and the claim that pig bones reflect functional-ecological realities rather than cultural-ethnic priorities (Faust 2006).

While the advocates of covariance for the highlands of Israel have made a repeated and sustained case, questions still linger, especially in light of the distributional data from Transjordan. The many subtypes in the four-room house layout (see Faust 2006: 72) compound the difficulties in singling one particular group connected to this style. It seems instead that such a generic layout, with antecedents in prior phases of the settlement history of the region, was adopted and adapted by the variegated elements of the population, whether indigenous or newcomers on both sides of the Jordan River (see Ji

---

6. Relying on Barth, Dever views ethnic groups as "biologically self-perpetuating." They share a "fundamental, recognizable, relatively uniform set of cultural values, including language." They constitute a "partly independent 'interaction sphere'"; have "a membership that defines itself, as well as being defined by others"; and perpetuate a "sense of separate identity both by developing rules for maintaining 'ethnic boundaries' as well as for participating in inter-ethnic social encounters" (Dever 2003: 192–93; see 1995: 201).

1997a).[7] Thus, the probability that this type of house would be generated by an Israelite ethnic group *exclusively* is too low to be historically meaningful (see Bloch-Smith 2003: 406).

Likewise, to single out Israelite ethnic identity on the basis of a cluster of ceramic types within a particular region is not without problems (see R. D. Miller 2004). Since the excavations at Tell el-Fûl (Albright 1924), the central highland regions have been identified as the distributional heartland of the collared pithoi (Shiloh: Finkelstein 1993: figs. 6:48–49, 51, 58; south Samaria region: Finkelstein 1997: fig. 8.268:4, 5, 7, and passim; Giloh: Mazar 1981; el Burnat/Mount Ebal: Zertal 1986–87). However, Megiddo Stratum VI points to a diversified assemblage in some parts of the lowlands.[8] Though not predominant, collared store-jars are nevertheless a significant part of the corpus (about 10%; see Esse 1992: table 1; Harrison 2004: 31–32). Collared pithoi are attested at Dan (Biran 1989), in the Galilee region (at Kinnereth: Fritz 1999: fig. 9:1–2; Gal 1992: fig. 5:1), and on the coast at Tel Nami (Artzy 1994; 1993: 1097). Ongoing excavations at central Transjordan sites (see chap. 5) continue to confirm the presence of this ceramic type so that the question posed by the four-room house is duplicated with respect to collared pithoi: should we view this archaeological trait as uniquely Israelite? Arguably, a case can be made (as Faust and others do),[9] but its presence outside the traditional Israelite boundaries requires that these conclusions remain tentative.[10]

Turning to the question of foodways as an ethnic marker, an *argument de taille* is the presence or absence of porcine remains in the archaeological record. It is argued that the virtual absence of pig bones in the highland sites and their well-attested presence in lowland sites speak to ritual taboos enforced in the highland culture regarding pork consumption (see Faust 2006: 35–40 for a solid discussion). It is worth noting the underlying assumption that these settlers abided by some dietary restrictions available to them. Nevertheless, the case that the distributional data speak more of ecological than socioethnic categories (Hesse 1995: 217–20) will be hard to dismiss for some.

---

7. As an illustration from a modern context (with its inherent limitations as an explanatory model), the famous timber house of the Alps, the "chalet," may a priori signal Swiss ethnicity until one realizes that the architecture is also typical of Savoie (France), Tirol (Austria and Italy), and Bavaria. As such, many subtypes do exist (even between cantons in Switzerland), but the generic architecture, adopted and adapted by various groups, transcends ethnic boundaries.

8. As Faust notes, collared pithoi are virtually absent at ʿAfula Stratum III (Iron I) a site west of Megiddo in the Jezreel Valley (Faust 2006: 195).

9. Faust cautions against identifying the collared pithos as a direct ethnic marker. Instead, he views it as a symbol of "ethnic behavior." Even if one disagrees with his co-variant approach, this kind of nuancing is precisely what is needed to move forward in this protracted debate (Faust 2006: 202).

10. At the risk of redundancy, I make the same observation about cooking-pot morphology. These ceramic groups reflect broad regional trends that extend beyond the central highlands of Cisjordan (Finkelstein 1996; Schloen 2002; Routledge 2000a; Stager 1998).

The stylistic distinctiveness of the Philistine material culture is not in question. Nevertheless, even though the Philistine settlement supports the "pots and peoples" connection, caution must be exercised and conclusions will vary, *depending* on the particular cultural zone under investigation. For instance, it is true that covariance is found in the heartland of Philistia proper (Killebrew 2005; Stager 1995), but in the Jezreel (Megiddo) and Jordan valleys and the Akko plain, where mixed horizons are present, Philistine ware may not necessarily reflect Philistine ethnicity. Similarly, during the Iron II, the presence of so-called Samaria Ware and locally produced Assyrian Palace Ware at Tell Keisan does not automatically mean ethnic Assyrians were present on site (Humbert 1993: 864–67). Thus, the link between ethnic identity and stylistic variations in *transitional zones* is much more difficult to establish. Consequently, Philistine covariance on the coastal plain may not necessarily "work" for the highland frontier (contrast Dever 2001: 115–16).

In summary, while for some the question of covariance is settled, for others there are enough departures from the proverbial "one-to-one" relationship to create suspicion that other dynamics should be considered to explain the available data. For instance, how do primordial-leaning definitions of ethnicity fit within the social dynamics present in tribal frontier zones (see Dever 2003: 180–81)?

The Case for Functionalism

G. London's research has pioneered the functional study of Iron I ethnicity in the highlands of Cisjordan (London 1989). In her case for the functional use of the collared pithos, London draws on comparative data from the Mari texts, North African pastoralism (1989: 40–41), and her own ethnoarchaeological research on Cyprus concerning pottery manufacturing technologies (1989: 43). With M. Ibrahim's publication of the collared pithoi in Transjordan (Ibrahim 1978), her (and Ibrahim's) conclusions were the first cracks in the rigid correlation between material culture and Israelite ethnicity in biblical archaeological circles (London 1989; see Albright 1940). On the basis of distributional evidence, she reached the conclusion that the collared pithos reflects a highland rural lifestyle rather than ethnic identity.

As we have seen, however, an argument based on presence-absence, whether cultural or functional, does not appear to be an open and shut case. Esse's reexamination of Megiddo Stratum VI (urban phase in the 11th century B.C.; Esse 1992: 95; Harrison 2004) undermines this dichotomy between rural and urban lifestyle. As Esse observed, Stratum VI contained a larger number of collared pithoi than previously indicated, although still a smaller amount proportionally than at highland sites (Esse 1992: 93–94; see Artzy 1993). Thus, while this presumed rural vessel type appears predominantly in the rural highlands, it should not be seen exclusively as a socioeconomic marker.

The main proponent of a functionalist perspective on Iron I ethnicity is I. Finkelstein. He defined ethnic identity according to an instrumental approach, although primordial traits such as phenotypical features were not excluded (Finkelstein 1996: 203). This balanced perspective, however, is not demonstrated with respect to textual sources. Relying on Cohen's instrumental view (1978: 397–98), which emphasizes the manipulation of descent, Finkelstein dismisses Israel's own version of its past as impossible to retrieve (Finkelstein 1996: 204). Consequently, in his view, biblical data are irrelevant to the discussion of Iron I ethnicity (Finkelstein and Mazar 2007: 55, 74). In an earlier study, citing a lack of consensus concerning the nature and location of "Israel" in the Merneptah Stele (ca. 1206 B.C.), he dismissed the evidence outright (Finkelstein 1996: 200). He has now returned to a more moderate view (contrast with Finkelstein 1988) and acknowledges the existence of "proto-Israelites" on the basis on the Egyptian epigraphic data (e.g., Finkelstein and Mazar 2007: 74).

Another way to interpret the instrumental understanding of descent, however, is to recognize that these manipulated notions may be based on actual realities. In other words, manipulation does not necessarily equal wholesale fabrication. R. Schermerhorn's standard definition of ethnicity emphasizes the social reality of the past in ethnic consciousness. Ethnicity is a collectivity with either real or putative common ancestry, which includes *"memories of a shared historical past"* (Schermerhorn 1970: 12 [emphasis mine]). In Finkelstein's approach, since the biblical data (both the "Conquest stories" and the book of Judges) come from the late Judean Monarchy (Finkelstein and Mazar 2007: 55, 73–74), he assumes that Israel could not possess accurate memories of Schemerhorn's "historical past." For Finkelstein, the bulk of the evidence to reconstruct Israel's ethnic past comes from the material culture. Since stylistic variations are minimal, however, and their distribution is widespread across the highland regions on both side of the Jordan River, the material cultural record is mute with respect to ethnicity. Instead, "pottery and architectural forms in Iron I sites on both sides of the Jordan River reflect environmental, social, and economic traits of the settlers" (Finkelstein 1996: 206; Finkelstein and Mazar 2007: 77–78). As a result, Finkelstein leaves little room for a premonarchic Israelite ethnic identity. Instead, in keeping with his low chronology of the emergence of the Israelite Monarchy, genuine ethnic identity is linked to state formation in ca. 900 B.C.

In a somewhat more nuanced tone, D. Edelman follows in his footsteps. She also highlights the widespread distribution of the so-called ethnic markers, with the resulting collapse of the case for covariance. Her approach toward the text seems to reflect similar skepticism, although she allows for warfare poems such as the Song of Deborah (Judges 5; Edelman 1996: 26–35) to reflect situations that may be premonarchical. Nevertheless, for her, this corpus remains suspect for historical reconstruction, as does the identity of "Israel" in the Merneptah Stele (1996: 35–38). In the end, these texts do not really influence her interpretation of the material record. Significantly, however, there may be hope for delineating ethnicity in burial practices, since these reflect stylistic features that are known to be conservative (Edelman 1996: 53; see Finkelstein and Mazar 2007: 78).

The *"Text-Only" Approach*

K. Sparks's *Ethnicity and Identity in Ancient Israel* (1998) represents the most developed textual study of the subject of ethnicity in recent years (see Mullen 1997; Ahlström 1986). His definition of ethnic identity displays a solid grasp of ethnic theory. He relies on elements that include self-definition, perceived common ancestry, kin-related ties, inherited physical features, and political and social context (Sparks 1998: 16–22). However, Sparks's primary interest is in biblical notions of "common ancestry." In this scheme, the organizing principle is kinship (Sparks 1998: 2–3). By balancing primordial and instrumental considerations, his construct of eclecticism comes close to mine, which is articulated in this book (see McKay 1997).

As an introduction to the topic of ethnicity in ancient Israel, Sparks's locus of research is Israel as a polity from the beginning of the 8th century B.C. to the period of the Exile.[11] During this period, Sparks concludes that ethnicity was expressed as a "corporate experience of the Israelite communities" (Sparks 1998: 16). His analysis of other polities in the ancient Near East and beyond (Neo-Assyria, Egypt, and Greece) leads him to conclude that ethnicity played a relatively minor role elsewhere in comparison with Israel. Thus, in Iron II Israel, ethnic identity was closely related to national identity. Kinship remained an important index, but it was not the only one. Furthermore, there seems to have been a dynamic interplay between ethnic and religious identity. Phenotypical features, however, would not have been considered a determining ethnic marker (Sparks 1998: 18–21, 328).

The above conclusions concerning ethnic identity during the Iron II require further testing and analysis (see Faust 2006). However, since the concern here is for the beginnings of ethnic identity in the region, it is his treatment of pre-Iron II that deserves closer examination. Sparks uses the failure of the traditional models of Israelite settlement, including the Conquest (see Albright 1939), Peasant-Revolt (Mendenhall 1962; Gottwald 1985) and Amphictyony models (Alt 1968) to build his case that a pre-Iron II notion of Israelite ethnicity cannot be recovered (Sparks 1998: 11; see McKay 1997). Unfortunately, his discussion omits crucial textual and archaeological studies (Cross 1988; Finkelstein 1988; 1995; Dever 1991; 1995; LaBianca and Younker 1995). One cannot attempt to deal with the question of ethnic identity seriously without interacting with these syntheses.

Sparks's lack of engagement with archaeological research seems to be based on the view that archaeological data cannot be used as an analytical

---

11. This limited scope reflects Sparks's own minimalist convictions (Sparks 1998: xiii).

tool to identify ethnic identity. This functionalist stance, taken from D. Edelman (Sparks 1998: 4), fails to develop the problems connected with the "functional-only" view of material culture (see pp. 17–19 above). That a cultural assemblage may not correspond with certain ethnic boundaries does not necessarily rule out the possibility that these two cultural domains did correspond at times. The situation may be more complex (or "dynamic") than either hard cultural or functional advocates have asserted.

In spite of these shortcomings, Sparks's analysis of Merneptah's "Israel" and the Song of Deborah in Judges 5 represents a useful point of departure for discussion. Unlike Edelman, Sparks sees in these sources valuable historical information for the period preceding the Monarchy. Accordingly, Merneptah's Israel was a group that shared both a common cultural identity and devotion to the deity El as early as the Late Bronze–Iron I transition (see Stager 1998; Bloch-Smith 2003: 420). Consequently, the earliest element of common identity in ancient Israel was *religious* in nature. Sparks finds additional support in the Song of Deborah. Though he dates the text following a low chronology (9th century B.C.), Sparks acknowledges traces of older traditions in the poem. Accordingly, Yahwism appears to have been the source of a common identity for these tribal groups. Furthermore, the documented conflict between the Canaanites and the Israelite tribal coalition in the Song of Deborah provided an additional sense of supratribal identity among the different factions. Tribal distinctives were set aside in order to face a common enemy. With a definition of ethnic identity framed in contrast to other groups, we may therefore have in these texts the earliest evidence of an ethnic identity in ancient Israel (Sparks 1998: 97–120). In this construct, considerable data are not introduced, on (presumably) ideological grounds. In the end, the setting aside of material culture in discussing ethnic identity in ancient Israel seriously undermines Sparks's arguments (Sparks 1998: 4). For instance, knowing Amos's view of ethnic identity (an important element of Sparks's reconstruction) says very little about the view that might have been espoused by the contemporary culture surrounding him.

In summary, the functional approaches described here illustrate a central problem—namely, the nature of the data that are admitted as evidence. Drawing a strict separation between textual and archaeological data sometimes results in minimal transfers of data for historical reconstruction. Obviously, there are ideological issues related to the inclusion of textual data. Scholars will continue to disagree about what may or may not be admitted as evidence. However, to rule out *all* biblical data seems extreme, especially concerning matters of ethnicity (Bloch-Smith and Nakhai 1999: 63). In the case of Finkelstein, the decision to ignore biblical texts goes contrary to his own methodological protocol. He is willing to use 19th-century ethnohistorical data (his adapted sedentarization model draws on traditional Bedouin practices; see chap. 1) but dismisses ancient texts that date to a time closer than these modern ethnographic accounts to the events that they purport to describe. In other words, even if his skeptical stance is adopted for the composition of the Conquest narratives and the book of Judges, from an ethnohistorical stand-point, to study Israel's own perception of an alleged very distant past should contain at least *some* information of value to reconstruct Israelite origins. The point is compounded when the cyclical/*longue durée* approach, which Finkel-stein embraces wholeheartedly, is applied to the question.

Comprehensive Approaches

Others have taken a softer approach to the functional-versus-covariance questions (such as Routledge 2000a; Schloen 2002; 1998). The genesis of this new perspective can be traced to D. Esse's study (1992) of the collared pithos. The argument he put forth was effective because several lines of evidence are drawn together into a historical synthesis: settlement patterns (highlands, coastal plain, lowlands, and Jordan Valley), textual (biblical), and ethnographic data. To explain the presence of collared pithoi in Transjordan (Esse 1992: 96–97), Esse argued his case from a social-organizational perspective, while also introducing economic considerations. Assuming a patrilocal structure for Israelite residence patterns in Iron I, we may explain the circulation of the collared pithos as resulting from intermarriage between the inhabitants of the highlands and the lowlands. The well-attested variations in collar and rim forms within contemporaneous collared pithos assemblages are explained as a result of exogamy (Esse 1992: 99).[12]

In an appraisal of Esse's work, Killebrew has questioned the specific claim that *women* were involved in the manufacturing process and, therefore, re-sponsible for stylistic variations to the collared pithos. She has identified the weight of these vessels as a deterrent to his female potter hypothesis (Kille-brew 2001). Nevertheless, Esse's proposal that the collared pithoi were circu-lated as a result of intermarriage remains plausible (see Faust 2006: 202). The case for itinerant potters rests on solid ethnohistorical data (Tibet, Cyprus, and Crete, all with relatively similar topographical contexts; Esse 1992: 98). Patrimonialism in ancient Israelite society (Esse 1992: 99–100) and the biblical evidence for the practice of intermarriage may be viewed as a likely way of life in Iron I highlands (Schloen 2001; 2002; Master 2001).

This welcome attention to social context also highlights the need for a definition of ethnicity that moves away from an exclusively primordial frame-work. The context of exchange and fluidity through intermarriage and trade relations requires a definition that contains instrumental elements (Esse 1992: 100). It is perhaps this attachment to a primordial viewpoint that led Esse to accept, at least tacitly, some level of covariance between Israelite ethnicity and the collared pithos (Esse 1992: 95, 103; see Faust 2006: 204).

---

12. For an evaluation of the chronological significance of these morphological varia-tions, see chap. 5 and appendix B.

In his synthesis of the emergence of Israel, L. Stager likewise refrained from adopting a strict cultural framework to interpret the highland data (Stager 1998; see Hackett 1998). Since the highlands were settled by heterogeneous groups (the closing of the frontier through lineage capture [Stager 1985a; 1998]), and elements of the material assemblage have been found outside the traditional boundaries of Israel, ceramics and architecture must reflect functional rather than cultural realities. However, Stager is not prepared to dismiss the possibility of a premonarchical Israel. He takes the data from the Merneptah Stele to establish the case for a distinct highland tribal group designated Israel in the late 13th century B.C. (Stager 1998: 124–25). Stager's contribution builds on F. M. Cross's revived Midianite hypothesis (1988; 1998) and identifies the primary ethnic marker of early Israel as followers of Yahweh (see Hackett 1998; Schloen 2002; see chap. 4 below).

D. Schloen's own version of the emergence of Israel represents the natural evolution of the Esse/Stager trajectory (Schloen 1993; 2002). Although a definition of ethnicity is not specifically stated, Schloen envisions ethnic identity to encompass both primordial and instrumental elements. Ancestry and common descent are important but do not come at the expense of the demands of the social context. Schloen's assumption is that ethnicity should be defined within a specific historical context, since in other phases of settlement, cultures may choose to highlight some markers that may not have been factored in previously or subsequently. In other words, ethnic identity may have looked quite differently during the Iron I and the Iron II periods (see Levy and Holl 2002: 85). Following Stager, Schloen espouses the idea that Yahwism may have represented a primary ethnic marker during the Iron I (Schloen 2002: 59).

In her treatment of Israelite ethnicity during the Iron I (the Philistine-Israelite context), E. Bloch-Smith reflects similar sensitivities to the fluid nature of ethnic identity. Primordial and instrumental traits are viewed in dynamic relationship. Thus, during the Iron I, different groups, each with its own primordial features, amalgamated and incorporated these ethnic distinctives into a "collective memory" (Bloch-Smith 2003: 404). In light of this fluid setting, recognizing an Israelite from a Canaanite on the basis of the material-cultural evidence is doomed to fail. Distributional patterns of collared pithoi and four-room houses reveal little of the ethnic identity of the highland populations. In her view, Israelite ethnic identity, while reflected in Merneptah's Israel within a religious framework cannot be set apart from Canaanite ethnic identity. The situation changes, however, when Israel is defined against Philistine ethnic identity. In the face of Philistine pressure, as documented in the Judges–Samuel narratives,[13] Israelite highland culture began to distinguish itself through instrumental traits. According to Bloch-Smith, these characteristics included short beards (from Merneptah's relief; see Stager 1985b), pork

---

13. For example, Judges 13–16; 1 Samuel 4–8, 13–14, 17–18, 23, 28–29, 31; 2 Samuel 5, 8, 21, 23.

abstinence (drawn from faunal analysis; see Hesse and Wapnish 1998),[14] and circumcision (the textual data from the Merneptah Stele).[15] Military inferiority (1 Sam 13:19–22) is also taken as a circumstantial trait of ethnic identity. Thus, ethnicity emerged in conjunction with Philistine imposition on Israelite territories in the highlands. I will review the crucial question of "otherness" in chap. 4.

Ethnicity in Transjordan

With the above as a backdrop, an analysis of the prevailing views of ethnic identity in Transjordan reveals that scholars are divided along similar lines here as well. The functional viewpoint (though not fully developed) is articulated by B. Routledge (2000a: 63–65) in his work on one of the Wadi Mujib's tributaries in south-central Transjordan. Set within the context of a discussion of the four-room house in Iron I Khirbat al-Mudayna al-ʿAliya, his definition of ethnicity encompasses both emic (objective) and etic (subjective) considerations and, following Jones (1997; see pp. 17–19), accepts material culture as a possible marker of ethnic identity (Routledge 2000a: 58). Social variables are included so that no ethnic correlation can be assumed a priori (Routledge 2000a: 58). Since Routledge takes a strictly archaeological approach to the question (2000a: 66), however, the picture provided is only partial.

The most complete analysis of ethnic identity in Transjordan relies on primordialism and covariance for its principal theoretical underpinnings (Herr 1999; see chap. 1). While L. Herr does not view certain material-cultural diagnostics as ethnic markers (for example, the collared pithos, four-room houses, written communication), he finds that the most convenient way to identify the settlement cluster in the northern Mādabā Plateau Region (MPR; for settlement analysis, see chap. 5) is to rely on F. M. Cross's Reuben hypothesis. According to this approach, the traditional territorial boundaries of Reuben (Josh 13:15–23; see Cross 1988: 48) must have somehow reflected cultural boundaries as well. Although Herr carefully qualifies his conclusions concerning the identity of the inhabitants of the MPR (Herr 2009: 196), the most likely candidate remains the Reuben tribal group (Herr 2000b: 177–78). This group headed a tribal confederacy called "Israel" (the same as the "Israel" of Merneptah), which in turn leads to the Iron II polity of Israel. In this construct, the Israel of Merneptah and the Israel of the Monarchy represent quite different social entities (Herr 1999: 72).

---

14. While Hesse and Wapnish argue against the use of pig bone data to draw ethnic conclusions, Bloch-Smith maintains that the presence-absence argument remains solid: highlanders did not raise pigs, but Philistines did. This difference would have been exacerbated during times of conflict between the two groups (Bloch-Smith 2003: 423).

15. "[Sher]den, Shekelesh, Ekwesh, . . . who had no foreskins." That the Peleset-Philistines did not make the list is interpreted to indicate that they were uncircumcised (see 1 Sam 17:26).

However, as C. Kramer warned, attaching ethnic value to a specific cultural assemblage within a tribal social context and in a transitional zone presents considerable problems (see LaBianca and Younker 1995). Hence, one central issue raised by the MPR covariance scheme is whether such an approach provides the best possible model to understand the cultural landscape of Iron I central Transjordan.

Summary

This survey highlights the benefits of a contextually driven definition of ethnicity that is based on the social particulars of a historically defined time period and, if possible, in light of possible interaction with other groups. Stylistic variations and distributional patterns will not necessarily indicate ethnicity, but they may be a factor. Likewise, linguistic, textual, and/or iconographic data may lead to an explanatory framework in which ethnicity fits as a social category. To be able to reconstruct the social context, an analysis of the available material culture is essential (e.g., Dion 1997). As we have seen in recent discussions related to Israelite religion, material culture has contributed enormously to the notion that Iron II Israel was not a monolithic entity with one religion but instead was highly heterogeneous with competing forms of religious expression (see Zevit 2001). Likewise, with the analysis of textual and archaeological data at Ugarit (Schloen 2001), the value of a contextual approach that takes advantage of every available line of evidence (whether textual, ethnohistorical, ethnoarchaeological, or archaeological) has been made effectively clear. Such syntheses of text and artifact nicely supply independent lines of evidence for historical reconstruction (Schloen 2002; Levy 2010).

In the next two chapters, I document the contours of tribal ethnicity from a textual perspective within the context of the frontier dynamics present in central Transjordan. Chapter 3 chronicles the contested nature of the region situated between the Wadi Mujib (Arnon) and the Wadi Zarqa (Jabbok; see maps 1–2) during Israel's early phases of settlement in the area. Chapter 4 maps ethnic dynamics present in early Israel's tribal frontier landscape.

CHAPTER THREE

Contested Histories of Northern Moab

Foundational texts that cover the broad topic of the settlement of Transjordan are Numbers 21, 32; Joshua 12–13; Deuteronomy 2–3; and Judges 11 (see Weippert 1979; 1983; Vyhmeister 1989; Levine 2000; Seebass 1999). In historical-critical studies, in spite of a renewed interest in Wellhausen's theory of the Hexateuch (Römer 2001), many scholars consider it axiomatic to view Joshua through 2 Kings as part of a Deuteronomistic History (DH; see Joshua 12, 13; Deuteronomy 2–3; Judges 11).[1] The consensus breaks down, however, with respect to the so-called JE (i.e., Yahwist/Elohist) narrative (see Numbers 21, 32), particularly as it pertains to its compositional history (see Peckham 1993). For both DH and JE, opinions continue to vary widely about their usefulness for historical reconstruction. V. Fritz was able to state that the book of Joshua is "eine literarische Fiktion" (Fritz 1994: foreword), while other scholars are willing to see them as genuine historical data, even in the case of notoriously difficult passages (see Numbers 21; Levine 2000: 115).

The Epic School under Fire

Viewing the Mādabā Plateau Region (MPR) as contested territory is not new (Glueck 1939: 243; see Harrison 1996a, 1997, 2009), but in light of recent minimalist approaches, I consider it helpful to elaborate on this dynamic due to the issues regarding admissible textual data that relate to the question of Israel's origins in Transjordan. The origin of the theory of an epic tradition can be traced to Hugo Gressman (1913; see Van Seters 1994; Cassuto 1975; Conroy 1980), but it was W. F. Albright and particularly his student F. M. Cross who formalized the concept in his programmatic *Canaanite Myth and Hebrew Epic* (Cross 1973; see 1998; see Rainey 2007: 42). In this scheme, the assumption of the presence of an Archaic Biblical Hebrew corpus (ABH; see Sáenz-Badillos 1993) is hard to overstate. Well-known poems such as the Song of the Sea and the Song of Deborah (see Cross 1973; Freedman 1960) from the JE narrative are explained on the basis of the presence of an oral tradition from which these and other poems were derived. Following the traditional critical scheme, the J source is dated generally to the 10th century B.C., and, has been linked to the establishment of the Davidic Dynasty in Jerusalem

---

1. For a brief survey of the history of the field, see Butler 2009: xliii–xi.

(Anderson 1998). For Cross, the West Semitic oral tradition is not unlike the Greek epic tradition preserved in Homer's *Iliad*, where stories are said to have been circulated orally before being translated into written form as a narrative epic. In its West Semitic rendering, themes of the deity as divine warrior and hero, in addition to the covenantal league figure prominently. This model of Israelite history and religion lives on in the research of Cross's students (P. D. Miller 2000a: xviii; see Cross 1998 for a defense of this view).

By placing its composition in the 10th century B.C., Cross maintains that the epic narrative contains valuable historical data, particularly for the formative stages of Israelite history. Cross speaks of the Exodus-Conquest that is remembered in the old poetry. In his view, the events of Exodus 15 describe a premonarchic celebration at Gilgal, while the so-called P narrative of the preceding chapter (Exodus 14) comes from a 6th-century B.C. context. Thus, according to Cross, the epic poem does hark back to an older tradition of the march from Egypt into Canaan by early Israelites. Cross's synthesis of the early Iron Age settlement in Transjordan sounds remarkably sedate in today's charged minimalist climate, with a Moses group advancing north and settling the area of central and northern Transjordan, as the biblical narrative indicates in Numbers 21 (see Cross 1988).

The most articulate opposition to the Epic School has come from J. Van Seters (see Conroy 1980), who has consistently argued that what he views as D (Deuteronomist) is the earliest source available and that J drew his narrative from D later during the Exile (Van Seters 1972; 1994: 11–12). The notion of an oral "epic" tradition holds very little credibility in this construct. Since the earliest texts can be dated only to the 8th century B.C. prophets, any memory of early history in the biblical texts is considered so dimmed as to be essentially unrecoverable. Wenham has astutely observed that Van Seters has taken the Wellhausen notion of law to its logical outcome, with the law narrative coming after the prophets (Wenham 1999: 125). Although a thorough critique of this innovative thesis falls within the scope of another full monograph, there remains, in my opinion, a crucial problem with Van Seters's approach. In addition to the assigning of primacy to the DH data over J, the weakness of Van Seters's construct lies in his conclusions about history writing, which do not allow for the possibility of historiographic memory by nonliterate tribal societies. In other words, he does not account for the possibility that his first source, the Deuteronomist, could have used reliable ancient traditions for his reconstruction of Israel's past. Likewise, his Yahwist writes a history that is essentially a literary exercise (Van Seters 1994: 11).[2]

As B. Peckham has noted, embracing the theory of an epic narrative for the biblical sources also raises several questions concerning the relationship between oral and written traditions. Peckham suggests that traditions from which the texts were derived did not have oral but written origins. Thus poetic

---

2. John Van Seters's most recent volume on Israelite origins (*The Yahwist: A History of Israelite Origins*, 2013) appeared too late to be integrated into this discussion.

"lore" were works of *literature*, not the fruit of oral traditions (Peckham 1993: 21). Accordingly, Peckham's Yahwist Epic (700 B.C.) and its sequel 20 years later would all be included in the Deuteronomist's universal history, an exilic masterpiece of historiography (560 B.C.; Peckham 1993: 2, 15–20). While I do not agree with Peckham's late Judean reconstruction, his approach to questions of transmission has opened new avenues of discussion. He accounts for the sophisticated literary style of biblical literature and the dynamic feedback between "history" (that is, narrative) and "prophecy" (that is, poetry; Peckham 1993: 1–2). However, as he himself acknowledged, data were gathered from both "lore *and* libraries" (1993: 18 [emphasis mine]). Thus, even within a literary construct, we must allow for some levels of orality. As S. Niditch has shown in her study of orality and literacy in ancient Israelite literature, a continuum between the two may be a more accurate representation (Niditch 1996).

However, the reality of a possible continuum does not thereby provide a sure pathway to a consensus about historical reconstruction. Even if the quantification of any discernible chronological span between orality and literacy were achieved, opinions regarding the historiographic qualitative value of either (or both) the oral or the written records would obviously vary according to the well-known competing approaches in biblical-historical scholarship.[3] In the current climate in biblical studies, no one really expects any agreed-upon protocol. Nevertheless, if history writing is considered in cultural terms, the author's appeal to historical memory would be recognized by his audience. The wholesale dismissal of historical data (e.g., Cross's version of Epic Narrative or more-traditional biblicist schemes [Provan, Long, and Longman 2003]) for any pre-Iron II history essentially nullifies the cultural context of the Hebrew writers and relegates the entire corpus to verisimilitude—a stance that is still rejected by many influential scholars (see Stager and King 2001: 7–8).

The trend toward a low chronology of the sources is by no means an isolated phenomenon.[4] Ironically, this questioning of the 10th century B.C. as a high point of literary creativity in Israel provides an additional argument in a separate discussion concerning the nature of the Israelite settlement during the 10th century B.C. Proponents of a low chronology for the United Monarchy (e.g., Finkelstein 2005; 1996; see Levy and Higham 2005; also Master

---

3. In this respect, it is worth noting that even scholars who embrace late origins for some texts do not rule out the possibility that events described in these sources referred or related to earlier periods. L. Stager and P. King, in their sociocultural history of ancient Israel make the argument concerning materials typically attributed to the traditional Priestly source. In their view, these texts may have been written in the exilic period, but they contain "*many* earlier traditions" (Stager and King 2001: 2 [emphasis mine]). B. MacDonald mirrors this perspective in his comprehensive overview of the historical geography of ancient Jordan: "Biblical stories about Tranjordanian places and events best fit into the Iron II period and later. . . . This does not mean that the present writer denies that there are older traditions behind the biblical narratives" (MacDonald 2000: 4).

4. Friedman specifically links the writing of J to the independence of Edom from Judah during the reign of Jehoram but before the fall of Samaria (848–722 B.C.; Friedman 1987: 86–87).

2001) assert that if there was no monumental architecture in the 10th century
B.C., the notion of a literary center situated in 10th-century B.C. Jerusalem
seems unlikely (e.g., Finkelstein and Silberman 2001: 22–23). Thus, according
to this view, the rise of literacy and textual production should be placed in a
late Iron II setting, well after the traditional 10th-century B.C. Sitz im Leben
for the traditional, putative J. The very distance between their alleged time of
composition and the events they purport to describe creates a tension with
which some are unwilling to interact, resulting in the assumption that events
before the Monarchy are historically inaccessible.

Tribal Memories

One line of evidence that may provide a fresh perspective concerns documented patterns of recorded histories among tribal societies. A. Shryock's
ethnographic work on tribal historiography in the Hashemite Kingdom of
Jordan illustrates that historical memory in tribal societies can extend back in
time long before the present (Shryock 1997: 22–23). Even though the accounts
compete with each other (and sometimes conflict: van der Steen 2006: 31; see
below), oral traditions are carefully preserved and passed on through elders
(Shryock 1997: 150). In her brief overview of the tribal history of the Kerak
Plateau and the Belka (north of the Wadi Mujib) in Ottoman Jordan, E. van
der Steen documents similar patterns of shifting relationships between major
tribal protagonists (e.g., the Majali, Adwan, and Beni Sakhr). There are periodic confrontations, land reconfigurations, realignments, and resulting geographical dislocations and relocations (van der Steen 2006). In another tribal
context, E. Tonkin has gathered evidence of sophisticated oral traditions in
her study of the Jlao Liberian culture. She highlights oral historian Sieh Jeto's
(1899–1975) form of narrative. His description of the Jlao's migration from
the Ivory Coast to Liberia is organized in the form of a plot (from problem
to resolution). The narrative has 20 stages with elaborate turning points and
subplots. Thus, Jeto's oral history exhibits significantly more order and complexity than might be expected from oral traditions (Tonkin 1992: 29–30).
Likewise, J. Goody has documented the oral "tribal epic" genre as a common medium for communicating tribal historical memory among pastoral-nomadic and agricultural groups in West Africa (Goody 1987).[5] While the topic
cannot be developed fully here, this situation raises similar issues about social
organization in tribal societies (see chap. 1). Thus, the traditional evolutionary
band-to-state social development from less developed (i.e., little or no historical record) to more developed (i.e., organized archives) societies may not
apply any more than the assumption that ideals of kingship can only be found
in state-ordered societies. Tribal societies seem in fact to purvey sophisticated
historiographies based on both oral and written records.

Turning to ancient textual evidence, the minimalist claim that the production of texts was limited to the late Iron II presents obvious problems in light

---

5. See also A. B. Lord, *The Singer of Tales* (1960).

of the available epigraphic data. Well-known early evidence includes the Gezer calendar (10th century B.C.; Cross and Freedman 1952: 45), the Tel Dan Stele (9th century B.C.; Biran and Naveh 1993) and the Mesha Stele (9th century B.C.; Gibson 1971: 71–74; 2002).[6] The Mesha Stele offers especially valuable insights into Moabite tribal history writing (Dearman 1989; Smelik 1992). Its narrative includes a well-articulated historiography based on *ḥērem* warfare (Stern 1991; see chap. 4), an elaborate boundary/border schematic based on developed literary-syntactical symmetries (Routledge 2000b), and long-range memories of the settlement history of the region (see line 10 and discussion below). Finally, if there was an oral-written continuum, the process was abbreviated in the Mesha Inscription (MI), as many of the events seem contemporary to Mesha's time. Consequently, pursuant to an approach that takes Israelite tribal memories as historically meaningful (see Provan, Long, and Longman 2003), I am reviewing here a key text that relates to the early settlement history of Transjordan, the so-called Song of Heshbon in Num 21:27–30, in order both to examine its linguistic structure and to offer a suggestion about the sociohistorical context in which the song may have been situated.

Situating Numbers 21

The general focus of the book of Numbers is geographical, with its beginning at Sinai (chaps. 1:1–10:10), around Kadesh (10:11–20:13), and the journey from Kadesh to the "Plains of Moab" in the Jordan Valley (20:14–36:13). The narrative from chap. 20 to the end of the book deals with the emergence of Israel as an entity in the company of other tribal groups in the region. The Israelites are contrasted with the Edomites, Moabites, Amorites, and the Midianites.[7] Numbers emphasizes the special nature of the Israelites as "blessed" (see Num 24:10). Proleptically, this is first indicated in chap. 6, with the Aaronic blessing (vv. 24–26). The theme receives its climax with the blessing of Balaam (Num 22:6, 12; 23:8, 11, 20; 24:10).

Apart from this geographical structure, few critical scholars venture to claim the book contains much cohesion, so that Numbers is hailed as a good example of the garbled nature of Hebrew narrative, without unity or pattern. What particularly frustrates some commentators is the interchange between narrative and law (Noth 1968: 1–2). However, as J. Milgrom has noted, the fusing of narrative and law is attested practice in some Near Eastern literary conventions (Milgrom 1992: 1148; see Lee 2003). In Numbers, several narratives are integral to the legal rulings. In the case of Zelophehad's daughters, for example, the narrative (Num 27:1–4) provides the introduction to the legal ruling that protects clan inheritance (Num 27:5–11; 36:5–12). Similarly, the ruling about Reuben, Gad, and the half-tribe of Manasseh provides the

---

6. To this list of early epigraphic materials, we can also add the Khirbet Qeiyafa Ostracon (Misgav, Garfinkel, and Ganor 2009; Puech 2010; Millard 2011. For further discussions, see Rollston 2011; Finkelstein and Fantalkin 2012).

7. See also the appearance of Amalek in Exod 17:8–16.

backdrop to the Deuteronomic land-grant decree concerning Transjordanian territory (Numbers 32).

Literarily, Numbers 21 stands as a significant watershed in the book of Numbers. In this section, three episodes belonging to the Conquest narrative genre are introduced (see Younger 1990). In Num 21:1–3, a Canaanite "king of Arad" (who remains anonymous) ambushed the Israelites as they began their journey toward Transjordan. The Israelites retaliated, and the Canaanites suffered a crushing defeat (Num 33:40). As firstfruit of the conquest, the place was named Hormah (a play on *ḥērem*, meaning 'consecrated to destruction').

The thrust of Num 21:10–35, the setting for the Song of Heshbon, is its claim that the land north of the Arnon was available to the Israelites, since it was not Moabite territory. In this context, the "Book of the Wars of Yahweh" (Num 21:14–15; see Freedman 1960) functions as documentary evidence concerning the division of northern Moab into two separate regions: Moab and the land of the Amorites. The border is clearly specified as the Arnon River (Wadi Mujib; see MacDonald 2000: 74–75). Likewise, the Song of the Well (Num 21:17–18) is used as tribal territorial evidence that Israel had staked its claim over the area.

Numbers 21 thus provides an explanation for an awkward situation in which Reuben, Gad, and the half-tribe of Manasseh—who were all supposed to have joined the rest of Israel across the river—had settled east of the Jordan (Numbers 32). Even though permission to settle outside the "promised land" was granted to the tribes (Num 32:33–41), the narrative in Numbers anticipated the perception of Gilead-Transjordan and its inhabitants as "outsiders" (see Josh 22:10–34).

Following the Song of Heshbon and the conquest account of Og in Bashan, the Balaam Oracles (Numbers 22–24) are the longest literary unit in the book of Numbers. These supply additional literary context for the narrative sequence of chap. 21. The Song of Heshbon as a taunt song against Moab provides the motivation (or *casus belli*) for Moab's stand against Israel in the Balaam texts and the ensuing conflict between Moab and Israel. In the context of the overall theme of "blessing" in the book of Numbers, the Song of Heshbon also serves as an introductory backdrop to Balaam's climactic declarations concerning Israel, "Blessed is everyone who blesses you" (Num 24:9, NRSV). Some other literary connections include:

- The narrative frame of Num 22:2–3
- In the Song of Heshbon, Chemosh abandoned Moab. The Moabites turn to Balaam for divine assistance in the Balaam pericope (Num 22:5, 7)
- The Song of Heshbon is a *māšāl*. Balaam speaks up with a *māšāl* four times. The Balaam and Heshbon traditions seem to have been fused in Jephthah's speech (see Judg 11:25) and by Jeremiah in the oracle against Moab (Jer 48:1–47).

Concerning the composition of Num 21:10ff., M. Noth assigned this segment to E on account of the designation "Amorite" (Noth 1968: 11). J. Van

Seters notes, correctly in my opinion, that there is another reason why the designation "Amorite" is used instead of Canaanite. Transjordan is never considered part of Canaan in the biblical record. Thus, it was probably on the basis of other concerns (such as geographical and ideological; see Gen 15:16) that "Amorite" was used in this context (Van Seters 1972: 182). Another assumption by critical scholars is that the Deuteronomist (D) probably emended the chapter with the addition of vv. 33–35 (see Deut 3:1–7; Gray 1903: 306). Some go further and see a Deuteronomistic framework in this chapter, since it concerns territorial claims (Deut 3:12–17; Josh 13:15–33; Peckham 1993: 105; see Vyhmeister 1989: 51–52).

This brief sketch highlights the distinct lack of consensus regarding the composition of the text, a situation also reflected in current discussions about the Nothian "Deuteronomistic History" approach to the historical books.[8] However, if Numbers 21 is viewed as part of the tribal collective memory of Israel's past, we may be able to view the chapter in more cohesive terms than traditional-critical analyses have proposed. These tribal recollections, accentuated by excerpts from "The Book of the Wars of Yahweh" (Num 21:14–15), the Song of the Well (21:17–18; see Freedman 1960), and the Song of Heshbon (21:27–30) include the following features: divine claim of ownership of the land, mediated either explicitly via the language of *ḥērem* (Num 21:1–3), or implicitly (Chemosh's giving up his progeny in Num 21:27–30; see below); records of armed confrontations between different *mlkym*/"tribal warlords" (as an inclusio in Num 21:1–3, 27–35; see Glueck 1939); officially recorded claims of territorial boundaries (i.e., the formidable geological barrier of the Wadi al-Mujib as duly recorded in the "Book [*spr*] of the Wars of Yahweh" Num 21:14–15); and claims to highly valued water sources ("The Song of the Well," Num 21:17–18). These records are carefully mediated and controlled by a tribal authority who, in the Moabite historical memory available to us, is identified as Mesha. Though largely abandoned in contemporary critical scholarship, Israelite texts also have a correlation to their own tribal head in the person of Moses, a reality previous generations of mainstream scholarship found hard to dismiss (Cross 1998; Albright 2006; Mendenhall 1961: 39; Eichrodt 1961). In Deut 2:24–37, the essential account of Numbers 21 is preserved with similar elements, including the *ḥērem* framework (Num 21:1–2, 27–30; Deut 2:37). The duplicate tribal records thus provide other dimensions that enrich the traditions of Israel's shared historical past. This harmonizing approach does not cancel the presence of competing accounts (see Shryock 1997; van der Steen 2006: 31). Instead, the provenience of contradictory claims shifts to opposing tribes, who also stake a claim to the area for themselves (e.g., modern tribes' view of warfare with their enemies; Niditch 1993). In this particular instance, the competing version emanates from the people of Chemosh, the Moabites. Thanks to the colorful and fortuitous discovery

---

8. Although T. Butler describes the context of the book of Judges, his discussion on the present state of the "Deuteronomistic History" approach to the historical books applies here as well (Butler 2009: li).

of the Moabite Stone/Mesha Inscription in the 19th century, modern scholars are privy to this version of the ongoing dispute between Israelite and Moabite tribes. In contrast, biblical sources, usually candid in their descriptions of internecine warfare (Judges 12; 20–21), do not characterize the Transjordanian Israelite tribes as engaged in episodic conflicts with each other (with the resulting competing versions of the events) during the early phase of the settlement in Transjordan.

The Song of Heshbon (Num 21:27–30)

(27) *ʿl kn yʾmrw hmšlym*
Therefore,[9] the *mošelîm*[10] used to say,[11]

bʾw ḥšbwn tbnh
Come,[12] may[13] Heshbon be built!

wtkwnn ʿyr syḥwn
May the town of Sihon be established!

(28) *ky ʾš ysʾh mḥšbwn*
For fire came out[14] from Heshbon,

lhbh mqryt syḥn
A flame from the town of Sihon.[15]

ʾklh ʿr mwʾb
It consumed Ar Moab,

bʿly bmwt ʿrnn
Baʿley Bamoth Arnon.[16]

(29) *ʾwy lk mwʾb*
Woe to you, Moab!

---

9. The subordinating conjunction *ʿl kn* dicates the syntactic dependence of v. 27 on v. 26. The poem proper begins with the imperative *bʾw*.

10. 'Those who speak/sing in verse' (see below).

11. If archaisms are present in the poem, the prefixed conjugation may be the short form *yaqtul* (see Exod 15:1, *ʾz yšyr*; Exod 15:5, *yksymw*).

12. The imperative invites the hearers to "listen in," as it were. Some translations prefer "Come [to] Heshbon," but this expansion seems unnecessary and is not supported by the parallelism of the lines (see Stuart 1976: 95).

13. The favored translation among exegetes is 'let', which is of course syntactically acceptable. The translation suggested here attempts to reflect what may have been a more formal tone of extolling the importance of Heshbon (see Levine 2000: 83).

14. The *qatal* sequence in this relative *kî* clause is taken as a signal of anteriority. Thus, a future tense value seems less likely (see Ottosson 1969: 63–64). See discussion below.

15. The verb is elided in the second line.

16. Another possible translation is 'the cities of Moab' and 'the high places of Arnon' (Stuart 1976: 94). However, Ar/Ir and Bamoth are mentioned elsewhere as toponyms (Num 21:15, 19; see MacDonald 2000: 70–79, 90–98).

ʾbdt ʿm kmwš
You were destroyed,[17] people of Chemosh!

ntn bnyw plyṭm
He[18] gave his sons as fugitives,

wbntyw bšbyt
And his daughters as captive

lmlk ʾmry syḥwn
To an Amorite king, Sihon.

(30) *wnyrm*[19] *ʾbd*
Their lamp perished,

ḥšbwn ʿd dybwn
Heshbon as far as Dibon,

wnšym[20] *ʿd npḥ*
The women as far as Nopha,

ʾšr ʿd mydbʾ
Which is by Medeba.

Exegetical Problems

Num 21:27–30 clearly is a difficult text, and the literature on the song reflects these complexities and the resulting lack of scholarly consensus (see Vyhmeister 1989). Salient issues include the relationship between the poem and the preceding narrative frame of v. 26. There are also questions whether the phrase of v. 29e, "to an Amorite king, Sihon," should be retained in the original. A third issue concerns the literary dependence of Num 21:27–30 on Jer 48:45–46, which deserves a reappraisal in light of Van Seters's primacy-of-Jeremiah hypothesis (Van Seters 1994: 398–402).[21] Finally, there is disagreement about the reading of v. 30 and how the text may be reconstructed.

The Role of Verse 26 in Relationship to the Poem

The relationship between "epic" poems and narrative has preoccupied many exegetes. Some see a close relationship, even if the texts are thought to be from different literary contexts (Cross 1973; Halpern 1988: 76–82). Each occurrence (among others, Exodus 14–15; Numbers 22, 25; Judges 4–5;

---

17. The *qatal* sequence continues to describe anteriority as it does in v. 30.

18. The antecedent is most likely Chemosh.

19. Taken as 'their lamp', which would parallel 'sons' in v. 29; compare with 'lamp' as male progenitor in 2 Kgs 11:36 (see discussion below).

20. Taken as 'their women', which parallels 'daughters' in v. 29d (see discussion below).

21. For a short critique, see Vyhmeister 1989: 51. Concerning the literary interdependence of Num 21:21–25 with Deut 2:26–37 and Judg 11:19–26, see Van Seters 1972; Bartlett 1978; and Vyhmeister 1989: 46–51.

passim) seems to present its own distinctive characteristics in terms of this relationship and should be examined on its own merit.

Concerning Numbers 21, however, the literary situation is unique. The narrative and poetics of the chapter are probably the most integrated of this "narrative-poetry corpus," which consists of poetic excerpts used as supportive evidence for the narrative rather than full poems. In the case of the first two poetic excerpts of Numbers 21, the sources are delineated by the syntactic markers *ʿl kn* (v. 14, introducing the "Book of the Wars of Yahweh"; note also the possible preterite *yʾmr*):

ʿl kn yʾmr bspr mlḥmt yhwh
ʾt whb bswph
wʾt hnḥlym ʾrnwn
wʾšd hnḥlym ʾšr nṭh lšbt ʿr
wnšʿn lgbwl mwʾb

Therefore, it is said in "The Book of the Wars of Yahweh":
"Waheb in Suphah,[22]
The wadis of the Arnon,
And the slopes of the wadis that extend to the seat of Ar,
and lie on the border of Moab."

And *ʾz* (v. 17, introducing the Song of the Well; compare with preterite *yšyr*):[23]

ʾz yšyr yśrʾl ʾt hšyrh hzʾt
ʿly bʾr
ʾnw lh
bʾr ḥprwh śrym
krwh ndyby hʿm
bmḥqq bmšʿntm

Then, Israel sang this song:
"Spring up, O Well!
Sing to it!
The well the princes sank,
The nobles of the people dug,
With the scepter, with the staff."

The narrative frame introducing "The Song of Heshbon," the longest poetic inclusion of the passage, is itself a *kî* clause explaining the situation of Heshbon prior to its defeat at the hands of the Israelites (v. 26). The default *wayyiqtol*, last used in v. 25, resumes in v. 31. Thus, each of the three poems is syntactically embedded directly within the narrative. In this context, their function may be

---

22. The precise location within the Arnon area is unknown (Ashley 1993: 412).

23. The vocalization of this preterite is problematic. Instead of a long *yaqtulu* form, it should probably be vocalized as a short form, *yāšer*.

seen in the same light as reported speech, which carries forward the narrative (Alter 1981: 66; see C. L. Miller 2003). In other words, these excerpts, as a form of "speech," supply additional semantic data deemed useful to the author.

The importance of the Heshbon poem to the narrative frame is highlighted in particular. Syntactically, the *kî* clause of v. 26 is meant to provide additional background information to the town of Heshbon by harking back to earlier times. This appeal to historical memory is achieved by the use of the lexeme *r'šwn* (probably meaning 'former'; see Levine 2000: 101). Prior to Sihon's reign, the Moabites claimed northern Moab for themselves. Based on these considerations, the syntactical context appears to indicate that our investigation should include the surrounding narrative perspective (see Ottosson 1969: 57–59).

The Problem of Verse 29e

There are problems with the inclusion of the phrase in v. 29e, *lmlk 'mry syḥwn* 'to an Amorite king, Sihon.' First, it has been asserted that the meter of the poem is disrupted by this prepositional phrase: 3:3 for vv. 28 and 29a is followed by 3:2 for vv. 29b and 30 (Weippert 1979: 19–20). Likewise, Van Seters (1972: 195) has maintained that the phrase overbalances the line. However, D. Stuart (1976: 33, 95) has explained this alleged imbalance on the basis of mixed meter: v. 29 is a combination of a 6:6 couplet and a 7:7:7 tricolon.

Apart from meter, a syntactic case can be made for the inclusion of v. 29e as an integral part of the poem. The finite verb *ntn* requires an indirect object. Without *lmlk 'mry syḥwn*, we would not know to whom the captives were given. The semantic parallelism of the poem also favors inclusion. In the first part of the poem, the focus is on the land. The conqueror is "the town of Sihon," and the vanquished is "Ar Moab." The second part concerns people, with the designation "people of Chemosh" and "his sons/daughters." If we leave out "an Amorite king, Sihon," then the line is incomplete. We do not know who the conqueror was, especially when the line is compared with the first part, where the two warring parties are clearly mentioned. There is an imbalance if the aggressor is not mentioned in the second strophe. Of course, one could suggest that a later redactor inserted v. 29e to fill in the "gap" on account of the linguistic feature of ellipsis. However, it is more reasonable to assume that no gap was ever present and that the writer clearly wanted to highlight the identity of the victor through the use of parallelism.

M. Weippert sets v. 29e aside based on his observation of the orthographic variations of *sîḥon*. In vv. 27b and 29b, Sihon is plene, *syḥwn* with a *ḥolem waw*, while in the body of v. 28 it is defective, *syḥn* with a *ḥolem*. Weippert sees the original text as containing defective spelling, with the longer form reflecting a later text (Weippert 1979: 19 n. 15). He claims that later Deuteronomistic texts tend to have a greater frequency in the use of plene spelling. However, the personal name Sihon does not seem to follow a given pattern. In Deut 2:24, it is defective, but in Deut 2:26, it is plene. As S. Gogel (1998) has discussed, dating texts based on presence-absence of *matres lectionis* is a difficult exercise. There are tendencies, but we should not build a case on these alone.

Finally, the syntax of the phrase *lmlk ʾmry syḥwn* ('to an Amorite king, Sihon') is said to be at odds with attested compound designations of Sihon, with respect both to the definiteness of the gentilic epithet and to word order, which appears to support the gloss hypothesis further (e.g., Levine 2000: 107).

- Deut 2:24, 26: *syḥn mlk ḥšbwn hʾmry* ('Sihon, king of Heshbon, the Amorite')
- Num 32:33, *syḥn mlk hʾmry* ('Sihon, king of the Amorite')
- Josh 12:2, *syḥwn mlk hʾmry hywšb bḥšbwn* ('Sihon, king of the Amorite, who dwells in Heshbon')
- Judg 11:19, *syḥwn mlk hʾmry mlk ḥšbwn* ('Sihon, king of the Amorite, king of Heshbon')

However, as is well known, definite articles do not occur in poetry as frequently as they do in narrative passages. The narrative dictates of definiteness do not always apply in poetry. Likewise, the question of word order may be considered from the view that word order tends to be more fluid in poetry than in narrative.

This poetic consideration is confirmed when we look at the *only* other occurrence of the indefinite gentilic *ʾmry* (Amorite) in Ezek 16:45. Ezekiel 16 has been characterized as a judgment speech against Jerusalem's idolatry (Block 1997: 460). In this literary unit (the longest in Ezekiel, 63 verses), Jerusalem is portrayed as an adulterous wife. The tone of the text is set immediately when it refers back to Jerusalem's ancestral origins in v. 3: *mkrtyk wmldtyk mʾrṣ hknʿny ʾbyk hʾmry wʾmk ḥtyt* ('your origins and your birth are from the land of Canaan; your father was Amorite and your mother a Hittite'). Here, the designation of the father as *hʾmry* ('Amorite') is definite, which is the typical usage. However, in v. 45, now as part of a *māšāl* (Ezek 16:44), the same quotation is repeated, but this time *ʾmry* is indefinite: *ʾmkn ḥtyt wʾbykn ʾmry* ('your mother was a Hittite, and your father was Amorite'). Thus, definite/indefinite variations of this sort do exist in the BH corpus, and they raise the question whether Num 21:29e must inevitably be viewed as an editorial gloss.[24]

---

24. It is difficult to explain why 'Amorite' shifts from definiteness to indefiniteness in Ezek 16:3 and 45 (where *ḥtyt* 'Hittite' does not). A possible answer lies in the *māšāl* genre, shared by both Num 21:29e and Ezek 16:45 (see v. 44). *Māšāl* means several things in BH (see Levine 2000; Schöpflin 2002). Generally speaking, the term can be translated 'balanced line' (Levine 2000: 102–3). When the *māšāl* genre is used, irony is sometimes implied, as in the case of Balaam, the foreign diviner speaking Yahweh's words (Num 23:11–12; observe the default frame in the Balaam cycle: Num 23:7, 18; 24:3, 15, 20, 21, 23). Clearly irony is in view in both contexts of Numbers 21 and Ezekiel 16. But perhaps there is an added tonic to the nuance that was signaled by the indefinite use of the gentilic. In Numbers 21, it might be conveyed as 'Moab was destroyed by whom? Why, an Amorite king!' Similarly in Ezekiel 16, the taunting nature of the poetic line might be paraphrased 'Your mother was Hittite, and your father? Oh my, an Amorite!' (Ezek 16:45). Such irony

Jeremiah's Use of the Song of Heshbon

In his oracle against Moab, Jeremiah uses excerpts from the Song of Heshbon as well as from the Balaam oracle (Num 24:17). This borrowing of traditions appears to have been standard practice in prophetic literature. The prophets used and adapted available literary traditions to bolster their arguments. There are numerous examples of intertextuality in prophetic literature (such as Hag 2:22//Exod 15:1; see Schultz 1999; Kessler 2002; Fishbane 1988). The evidence usually supports the claims that the prophets borrowed from established literary traditions or stock phrases. This tendency seems to be the case with Jeremiah as well. The following analysis indicates that Jeremiah borrowed from the Song of Heshbon and the Balaam oracle in order to generate a new oracle against Moab. For the sake of clarity, the complete text of the Moab oracle in Jeremiah 48 is presented here, with commentary in footnotes.

(45) *bṣl ḥšbwn ʿmdw mkḥ nsym*
In the shadow of Heshbon, fugitives stood without strength.[25]

ky ʾš yṣʾ mḥšbwn
For a fire went out from Heshbon,

wlhbh mbyn syḥwn
and a flame from[26] Sihon,[27]

wtʾkl pʾt mwʾb
and it consumed[28] the forehead/edge of Moab

wqdqd bny šʾwn
and the crown of head of the sons of tumult.[29]

(46) *ʾwy lk mwʾb*
Woe to you, Moab.

related to gentilics also appears to be present in the David and Goliath narrative: 'Who is *this* [*hzh*] uncircumcised Philistine [*hplšty*] . . . ?' (1 Sam 17:26; also v. 32; Alter 1999: 103).

25. This first line is not drawn from "The Song of Heshbon." Jeremiah is setting a different context—namely, an oracle of judgment against Moab.

26. There is no need to change the well-attested compound preposition (28 occurrences in the Hebrew Bible) to *mbyt* (see NRSV).

27. The author here alters the parallelism found in Numbers 21 and makes Sihon himself the source of the flame, not the city of Sihon as in Num 21:28. The meaning remains generally the same, however. Sihon was used to judge Moab, and Jeremiah recalls this incident in the past to speak of a future judgment against Moab. Recalling past judgments in order to proclaim new ones is attested elsewhere in the Jeremiah corpus (such as Jer 7:14).

28. A *wayyiqtol* replaces the *qatal* of Numbers 21.

29. Note the possible pun on "Sihon." Here, the author borrowed the phrase from Balaam's fourth oracle (Num 24:17). This is perhaps the clearest literary evidence that Jeremiah had access to several traditions from which he built his oracle. Van Seters's argument begs the question of the provenience of this fragment. It is almost impossible to imagine that the Balaam oracles were derived from this excerpt in Jeremiah!

ʾbd ʿm kmwš
The people Chemosh has perished,[30]

ky lqḥw bnyk bšby
for your sons have been taken[31] as captives[32]

wbntyk bšbyh
and your daughters into captivity.

In his case for the primacy of Jeremiah, Van Seters takes the fire that went out from Heshbon (*yṣʾ*) to encompass the destruction of Heshbon itself. He identifies the "fugitives" of Jer 48:45 as inhabitants of Heshbon who fled their town after its destruction (Van Seters 1972: 194). While a case can be made that this was the fire that destroyed Heshbon itself, the literary context in Numbers 21 seems to indicate that the fire of judgment was directed away from Heshbon and toward Moab. Also, it is worth noting that Van Seters's argument for dismissing Num 21:29e on the basis of its absence in Jeremiah loses its appeal considerably (Van Seters 1972: 193). Thus, it seems preferable to assume that the author of the oracle in Jeremiah borrowed from the Song of Heshbon and from a fragment of the Balaam pericope (see Num 24:17), rather than the reverse (see Boling 1988: 46).

The Problem of Verse 30

The last verse of the Song of Heshbon is difficult, particularly MT *wayyiqtol*, *wnyrm* 'we shot them' (*yrh* with pronominal suffix) and *wnšym* 'we laid waste' (*šmm*; see Ashley 1993: 417, 427; Netzer 1973; Hanson 1968). In support of this verbal construction, *wayyiqtol* forms, though rare, are attested in speech (Smith 1991: 21–27; see 1 Sam 30:13, *wyʿzbny*) and in poetry. In the Song of the Sea, a *wayyiqtol* is used at the end of the poem (Exod 15:19, *wyšb*) within a *kî* clause that functions as an inclusio (see Exod 15:4). Even if the reconstruction of these verbs remains difficult, there seems to be agreement on the observation that in general terms the verse reflects the destruction of Heshbon (*ʾbd*).

However, there is another way to read the text without substantial emendations. The verbal *wnyrm* could be read as nominal 'their lamp' (*nyr*). This reconstruction is parallel with "the sons of Chemosh" of v. 29c. A similar parallel sons/lamp is found in 2 Kgs 11:36 (Hanson 1968). Likewise, verbal

---

30. *ʾbdt* in Num 21:29b. The shift to a 3rd-person singular for the verb *ʾbd* (v. 46b) followed by a return to 2nd person (v. 46c) alters the parallelism of Num 21:29, namely: 29a, b = 2nd person; 29c, d = 3rd person. No conclusion as to which is more original can be drawn from this change. However the parallelism of Numbers 21 seems more balanced with two lines paralleling each other—that is, 'you/you // he/he'.

31. The *qatal* substitution for a relative *kî* clause with a Qal passive reflects Jeremiah's "freedom" with the verbal system of the poem.

32. Num 21:29c, d has parallelism: *plytim // bšbyt*. These alterations do not represent significant changes for our discussion.

wnšym can be rendered 'women' in parallelism with the daughers of Chemosh of v. 29d (with an ellipsis of the verbal *'bd*).

Thus, v. 30 would claim:

Their lamp has perished, Heshbon as far as Dibon;
and [the] women [ellipsis of the verb 'perish'] as far as Nophah,
which is by Medeba.

Concerning the *puncta extraordinaria* (attested 15 times in the Leningrad Codex) above the *r* of *'ăšer* in v. 30b, one possible solution is to emend *'ăšer* to read 'fire as far as Medeba' (thus the LXX). This suggestion has the advantage of allowing the lexeme to form an inclusio with the fire of v. 27b. However, no definitive solution can be provided, and in the reconstruction presented here, *'ăšer* is retained.

Finally, the general structure of the poem may be used to favor the inclusion of v. 30 in the poem: the first part focuses on the city of Heshbon and the conquered land (vv. 27b–28); the second part focuses on the conquered people (v. 29); the third part returns to geography (v. 30). A chiastic ABBA structure is yet another way to examine the symmetry of the poem:

Destruction of Heshbon (v. 27)
   Against Moab (v. 28)
   Against Moab (v. 29)
Against Heshbon (v. 30)

Literary and Historical Implications

Based on the above arguments for its literary and syntactical integrity, the central points of the poem are developed as follows:

(1) Heshbon Is Exalted as the Conqueror of Moab (vv. 27–28). The injunction to build Heshbon consists of two parallel lines in v. 27 (synonymous). This relationship is clarified when we examine the parallelism linking the lines in vv. 27–28,

ḥšbwn / 'yr syḥwn (v. 27b) nominal / construct //
mḥšbwn / mqryt syḥn (v. 28b) prep.+ nominal /prep. + construct

The subordinate *kî* clause (v. 28) explains why Heshbon should be built/established.[33] The line could be understood either as a statement projecting Heshbon's power against Ar Moab, in the future, or as a description of the fame of Heshbon, which destroyed Moab in the past. With v. 26 incorporated into the analysis (signaled by *'l kn* 'therefore' [v. 27] as the narrative-poem literary connective), the text manifests knowledge of a conflict between the Amorites and the Moabites in the region, prior to the Israelites' encounter with Sihon of Heshbon. Accordingly, this particular *qatal kî* clause can in fact be given a

---

33. There is no need to dismiss *ky* as a gloss (Weippert 1979). It is attested elswhere in poetry (Judg 5:23, emphatic; Isa 3:1).

past tense value. Heshbon is lauded here as a great city in the region, because it has defeated Ar Moab.

(2) Explanation for Moab's Defeat: Chemosh's Retribution. This section stands at the heart of the poem, because it provides the explanation for Moab's defeat at the hands of Sihon. It can be subdivided into two parts. In the first part, in language evoking the concept of *ḥērem* (see chap. 4), the Moabite deity Chemosh exercises his right as the divine kinsman (see Cross 1998: 7) to disown his sons and daughters, who are sold into slavery to Sihon, the Amorite king. Thus, while v. 29 is semantically independent of v. 28, together the verses form a *qatal* sequence, and the parallelisms complement each other:

> *mḥšbwn / mqryt syḥn* (v. 28b) // *syḥwn* (v. 29e)
> *ʿr mwʾb* (v. 28c) / *mwʾb* (v. 29a)

The second part of this rationale is found in the last verse of the poem (v. 30), which further describes through the use of "lamp" as metonymy (= Chemosh's sons of v. 29) and the designation "daughters" the complete devastation wrought against the Moabites in the territory north of the Arnon. Their defeat extends south from the heartland of the *mishor* ('plateau'), represented by the town of Medeba, to the heartland of the Dibon Plateau, north of the Arnon, represented by the town of Dibon. The geographical focus of v. 30 completes the picture provided in the narrative prose and supports the key argument in Numbers 21 that legitimizes the Israelites' claim to northern Moab.

Is the Poem Archaic?

The corpus of what has been identified as Archaic Biblical Hebrew (ABH) is well known (see Sáenz-Badillos 1993: 56–57; Cross and Freedman 1997; Freedman 1960; Robertson 1972; see Bloch 2012) and includes the following: Genesis 49; Exodus 15; Numbers 23–24; Deuteronomy 32, 33; Judges 5; 2 Samuel 22/Psalm 18; Habakkuk 3; Psalm 68; as well as a few other psalms and excerpts in narrative passages (such as 2 Samuel 1 and Numbers 21). Salient morphological features deemed early include:

- The 3rd-person pronominal suffix *-mô* (Exod 15:5)[34]
- Third-person masculine suffix *-h* instead of *-w* (Gen 49:11)
- Relative particles *ze, zô, zû* (Exod 15:13; Judg 5:5)
- Relative pronouns *še, šā* (Judg 5:7)
- Third-person feminine verbal suffix *-at* (Deut 32:36)

With respect to verbal forms, the use of the prefixed conjugation ("imperfect") to express the default past tense (see 2 Sam 22:5) is regularly noted among proponents of ABH (see Bloch 2009). Vocabulary variations also identify ABH texts as earlier texts than SBH. The variations occur in terms of both ABH roots found in other Northwest Semitic dialects (such as, *ḥārūṣ* 'gold' //

---

34. For a recent critique of this diagnostic, see Y. Bloch 2012.

Ugaritic) and hapax legomena. Thus, the presence of Ugaritic (or other West Semitic) features can be indicative of early cultural contacts.

In "The Song of Heshbon," possible archaic features include the following: the presence of a **yaqtul* in the introduction of the poem (v. 27), the mixed meter of the poem (Stuart 1976: 95), the absence of definite articles in the poem itself, the use of particles for emphatic purposes (see Sáenz-Badillos 1993: 59–60), and the presence of foreign personal names—all offer clues that could be used to accept the poem as part of the ABH corpus (Freedman 1960; Hanson 1968; Stuart 1976: 93).[35] Indirect support for the antiquity of the poem may also be derived from the textual-critical problems of v. 30 (see above).

However, recent studies have raised some doubts whether linguistic variations in poetic texts necessarily signal chronological phasing (Young and Rezetko 2010: 335; Young, Rezetko, and Ehrensvärd 2010). Variations may also reflect semantic considerations on the part of the writers, quite apart from any chronological significance (Young 1993: 123; see Gogel 1998: 49–74). The case for archaisms also weakens when one considers the variations in usage for forms usually categorized as archaic (see Young and Rezetko 2010: 335). Nevertheless, it would also be a mistake to lump all noted variations as the result of stylistic conventions, devoid of diachronic significance (Dresher 2012; see Holmstedt 2012: 112). In this regard, I. Young's earlier work is more cautious in retaining *both* archaic and stylistic realities as part of the dynamics present in these texts (Young 1993: 123–24). Turning back to our specific text: because of its brevity, it seems reasonable to assume that any case for its antiquity will need to rest on more than one line of evidence.

Who Are the Mōšĕlîm?

Following the above reconstruction, the question whether the poem is of Israelite origin is relevant (see Geraty 1993: 627). Our limited understanding of the Amorite language makes it impossible to isolate possible Amorite lexemes or syntactical features. Nevertheless, some interpreters have suggested that the personal name *sîhôn/sîhōn* is Amorite in origin (Mendenhall 1992; Hanson 1968). Similarly, the woe against Moab/the people of Chemosh (v. 29a, b) reveals knowledge of Moabite culture on the part of the *mōšĕlîm*, in terms of both the Moabite religious context and its theological understanding of divine retribution. This sentiment is reflected in the opening lines of the Mesha Inscription: "Chemosh was angry with us." In addition, the vocalization *ʿār môāb* (v. 28c, paralleled in the related poetic excerpt in Num 21:15; compare with *ʿîr*, Num 22:36) perhaps reflects local Moabite realities.[36]

In his article on the presence of northernisms in 2 Kings 20, I. Young notes that sometimes linguistic variations follow what appears to be an intentional

---

35. Hanson's work has rightly been criticized on account of the sometimes drastic emendations necessary to "fit" a Canaanite scheme of poetry (Weippert 1979: 21). On meter, see also O'Connor 1997: 65.

36. In the Mesha Inscription, the lexeme 'town' is uniquely designated *qr* (*qar*), as opposed to *ʿr*. This could further indicate that here it refers to a toponym.

pattern in direct speech—namely (in the context of discussion for 1 Kings
17-2 Kings 10), "Aramaisms in the mouth of Arameans" (Young 1995: 65).
The problem, in the context of Numbers 21, is that we have far too small a
sample to make such a judgment, as is the case when attempting to identify dialect in the corpus in general (Young 1993). Nevertheless, in light of the available evidence, the poem does seem to reflect evidence of contact between
these neighboring cultures. The Hebrew version makes use of local sources
to support the particular point about the legitimacy of the Israelite claim over
northern Moab. Amorite poets (mōšĕlîm) had a song to commemorate Moab's
humiliation at the hand of Sihon (and as the song emphasizes, ultimately at
the hand of Chemosh). The writer simply assimilated this textual tradition
to his own purpose. The Moabites had lost northern Moab to the Amorites,
and now, the same Amorites had lost this territory to the Israelites. This ac-
quaintance with different literary traditions is also represented in the Balaam
oracles. Although the Balaam texts in Numbers 23–24 are written in Hebrew,
the Dayr ʿAlla plaster inscriptions point to interaction between indigenous
traditions in the region of Transjordan and Hebrew writers (Hackett 1980;
McCarter 1980; Hoftijzer and van der Kooij 1990).

In summary, this intertextuality seems to indicate knowledge of the region
on the part of the writer. He was clearly aware of the contested history of the
region and that the territory north of the Arnon had changed hands several
times. His awareness of an Amorite defeat of Moab is supported by a victory
song that may have derived from Amorite, and perhaps even Moabite sources.
Regardless of what was adopted from elsewhere, however, as in the case of
the Balaam oracles, the final product was a distinctly Hebrew edition of the
poem.

The Amorite Question

This reading of the Song of Heshbon appears to support G. E. Mendenhall's long-argued hypothesis of an Amorite presence in the region (Mendenhall 1973: 159–60).[37] The evidence cited includes the etymology of *shn*, which
may be Amorite in origin (Mendenhall 1992: 201). Geographically, cultural
interaction between the northern and southern Levant within the steppe region of Transjordan falls within the realm of possibility (see Boling 1988:
35). Documentary sources from Alalakh attest the existence of a Late Bronze
polity named Amurru (Whiting 1995: 1236). At Ugarit, a connection is made
between the *rpʾum* as deified ancestors and the region of Ashtharot and Edrei
in Transjordan:

---

37. In a previous generation, K. Kenyon proposed that an Amorite invasion took
place at the end of the urban Early Bronze as an explanatory model for the destruction
of EB III sites and the ushering in of the transitional EB IV (Kenyon 1966). This view has
now largely been discarded in favor of a similar process at the beginning of the MB II
(Mazar 1990b: 188–89).

[Lo], may Rapiu, the eternal king, and may [the god] Gathar-and-Yaqar drink, the god who is dwelling in *Athtarot*, the god who is judging in *Edrei*. (KTU 1.108.2; Noort 1987: 128)

Apparently, this tradition was known to the Hebrews. In Josh 13:12, Og, the Amorite king in Bashan, is described as being from a remnant of the Rephaim (see Noort 1987: 128–29). Finally, if the Mari model of social organization (Whiting 1995: 1238) for the Amurru is applied to the Hebrew gentilic *h'mry*, we could perhaps view the Amorites as tribally organized, with the incumbent fluidity of both social and territorial boundaries that typify such social groups.

The Moabite Perspective

The fluid nature of the region of northern Moab, as portrayed by the Hebrew text, seems to be echoed by Moabite traditions in the Mesha Inscription (MI) line 10, "[T]he men of Gad had lived in Ataroth *m'lm*." Setting aside the question of the specific identity of the men of Gad for the moment (see chap. 4, p. 72), we may assume that these men were affiliated in some way with the biblical tribe of Gad (see Num 32:34). The crucial question for our discussion is: when should we situate this settlement in the "land of Ataroth"? We do not have comparative data in the inscription to ascertain a possible range of meaning for the adverbial *'lm*. However in BH, *'lm* with the prepositional *m-* occurs 16 times.[38] Close to the MI semantic context are examples in Josh 24:2 and 1 Sam 27:8, where the phrase clearly means 'of old' or 'originally'. Elsewhere, meanings include the longest time span possible, *m'wlm w'd 'wlm* (Ps 103:17) or going back to the very beginning of creation (Prov 8:23). What is important to retain is that, rhetorically, the phrase is always used to convey long periods of time (see Jer 2:20). It seems fair to assume, therefore, that the term probably shared an equivalent semantic value in the MI (see Cross 1988), so that according to Moabite historical memory, the men of Gad not only resided in Ataroth (Num 32:34; see McDonald 2000: 144; Dearman 1992: fig. 8.1) but had done so since the beginning of recorded history. The Moabite author could not remember a time when the region was not inhabited by the "men of Gad." Thus, in light of the long-range time posited by *m'lm*, while still allowing for a certain degree of hyperbole (i.e., 'forever') in the context of MI, lines 10–11 (see chap. 4, p. 72), we should search for a setting as far removed from Mesha's present as is reasonably possible.

Sitz im Leben

Whether a consensus can be reached regarding a specific Sitz im Leben for the Song of Heshbon remains doubtful. Salient proposals tie the poem to Mesha's war with the Omrides in the 9th century B.C. (Meyer 1885). That the settlement was known as the "city of Sihon" in v. 27c only referred to a prior historical situation, in the same way that Jerusalem is called the "city of David"

---

38. Gen 6:4; Josh 24:2; 1 Sam 27:8; 1 Chr 29:10; Ps 25:6, 93:2, 103:17, 119:52; Prov 8:23; Isa 42:14; 46:9; 63:16, 19; Jer 2:20, 5:15; Ezek 26:20.

(e.g., 2 Sam 5:7). M. Noth (1940) linked the setting to the 11th century B.C. and a Gadite/Moabite conflict. Bartlett connected the Song to David's wars with Moab (1968). A more recent analysis revives Meyer's 9th-century setting of Mesha's conflict against the Omrides (Levine 2000: 132–33).

However, by relegating the context of the Song of Heshbon to the 9th century B.C., with two protagonists (Israel and Moab), we limit the dimension of the poem to a strictly Israelite perspective, and we mute the competing voices that are embedded in it. According to the reading proposed above, both Amorite and Moabite views are present in the poem. If the setting were to be placed even later, the presence of the Amorites becomes an added problem. The most simple and effective explanation for the presence of these elements is that they reflect a premonarchic social and cultural context that had disappeared by the later Iron II.

The above reconstruction also raises the question of the presence of borders between pastoral nomads and early agriculturists in this pre-Iron II setting (see chap. 1; Routledge 2000b; Levy and Holl 2002). In its detailed description of the Wadi al-Mujib, the poetic excerpt The Book of the Wars of Yahweh (Num 21:14–15) clearly separates northern Moab from Moab proper and provides specific boundary markers (vv. 14–15): the mysterious *whb bswph*,[39] the Mujib's tributaries (*hnḥlym 'rnwn*) and its banks (*'šd hnḥlym*). In literary proximity, the Song of the Well (Num 21:17–18) makes a similar territorial argument on the basis of the digging of wells.

It appears that these poems reflect the common tribal practice of defining territorial boundaries according to control of established water sources (see van der Steen 2006: 30). In addition, boundaries remembered in Numbers 21 seem to incorporate the reality of the formidable barrier that the Wadi al-Mujib represents. Because of the ecological attraction of the tableland north of the Mujib (van der Steen and Smelik 2007: 155), processes of incursions, accommodations, alliances, and assimilations were probably at work during different periods of settlement history, which would also include contexts preceding and following the Iron II. Furthermore, if we follow the lead of Israel's own tribal literary tradition, these texts were perceived as one of the earliest witnesses to an Israelite presence in the highlands of Transjordan, harking back to times that long preceded the Iron II Monarchy (Ashley 1993: 6).[40]

---

39. See discussion in MacDonald 2000.

40. From a historical-archaeological standpoint, Numbers 21, with its descriptions of the attack on Arad and Heshbon, has come to represent one of the key passages illustrating the failure of the so-called conquest model of Israelite settlement (Finkelstein and Mazar 2007; Mazar 1990b: 329–30). According to this viewpoint, in the case of Arad (22 miles east-northeast of Beer-sheba), excavations at the site of Tel Arad and other sites in the region have failed to uncover Late Bronze levels, which, following biblical chronology, would correspond to the events of the earliest settlement of Israel in Canaan (Glueck 1959; see Petter 2005a). Likewise, Tall Hisban does not preserve a significant Late Bronze or Iron I settlement (Herr and Clark 2002; Merling and Geraty 1994). While no one denies

Summary

The implication of this analysis of the Song of Heshbon is that there were several protagonists in the region, with the region changing hands on several occasions. Supplemental data from the Mesha Inscription confirm that the contested nature of the region began in the earliest phases of Israelite settlement in Transjordan. This last point is especially important when set against the broad, historically attested dynamic of sociopolitical interaction that characterizes the *mishor* throughout its settlement history.

With this groundwork in place, a question arises: how did the frontier setting affect perceptions of tribal ethnic identities? As I argue in chap. 4, the textual perspectives suggest that, from both Israelite and Moabite viewpoints, a similar history of competing identities existed in the region. These shifts in tribal identity were not limited to one particular historical period but reflected *longue durée* trends inherent in the frontier setting of Transjordan.

---

the absence of Late Bronze levels at Arad and Hisban, there may be other ways to interpret the data, especially in light of the tribal dynamics in transitional frontier zones such as the Negeb and northern Moab. Terms such as *mlk* ('king') and *ʿyr* ('city') will transmit different realities on the ground in these areas than what might be expected in zones with demonstrated multitiered settlements. Thus *mlk* could mean 'tribal head' and *ʿyr* 'a large permanent encampment' (see Num 13:19; Petter 2005a: 39–40). Likewise, in the case of Heshbon/Hisban (see Lemaire 1995), the *ʿyr* of Heshbon may not have been a fortified permanent settlement with Sihon seated in some Late Bronze–like palace. Indicative of the typical mobility of tribal settlements, we are told Sihon 'resided' (participle *yšb*) in Heshbon but 'ruled' (participle *mšl*) from Aroer (Josh 12:2). In this regard, the presence of Late Bronze and Iron I sherds at Hisban may tell its own story of *both* a "people" presence *and* an absence of structural features. However, this does not mean that we should equate tented settlements with primitive and unsophisticated lifeways. In New Kingdom Egypt, Ramesses II's battle camp demonstrates that substantial and elaborate structures were available while in the field (Homan 2002). Ethnohistorical data in tribal Jordan suggest settlements more akin to tensile palaces with semipermanent occupancy.

CHAPTER FOUR

Localized Identities

In her discussion of ethnic identity in early Israel (2003), E. Bloch-Smith abandons the possibility that texts may be able to yield information relevant to ethnicity prior to the emergence of the Philistines. In her view, the Canaanite-Israelite cultural matrix is too uniform for textual evidence to draw meaningful separations during the earliest phases of the Iron I period. This approach, of course, appears to be supported by the material cultural evidence: highland material culture seems remarkably homogeneous on both sides of the River Jordan. Hence, she concludes that we cannot distinguish Canaanites from Israelites (Bloch-Smith 2003: 402; see Hess 2007: 20).

However, there is a possible way out of this "impasse" (Bloch-Smith 2003). We may be able to draw on textual evidence to reconstruct the social currents that may have shaped ethnic identity in early Israel. Within the social context of dynamic, shared dispositions (*habitus*), statements of origins may represent important primordial markers governed by a perceived common ancestry (e.g., tribal genealogies; see Shryock 1997; King and Stager 2001: 37), as is clearly the case in the biblical framework. However, if the social conditions are met in which a certain group or individuals reflect a set of practices as "lived," we may accept the notion that a particular social expression represents the core or ethnic identity of the group or individual in question. This is especially true if identity is defined in contrast to other groups (see chap. 2; Routledge 2004: 42–43).

Early forays into the instrumental-primordial continuum have included several foundational studies. In his 1993 article on the Kenites' involvement in Judges 4–5, D. Schloen made some initial statements about the instrumentalist nature of ethnicity during the Iron I period. His analysis of the Song of Deborah led him to the conclusion that threatened caravan trade routes probably caused the war described in the poem in Judges 5. These caravan traders (for instance, the "Midianites") were probably organized according to kinship ties. Through intermarriage with the highland population, southern caravaneers may therefore have affiliated with the early Israelites (Schloen 1993: 27, 35–37). B. McKay's University of Toronto dissertation plots ethnic identity in the book of Judges from the standpoint of an "integrative synthetic approach" (McKay 1997: 53), in which he takes into consideration both the primordial and the circumstantial elements in select individual stories of the Judges. While he refrains from drawing historical conclusions from his findings,[1] his articulation represents the most comprehensive survey on the question to date. Focusing on the Moabite perspective, M. Weippert also broaches the notion of an instrumentalist perspective in a footnote about the identity of the men of Gad in line 10 of the Mesha Inscription (Weippert 1997).

Building on these preliminary observations, I propose in this chapter to view early Israelite ethnicities as localized expressions of shared ideals of eponymity and covenantal Yahwism within a broader Israel group. In support of this suggested model, I examine the stories of Jael (Judges 5), Ruth, and Jephthah (Judges 11). I conclude the chapter with a reevaluation of the notion of the primacy of Reuben as suggested by F. M. Cross (see chap. 1).

Yahwism as Primordial and Instrumental Impulse

Ḥesed-Loyalty as Primordial Marker

While my purpose here is not to provide an examination of the scholarly debates concerning the origins of Yahwism in ancient Israel (e.g., Smith 2002; van der Toorn 1996; Dever 2005; Hess 2005; P. D. Miller 2000a; Albertz 1994; Albright 2006; passim), it is nevertheless important to situate some of the discussions as they pertain to ethnic identity in Transjordan. In this respect, F. M. Cross's essay on the relationship between kinship and covenant in Israelite religion (Cross 1998), set against the backdrop of his revived Midianite hypothesis (Cross 1988; see chap. 1 above), provides a helpful framework of discussion in which to understand early Israelite identities. To summarize again, he traces the origins of Yahwism to the northern parts of the Arabian Peninsula (Hijaz/biblical southern Edom). In their march northward (see P. D. Miller 1973: 7), tribal groups connected to Moses, particularly the Reubenites, settled in central Transjordan. This led to the formal establishment of Yahweh religion in the heart of Reubenite territory at Baal Peor, which Cross believes could be connected to the later Yahwistic cultic installation that Mesha conquered in the 9th century B.C. (Cross 1988: 51). Then, the cult of Yahweh presumably spread into the highlands of Cisjordan.

In returning to a long-standing assumption that the ethnic identity of early Israel was greatly shaped by its covenantal relationship with Yahweh (Albright 1963; Bright 2000; Halpern 1983; Eichrodt 1961; passim), Cross catalogs the close lexical relationship between the language of kinship and of covenant in both biblical and West Semitic sources. In support of this kinship/covenant connection, Cross lists among others the covenant between David and Jonathan (1 Sam 20:14–20), *ḥesed* as a covenantal term rooted in kinship obligations, and theophoric names connecting kinship terms to the deity (such as, *ʾabī-ʾil* 'my father is El'; Cross 1998: 6). Significantly, he highlights several features that characterized early Israel and gave it its identity: military conflicts

---

1. McKay does not thereby deny the need to situate ethnicities within a historical context. In this regard, he cites Cornell, whose own claim to the need for historically driven analyses is explicitly stated (McKay 1997: 58; see Cornell 1996: 266).

with opposing groups, kinship ties formalized through segmented genealogies, and religious identity as the "kindred of Yahweh." In language evoking
ethnographic observations of tribal social structures (see chap. 1)—these three
elements of identity overlapped and shifted according to the specific situation
(Cross 1998: 11–12).

L. Stager's adaptation of Max Weber's patrimonial model of social organization[2] adds further building blocks (Stager 1998; 1985a). In plotting the origin of Yahwism, Stager also relies heavily on several poetic excerpts attributed
to the ABH corpus that identify the location of Yahweh's theophany to Israel
in southern Edom: Seir/Edom (Judg 5:4–5), Seir/Mount Paran (Deut 33:2),
Teman/Paran (Hab 3:3; observe "Midian," Hab 3:7). Stager accepts Cross's
case for cultural covariance between Midianite groups/Qurayya Painted ware
and takes it as evidence of contacts between Moses and Midian (Stager 1998;
Exodus 4, 18, passim).[3] Thus, early Israel was "a religious federation" the allegiance of which was to the sovereign patriarch "Yahweh." To be sure, Israel
also recognized its tribal roots in Jacob/Israel, but this ancestral identity came
second (1998: 150–51). Coming from a different perspective, but with similar
conclusions, K. Sparks also focuses on religious identity as the principal trait
of early Israel. The conflict with a Canaanite coalition (in the Song of Deborah) brought them together as the "people of Yahweh" (*'am yhwh*; Sparks
1998: 116–17).

The baseline signal of identity, therefore, was tribal loyalty—*ḥesed* to Yah-
weh and to one another (Sakenfeld 2002)—which formed a unifying bond
between the different tribal groups. But the primordial bond of covenantal
Yahwism (see P. D. Miller 2000a; Mendenhall 1955; McCarthy 1978) was also
confirmed by recognition of a common ancestry carried via the eponymous
"Israel" or, in its full patrimonial designation, "sons of Israel." As Hasel (1994),
Yurko (1997), and others (e.g., Hoffmeier 1997) have argued, "Israel" of the
Merneptah Stele refers to a people group that, unless one takes an overly
skeptical stance, should be connected to the "Israel" mentioned in the biblical
sources (Finkelstein and Mazar 2007).

Ḥērem-Otherness as Primordial Marker

Israel, in typical tribal behavior (see van der Steen 2006: 28), also seemed
to identify itself in contrast to others (see chap. 2). In the biblical texts, these

---

2. See J. D. Schloen's comprehensive treatment from the perspective of Late Bronze
Ugarit (Schloen 2001).

3. The notion of a "Midianite trade route" has been developed more fully by P. Parr
(1988) and E. van der Steen (1996; 1999). Using survey data from the Wadi Hasa area
(MacDonald 1988) and the Moab Plateau (J. M. Miller 1991), van der Steen, in particular, identifies the following pattern: a population increase at the Qurayyat Oasis caused
some of the pastoralist elements of the population to move to new pastoral grounds
around the Wadi Hasa, which, in turn, caused another population movement northward.
Midianites are said to have been part of this south-to-north migration on account of the
"Midianite" Ware (Qurayyat painted pottery) present in Edom and at Amman (van der
Steen 1996: 66–67).

traits are reflected in the contest against "other gods" (see Josh 24:14, 17). Specifically, the "otherness" identity of the tribes as *ʿam yhwh* is expressed via *ḥērem* warfare. The topic of war in ancient Israel has been the subject of considerable attention both in classical critical studies and in recent discussions (Trimm 2012; Lyons 2010; Niditch 1993; von Rad 1991). B. Ollenburger (1991: 3), in his review of the history of scholarship (see also Lyons 2010: 14–21), quotes Wellhausen's framing of early Israelite identity:

> The name "Israel" means "El does battle,"[4] and Jehovah was the warrior El, after whom the nation styled itself. The camp was, so to speak at once the cradle in which the nation was nursed and the smithy in which it was welded into unity; it was also the primitive sanctuary. There Israel was, and there was Jehovah. (Wellhausen 1957: 434)

It is fair to say that this classical Wellhausian sense of early Israelite identity has had a profound impact on subsequent scholarship.[5] Whether fronted in the "conquest" models or deemphasized in the "peaceful"-infiltration approaches to Israelite settlement, the realities of conflict in tribal interaction (see chap. 1) are difficult to negate. Thus, the revelation of Yahweh as the divine warrior (e.g., P. D. Miller 1973: 92) appears to hold both religious and historical significance.

The shape and nature of war in ancient Israel according to documentary sources continue to be fiercely debated (Trimm 2012: 175–80), but no one seems to deny the considerable hold that the word and/or concept *ḥērem* seems to have on the biblical narratives (Niditch 1993; Stern 1991; Kang 1989; Monroe 2007). Evidence suggests that *ḥērem* was a widespread ancient concept with attested usage in Ugaritic (KTU 1.13), Sumerian, Hittite, Akkadian, and Egyptian contexts (Stern 1991: 5–17; see also Kang 1989).[6] In the available biblical and cognate data, *ḥērem* (verbal and nominal) carries the broad idea of "dedication" (MI, line 17; Lev 27:28) to the deity with, in most instances, the notion of "consecration to destruction" (Stern 1991: 16; e.g., Josh 6:17; Judg 1:17; 21:11; passim). Both the setting and the scope of destruction is debated because the record yields variegated dimensions to *ḥērem* warfare (e.g.,

---

4. For a review of scholarship on the etymology of "Israel," see van der Veen, Theis, and Görg 2010: 19.

5. As Ollenburger interprets Wellhausen, "War was not just a feature of Israel's experience, or even of its religion. Ancient Israel as the people of God was a military camp, and its God was a warrior. War was at the heart of Israel's religion and thus of *its identity*" (emphasis mine; Ollenburger 1991: 3).

6. See P. Stern's analysis (following J. Yoyote's) of an excerpt from the 9th-century B.C. Osorkon inscriptions at Karnak that attests the *ḥērem* concept (Stern 1991: 81–83):

> Thereupon (the governor of) Upper Egypt said, "Go and bring to me every (case of) transgression against him and the records of the ancestors . . . the Eye of Re." Then the prisoners were brought in to him at (once) like a bundle of pinioned ones (?). Then he struck them down for him causing (them) to be carried like goats the night of the feast of the Evening Sacrifice in which braziers are kindled . . . like braziers (at the feast) of the Going Forth of Sothis (i.e., the New Year). *Everyone was burned in the place of his crime. . . . Thebes.* (emphasis mine; R. Caminos 1958: 48, cited in Stern 1991).

Niditch 1993). In summary, *ḥērem* includes some destruction of life (but not always all human life; see Rahab and discussion below, contra Niditch 1993: 81), property, and territorial loss for those who incurred the 'anger' (*'p*) of the deity (e.g., MI, line 5). Hence *ḥērem* as a manifestation of divine judgment is a strong undercurrent throughout the available evidence. *Ḥērem* warfare is also tied to the deity's own otherness, typically expressed via the language of 'holiness' (*qdš* as 'consecration'; Kamrada 2009: 67–70; von Rad 1991: 42; Niditch 1993) and related notions of "sacred space" (e.g., Num 10: 35; Longman and Reid 1995). Consequently, efforts at separating *ḥērem* as divine judgment (Yahweh's just punishment against offenders) from *ḥērem* as Yahweh's own portion (e.g., that which is devoted to him; Niditch 1993: 29–37) have not been convincing (e.g., Smend 1970; Stolz 1972).

Because *ḥērem* warfare is used to characterize specific military confrontations in ancient Israel (see Kang 1989), the a priori implication is that we cannot view every conflict recorded in the biblical text as a *ḥērem* act. A posteriori, however, inasmuch as territorial armed disputes are involved, it seems difficult to disentangle the underpinnings of divine judgment and ownership that are the characteristics of *ḥērem* warfare. When the social notions of patrimonial inheritance bequeathed from the "father to the son" are considered, we may be exposed to a pervasive notion that reaches deep into conceptions of otherness identity in these tribal settings.

The emphasis on sacred space is evident in the dispute between Moabite and Israelite claims to the region of northern Moab (see chap. Three). Within the patrimonial social structure, the question becomes one related to inheritance and land: whose territory is it, Yahweh's sons' or Chemosh's sons'? In the Song of Heshbon, the argument is that in former times, Chemosh gave up his own claim to the area on account of an unstated grievance he held against his people (Kang 1989: 132). In Mesha's generation, the land was yet again given up on the basis of divine retribution. Mesha, "Chemosh's son" (MI, line 1) however, has now restored his relationship (loyalty) with Chemosh, which then enables him to reclaim the area (Chemosh's land, MI line 5) and devote to destruction (*wḥrmt*) the space that was hitherto the property of Israel (line 14–17). Thus, because territories were claimed by patrimonial heads, Yahweh (in Israelite texts) or Chemosh (in Moabite traditions),[7] tribal boundaries seem to have a significant impact on tribal identities as well.[8]

---

7. According to Deut 2:9, however, as a nod to Moab's ancestral ties to Israel (Gen 19), even the land grant to Moab was Yahweh's.

8. In this regard, a possible parallel also may be drawn from the Merneptah Stele (ca. 1206 B.C.) with the mention of "Israel":

Yenoam is made into nonexistence
Israel is wasted, its seed is not
Harru is become a widow (Hoffmeier 1997: 28)

The argument for seed-as-progeny can be made on the basis of the symmetry with the subsequent line, which describes judgment clearly as loss of human life ("widow"). Accordingly, Merneptah can claim the complete destruction of Israel as a people. In this language, the concept of *ḥērem* would thus be echoed in hyperbolic language typical of

Ḥērem-Otherness and Ḥesed-Loyalty as Instrumental Markers

Because of these *ḥērem* dynamics at work in both Moabite and Israelite contexts,[9] the fortunes of the different tribal groups and their territories were essentially tied to their own loyalty to the deity. In this respect, the well-known Deuteronomic evaluation of Judg 3:5–6 may be understood to extend beyond "religious syncretism" and go to the heart of the instrumental dimension of ethnic identity in Israel (see Deut 7:3–6):

> So the people of Israel dwelt among the Canaanites, the Hittites, the Amorites, the Perizzites, the Hivites and the Jebusites; and they took their daughters to themselves for wives, and their own daughters they gave to their sons; *and they served their gods.* (Judg 3:5–6, RSV, emphasis mine)

If patrimonial Yahwism served a unifying identity, then intermarriage (see Esse 1992) with non-Israelite tribal groups with the concomitant adoption of other religious practices had catastrophic consequences: patrimonial breakdown, disloyalty, loss of distinctiveness and dedication. This multifaceted and complex process of "Canaanization" (see Block 1999) is a pervasive motif in the book of Judges.[10] The resulting identity shift would set the stage for the "great reversal" in that the divine warrior (P. D. Miller 1973; Kang 1989) prosecutes *ḥērem* warfare against his *own* people (Josh 7:1ff.; Num 21:6; Kamrada 2009). One group could lose its good standing and thereby face banishment from the deity's sacred space with the resulting loss of identity: dislocation or, in more extreme situations, death. In the time of the Judges, the Israel confederation does act as a centripetal force, thanks in no small part to the Judges as prosecutors of Yahweh's wars. However, prospects for survival as an entity become gloomier in the prophetic corpus, with the Exile interpreted as the fulfillment of reversed *ḥērem* (Hos 1:9; Jer 7:15; passim). Thus, Ezekiel could speak ironically of the ancestral roots of his generation: "Your father was an Amorite and your mother was a Hittite" (Ezek 16:3).

So *ḥērem*-otherness, according to the model suggested here, becomes a literal and figurative two-edged sword as an identity marker. On the one hand, it signals patrimonial tribal identity. The deity owns the land and bequeaths it to his progeny (Yahweh to Israel; Chemosh to Moab). On the other hand, the contingency of the progeny's identity is equally tied to another "otherness," that of the deity, who as patrimonial head would not hesitate to disown his own children, should they transgress and become "common" by their disloyalty to him and to one another (e.g., Judg 21:11).

---

the conquest narrative genre (see Younger 1990). The specific use of the plow symbol for seed-as-crop (as opposed to the symbol seed-as-procreation; Hasel 1994) also leaves room for the agricultural meaning to be present in the destruction language of the stele. Thus, if we allow the metonymy to function as double entendre (see Hoffmeier 1997: 27–31), there might be enough (intentional?) ambiguity in the poetry to permit the meaning of a judgment that affected Israel as *both* progeny *and* territory.

9. The Chronicler also documents the practice among the Ammonites (2 Chr 20:23).

10. For a review of recent scholarship on Judges, see Butler 2009.

Movements away from Yahwism, however, are also balanced by shifting currents *toward* Yahwism. The "mixed multitude" of the Exodus (Exod 12:38; Num 11:4), the unhappy incorporation of the Gibeonites (Joshua 9), and the absorption of the Kenites, Kenizzites, and Yerahmeelites into the territory of Judah (Young 1993: 12–16) all document varying degrees of social interaction with Israel. When set against a frontier ecological backdrop, the process becomes more focused. Here individuals seem to undergo a dramatic shift to embrace Israelite Yahwistic identity. Non-Israelites could be the beneficiary of *ḥesed*/loyalty and avoid *ḥērem*/otherness as a result of their embracing of Yahwism.

With this broad conceptual framework in place, we now turn to several examples in the available documentary sources that appear to illustrate the dynamics of identity within the frontier tribal setting of early Israel in general and of Transjordan in particular.

Jael

Many studies still consider the Song of Deborah (Judges 5) to contain valuable historical data regarding premonarchic Israel (Albertz 1994: 80–82; Gottwald 1985: 281). The example of Jael (Judg 5:24–27) is taken to be a model illustration of the dynamic relationship between Yahwism and ethnicity during the Iron I, when *ḥesed* loyalty and separation from others (*ḥērem*) supply the conceptual underpinnings of early Israelite identity.

While this war song commemorating Yahweh's victory (Judg 5:1, 4–5, 10) seems to reflect remarkable literary symmetries (see Vincent 2000: 62; for a more-critical approach, see Peckham 1993: 603, 647–48), commentators differ in ways to portray the poem's syntactical and literary cohesiveness (e.g., Butler 2009; Soggin 1981). Nevertheless, as a baseline, the poem may be outlined generally as follows:

- 5:1–3:   Introduction lauding leaders who volunteered to engage in Yahweh's war
- 5:4–5:   Description of the appearing of Yahweh from Seir/Edom
- 5:6–11:   The cause of the conflict
- 5:12–18: Loyalty/disloyalty of the tribes
- 5:19–23: Description of the victory (Yahweh's control over the elements)
- 5:24–27: Sisera's death at the hand of Jael
- 5:28–31: The celebration of Sisera's mother will turn into mourning

The first part of the poem describes the victorious intervention of Yahweh and the loyalty of the leaders in Israel. This loyalty is reflected chiefly by the courage of Deborah. In contrast, some tribal groups are singled out for their exclusion from the conflict. The second part of the poem (vv. 24–31) directs its attention to another woman, Jael (with the specific designation "wife of Heber, the Kenite") and her victim, Sisera. Her loyalty is also established as being "most blessed among women" (v. 24), which results in her being a friend of Yahweh (v. 31). In the concluding lines, the mother of Sisera is also given space as a woman who thought she could celebrate her son's return. However, she will instead become a mourner (vv. 28–30). There are structural markers in vv. 2 and 9 ("that the people offered themselves willingly") that loosely frame the lengthy introduction.

Overall, the account lists those who participated in the conflict—namely, various groups that are affiliated with the designation "Israel" (Ephraim, Benjamin, Machir, Zebulun, Reuben, Gilead, Dan, Asher, and Zebulun [vv. 14–17]). The emphasis lies on the commanders. The poem also highlights those who did not participate (vv. 15–18). In typical divine warfare language, the actual battle account (vv. 19–23) puts the attention on the intervention of Yahweh in directing the heavens and watercourses against the kings and their chariotry (Block 1999: 218). Very little attention is devoted to the enemy (v. 19, "The kings came, they fought; they fought the kings of Canaan"). However, the most vivid description of the poem belongs to the killing of Sisera (vv. 24–27). Jael's bravery is highlighted in particular. She single-handedly kills the Canaanite general. Like a predator, she stealthily approaches her prey and overtakes him by surprise (while he is asleep? see 4:21).[11]

Significantly, along with "people of Yahweh" (vv. 10, 13), the designation "Yahweh" and "Israel"[12] are closely connected in the poetic symmetry of the song (vv. 3, 5, 10). Consequently, it may not be possible to draw precise distinctions between Israel and the people of Yahweh within the literary context of the song; "Israel" as the tribal-origin designation and "people of Yahweh" as a covenantal designation seem to represent different facets of the same primordial identity in the Song of Deborah (see McKay 1997: 145–49).

Commentators have long noted Yahweh's characterization as the divine warrior who defeats his enemies on his people's behalf and thus acts as a unifying supratribal force (P. D. Miller 1973; Block 1999; Kang 1989). Yahweh's "mighty acts" perform a dynamic function to recall the various tribal groups/ heads back to an ancestral unity, appealing to their covenant loyalty. Serving in Yahweh's army "forges" (Stager 1998) the ethnic identity of the individual tribes. However, to leave the discussion here would be to impose too-rigid a primordial framework on the text. If eponymous ancestry and covenantal Yahwism were indeed a primary ethnic trait, what the poem also emphasizes is the diversity of the confederation. The fact that some groups did not participate in the conflict indicates that allegiance to a supratribal "Israel" was subjected to personal/group concerns and priorities. It is possible that the reference to the leaders in the poem underlines this perception. Significantly, the "clans" (or 'divisions' *plgwt*; Block 1999: 233) of Reuben (vv. 15–16) did not elect to get involved, nor did Gilead (v. 17, perhaps an intentionally territorial designation for "Gad" in this context; Ottosson 1969: 29). In contrast, Machir (v. 14), also a territorial designation for Transjordanian Manasseh, and "the princes" of Issachar (v. 15) did. Allegiance to local rulers (or tribal heads) came before allegiance to any other entity, whether primordial or otherwise. Ties to an

---

11. For a discussion of the contrasts between the accounts of Judges 4 and 5, see Halpern 1988; on the role of Jael, see also S. Ackerman 1998; and T. Butler 2009.

12. The designation occurs in vv. 2, 3, 5, 7, 8, 9, and 11.

ideal, primordial root ("Israel") could therefore be subject to other, perhaps more-pragmatic considerations (see Schloen 1993). The linguistic evidence also appears to support this diverse and heterogeneous framework. In his earlier views (see chap. 3), Young singled out the Song of Deborah within ABH as the text that is most illustrative of the presence of several dialects prior to the establishment of SBH during the course of the Iron II (Young 1993: 124). In light of this background, the surprise in the poem is not that some tribes did not answer the call to arms but that *any* reported for duty at all.

The section of the song that concerns Sisera and Jael further illustrates the instrumental impulse of tribal identities in early Israel. According to the available sources, Kenites as pastoral-nomadic groups are generally located in the southeastern frontier regions of Israel (see Judg 1:16; 1 Sam 27:10; 30:29) or as far south as the Sinai region (Exod 3:1; Judg 1:16; see Halpern 1992). While biblical sources point to the shared ancestral ties with the Israel group (Judg 4:11; Exod 2:15–22; see McKay 1997: 129, 142–43), these primordial bonds may not necessarily have translated into loyalty. The biblical account of Heber's geographical "separation" from his kinship group (Judg 4:11) coupled with the establishment of "peace" between Heber's "house" and "Jabin, king of Hazor" (Judg 4:17), seems to reflect a socioethnic background of shifting localized loyalties not unlike the one described in the poem of Judges 5 itself.

The significance of Jael in the poem may be partially indicated in terms of the level of details concerning the incident and the manner in which she disposes of Sisera in Judges 5. Her deed offers some parallels to the heroic acts of Ehud who, by deceit and stealth, stalked and killed his prey for Israel (Eglon of Moab), along with recounting the graphic details (Judg 3:15–25; see Halpern 1988). But the emphasis of the poem seems to rest in her characterization as 'most blessed' (*tbrk mnšym*, v. 24). In the concluding line of the account, by implication, she is counted among the friends of Yahweh (*ʾhbyw* 'the ones who love him [= Yahweh] v. 31). Thus Jael's identity as one who loves Yahweh and, by implication, the people of Yahweh could be perceived as a return to her true, primordial, Kenite identity. This image would then be cast in contradistinction to Heber, who is portrayed as a man who is disloyal to his ancestral ties (by relocation and by his alliance with Canaanites, "the enemies"; cf. Judg 5:31). If we allow the "house-of-the-father" social metaphor to weigh in (see Schloen 2001: 54), her blatantly deceptive and ruthless actions seem to signal an actual transfer from one patrimonial head (Heber's house) to another (Yahweh's), which translates into her socioreligious reintegration rather than exclusion. As the narrative account of Judges 4 states, victory has indeed come by the hand of a woman (Judg 4:9).[13]

---

13. The Rahab narrative in the book of Joshua provides some obvious thematic parallels in terms of identity shift: the act of loyalty to Israel (*ḥesed*, Josh 2:12, 14) of Rahab, the Cananite prostitute, is expressed through words of deception to her own people (the "king of Jericho" [Josh 2:3]), which in turns leads to the destruction of Yahweh's enemy (*ḥērem*, Josh 6:12, 18, 21). Thus, in both narratives, salvation is secured by a deliberate abandonment of allegiance, either to a husband or to a king, which in a patrimonial framework

To summarize the data from the Song of Deborah: there probably were many underlying socioeconomic reasons why some tribal groups did not come to join the fight (see Stager 1989). However, perhaps the main reason some tribes were not mentioned was to highlight their lack of religious commitment. When these tribal groups failed to join "the tribes of Yahweh," as in the case of Reuben and Gad, their action underscored their tenuous commitment to an Israelite identity at that time. In contrast, a female standing on Israel's tribal periphery (a duly noted fact within a patrimonial social structure; see Judg 4:4–5, 9) was incorporated among Yahweh's friends during this time of crisis. Thus, with Yahwism as the primary ethnic marker of shared dispositions (expressed through loyalty), along with "otherness" (expressed through destruction of Israel's enemy), Jael effectively embraced an Israelite identity, while tribal groups such as Reuben and Gilead/Gad functionally ignored their identity or deliberately turned away from it.[14]

Ruth

Ruth's setting in the central Transjordan shifting frontier zone seems especially well suited to being included in this discussion. Her switch of allegiance is not unlike Jael's experience in the Song of Deborah. However, whereas Jael might have had ties to Israel's ancestry in the story line, in the case of Ruth, the text makes no such claim and does not wish to trace Moab's common origins with Israel (e.g., Genesis 19; Deuteronomy 2; see Routledge 2004: 43–44). On the contrary, in the general setting of the book of Judges (e.g., Judges 3), Moab is viewed as an enemy of Israel. Ruth, however, evokes a different viewpoint of the period preceding kingship in Israel (Ruth 1:1).[15] One glaring contrast between Judges and Ruth that is relevant to our discussion concerns Ruth's marriage (and Orpah's, 1:4) into an Israelite 'family' *mšpḥh* (see Cross 1998). While this practice is clearly condemned in the Deuteronomic framework of Judges and brings curses on Israel (Judges 3; Deuteronomy 28), in Ruth, intermarriage turns into a blessing and eventually spawns the Davidic line.

---

carries considerable significance in terms of social identity. The narrative also emphasizes Rahab's role as what appears to be a proxy patrimonial head in securing the salvation of her own "house" (Josh 2:13; 6:23). While the Song of Deborah focuses solely on Jael's actions, Rahab's confession of Yahweh's mighty acts is explicit ("I know" could be taken as covenantal knowledge in this context, Josh 2:9). Finally, the narrative summary "she has lived among the Israelites to this day" (Josh 6:22) characterized her shift in identity as permanent, extending beyond an ephemeral machination based on self-preservation (see Hess 1996: 134).

14. Scholars differ with regard to the reason that Judah and Simeon did not participate (see the summary in Butler 2009: 146), but it is not unreasonable to surmise similar currents affecting Judah and Simeon, both geographically (part of their territories in transitional zones) and religiously (as members of the tribes of Yahweh).

15. While studies routinely divorce Ruth from the period of the Judges (e.g., Driver 1956: 454; passim), there is no compelling reason to dismiss the story as unrelated to an Iron I setting (see Hackett 1998).

The theme of kinship obligations forms the backbone of Ruth's story. In this context, kinship designations abound. The narrative sections designate Naomi as Ruth's 'mother-in-law' *ḥmwt* (2:11, 18, 19 [twice]; 3:1, 6, 16, 17). In the interactions between Ruth and Naomi, the narrative designates Ruth a 'daughter-in-law' *klh* (1:6, 7, 8, 22; 2:20; 3:1, 6; 4:15), but in reported speech, Naomi addresses Ruth as 'my daughter' *bty* (1:11, 12, 13; 2:1, 22; 3:1, 16, 18).[16] Boaz (2:4, passim) is 'from the family of Elimelech' *mmšpḥt ᵓlymlk* (2:1, 3; see also 4:3), as 'our relative' *mgᵓlnw* (2:20), *mdᶜtnw* (3:2), and of course, as a 'kinsman redeemer' *gᵓl* (3:9, 12; 4:14).[17]

This kinship language should be viewed in a primordial light in the narrative. The gentilic phrase 'Ruth the Moabitess' *hmwᵓbyh* is the anchor designation for Ruth (1:22; 2:2, 21; 4:5, 10). [18] A variant is the 'Moabitess maiden' *nᶜrh* (2:6). Otherwise, she is simply Ruth (1:14, passim). This general geographic designation, "Moabitess," reflects typical use of gentilics to describe foreigners in narrative. Specific patrimonial origins are reserved for individuals in the Israelite territory (see 'Ephratites from Bethlehem of Judah' *ᵓprtym*, 1:2; Revell 1996a; 1996b). Further evidence of primordialism is Ruth's own declaration concerning her ancestral home, the 'field of Moab' *śdh* (1:1; 2:6): 'I am a foreigner' *nkryh* (2:10). Likewise, Boaz assumes a similar perspective based on descent when he evokes 'the land of your generations' *ᵓrṣ mwldtk* (2:11). Clearly, the narrative follows the expected biblical trajectory of a primordial tribal view of identity.

This essentialist/primordial setting, however, only serves as backdrop to what appears to be deeper social realities in the story. Ruth's declaration to her mother-in-law is tantamount to a covenantal oath (see Cross 1998: 5) and states (1:16–17):

ky ᵓl ᵓšr tlky ᵓlk
wbᵓšr tlyny ᵓlyn
ᶜmk ᶜmy wᵓlhyk ᵓlhy
bᵓšr tmwty ᵓmwt
wšm ᵓqbr
kh yᶜśh yhwh ly
wkh ysyp
ky hmwt ypryd byny wbynk

Where you will go, I will go. Where you will live, I will live. Your people are my people and your God is my God. Where you will die, I will die; there I will be buried. May Yahweh do thus and more so to me, if even death separates me from you!

---

16. Plural forms are in 1:6, 7, 8, 11, 12, and 13 for "daughters" and "daughters-in-law," obviously referring to Ruth and Orpah. Boaz also calls Ruth "my daughter" (2:8; 3:11).

17. The nameless kinsman redeemer's designation as *gᵓl* is in 4:6, 8.

18. Her full legal status is probably indicated in 4:10, "Ruth the Moabitess, the widow of Mahlon."

Thus, her primordial roots are set aside for a new circumstantial identity. She adopts her mother-in-law's people, her God, and, by wishing to be buried in a foreign land, she effectively renounces her Moabite ancestry. In contrast to Orpah (1:15), she abandons her religious identity as a member of the "people of Chemosh" (see Num 21:29) and embraces a new identity as follower of Yahweh (2:12), which also includes the locus (and presumably practice) of her burial (I will discuss the relationship between mortuary practice and ethnicity in chap. 5). Boaz acknowledges the profound shift in her identity (2:11–12):

*wt⁽zby ᵓbyk wᵓmk wᵓrṣ mwldtk wtlky ᵓl ⁽m ᵓšr lᵓ yd⁽t tmwl šlšwm
yšlm yhwh p⁽lk wthy mśkrtk šlmh m⁽m yhwh ᵓlhy yśrᵓl ᵓšr bᵓt lḥswt tḥt knpyw*

[Y]ou left your father and your mother and the land of your birth and have come to a people that you did not know before. May Yahweh repay your deeds, and may you have a full reward from Yahweh, the God of Israel, under whose wings you have come for refuge!

The transformation is sealed after Boaz marries Ruth (no longer designated a Moabitess at this point, 4:13): the Davidic genealogy assumes Ruth's assimilation into Israel. She has lost her Moabite identity and gained full acceptance into Israel as one of King David's ancestors. Thus, on the one hand, while "otherness" here does not take the imagery of *ḥērem*,[19] the concept of separation is implied by the predominant designation "Moab" in characterizing Ruth. On the other hand, *ḥesed* loyalty forms the backbone of her newly found identity. Perhaps it is on the basis of this shift in her identity that she finds herself listed in the Davidic genealogy.[20]

---

19. Broadly speaking, covenant curses are implied in the famine and death motifs of the story.

20. In this context, it is perhaps helpful to consider the illustration provided by Uriah, the Hittite (2 Samuel 11). Even though Uriah's gentilic designation 'Uriah the Hittite' (*ḥḥty*) places him outside the ethnic boundary of Israel (and liable to Deuteronomic *ḥērem*, Deuteronomy 7), everything else we are told about him justifies an Israelite ethnic identity. Thus, in this case, the gentilic *ḥḥty* functions as a primordial designation of origin rather than a reflection of current ethnic identity (similar to Jael's Kenite origins). His name bears the apocopated theophoric suffix *yh*. This would indicate a religious identity that is no longer connected with his Hittite origins. In support of this interpretation, he marries an Israelite, Bathshebah, daughter of Eliam (2 Sam 11:3), and makes his home in the land of his wife—a clear example of matrilocalism (v. 8). His allegiance to Israel is further documented by his loyalty to the Davidic kingdom and his commitment to fight for David and his commander, Joab ("my lord Joab" [v. 11]). Finally, in his speech to David, he refuses to go down to his house, since "the ark (*hᵓrwn*) and Israel and Judah are dwelling in tents" (v. 11; see Alter 1999: 252). In the setting of *ḥērem* warfare, dedication through sexual abstinence was considered paramount (von Rad 1991: 42). On its own, the allusion to the ark would be slim evidence indicating his religious identity. However, in light of the total evidence gathered from the pericope, the example of Uriah perhaps provides another illustration of the instrumental impulse in ethnic identity in ancient Israel (perhaps also Zelek, the Ammonite, listed with Uriah among David's mighty men, 2 Sam 23:37–39).

Early Israelite Identities in Transjordan

With this proposed model of dynamic ethnicities, we now turn specifically to the context of the early settlement of central Transjordan and review textual perceptions of the region, examine the Jephthah story as a localized example of dynamic ethnicity, and reassess F. M. Cross's hypothesis of the primacy of Reuben in early Israel.

Defining Gilead

In terms of geographical boundaries, "the other side of the Jordan" falls outside the borders of the promise land. In typical tribal boundary fashion, it is a river that provides the natural border (Num 34:11, 12; Noort 1987: 125). In the well-known story of the altar of witness (Josh 22), it seems important to underscore that the closely avoided conflict (Josh 22:12) concerns the location of the altar in the "region of the Jordan on the *side of the sons of Israel*" (Josh 22:11, emphasis mine).[21] Thus territories are clearly contrasted: "the sons of Israel" are in 'the land of Canaan' *'rṣ knʿn*; "the sons of Reuben, the sons of Gad and the half tribe of Manasseh" are in 'the land of Gilead' *'rṣ hglʿd*, characterized as 'the land of their possession' *'rṣ 'hztm* (Josh 22:9; Ottosson 1969). Noticeably, the two and a half tribes are never designated "sons of Israel" in the story.[22] This sociolinguistic nuance appears to obtain elsewhere as well. It seems customary for the designation of individuals to switch from specific patronymics in the case of a "bona fide" Israelite (e.g., Elisha, "son of Shaphat") to gentilics in the case of a Transjordanian Israelite resident (such as "Gileadite"; e.g., Jair, Judg 10:3 [see Revell 1996b]).[23] Furthermore, the famous s/shibboleth incident (Judg 12:6) hints at the fragmented nature of the region, even in terms of linguistic differences (Young 1993). Similarly, the debate over the language of the Dayr ʿAlla inscription (in the Jordan Valley) perhaps attests that the region was a cultural fault line.[24]

Space does not allow for a review of scholarship on tribal settlements in Transjordan (see Hess 1994; McDonald 2000; Noth 1944), but even a cursory examination of the issues results in the strong impression that the land grant in Transjordan is regarded as a concession to the tribes of Reuben, Gad, and the half-tribe of Manasseh (e.g., Num 32:6–15; Josh 12:6). In Josh 13:8–33, the town lists (as opposed to boundary descriptions; Hess 1994: 190–91) for

---

21. See Boling and Wright (1982: 505) for a discussion of the textual problem. The LXX places the altar across the river on the Transjordanian side. However, v. 10 makes it clear that the altar was built "in the land of Canaan."

22. See Josh 22:11, 13, 15, 21, 25; Josh 22:30, 31 replaces "half tribe" with "sons of Manasseh"; Josh 22:32, 33, 34 exclude "Manasseh" in the designation.

23. "Elijah, the Tishbite . . . in Gilead" (1 Kgs 17:1) is a marked designation, perhaps due to Elijah's prominent role in Israelite records.

24. In spite of its affinities with Aramaic, the language of Dayr ʿAlla, Huehnergard concludes, represents another, independent branch of the Northwest Semitic family (Huehnergard 1991: 293).

the tribes in Transjordan are notably less clear than the boundary descriptions of the Cisjordanian tribes (Routledge 2004: 44–48; see Hess 1994). To be sure, in typical *ḥērem* warfare the tribes receive their grant from Yahweh (Deut 3:12–13; Num 21:31–35). However, perhaps as a nod to the complexities of the situation, on the (rare) occasion when the tribes of Transjordan are designated "sons of Israel," they are said to dwell "in the land of the Amorites" (Judg 10:8; Num 21:31). In the majority of instances, however, the fallback designation for Israelite Transjordan seems to be the geographical region of "Gilead" (e.g., Gen 31:21; Deut 34:1; Josh 22:9; Judg 7:3; 10:17; 20:1; 2 Kgs 10:33; see Ottosson 1969; McDonald 2000: 198). From this general designation, single tribes may also be in view: Manasseh, because of its patronymic ties to Gilead (e.g., Num 26:29) receives "half of the mountain of Gilead" with the Jabbok/Zarqa as its southern boundary (Deut 3:13; Josh 17:1). However, since it receives "all of Bashan" (which included the region of "Argob," Og's conquered land, Deut 3:4, 14; see McDonald 2000: 127), Manasseh is often linked to Bashan (Deut 4:43) or via its eponym, "Machir" (as in the Song of Deborah). Gad and Reuben share the other "half of the mountain of Gilead" (Deut 3:12; see Num 32:40; Josh 12:3, 4) from the Arnon/Mujib to the Jabbok/Zarqa (Deut 3:16; see McDonald 2000: 197). Specific boundaries between Gad and Reuben associate Reuben with the *mishor* (MPR; e.g., Deut 4:43), and "Gilead" with Gad (e.g., Ramoth Gilead, Deut 4:43; in the Song of Deborah). In summary, while there exist several variations in designations of Transjordan and the differing tribal groups in the available texts (see McDonald's thorough discussions, 2000), there is nevertheless a distinct separation between the tribes of Israel in Transjordan and the tribes of Israel in the heartland. In this regard, the story of Jephthah may illustrate some of the complexities connected with the emergence of Israelite identities in Transjordan.

Jephthah

In Judges 5, the tribes in the central highlands of Transjordan are clearly at odds with the broader Israelite tribal group. In the Jephthah story (Judges 11–12),[25] however, the perception of Transjordan appears at first to have shifted dramatically to a prestige status as a preeminent tribal grouping in the larger Israel confederation. Jephthah's own identity is unambiguous in the storyline. As the 'son of a harlot' *bn 'šh zwnh* (Judg 11:1; Butler 2009: 280), he has no patrimonial ties and no land ownership (v. 7, "Did you not hate me and drove me out of my father's house?"). Nevertheless, the elders of "Gilead" (the geographical designation that presumably encompasses the two

---

25. As in the case for the Song of Heshbon (see chap. 3), the story of Jephthah has its own "contested history" in biblical scholarship (B. G. Webb 2012: 15–52). Unsurprisingly, opinions differ sharply in terms of both the composition of the narrative and its value for historical reconstruction. From both a tribal-memory and ethnohistorical perspective, however, the Jephthah story contains rich and relevant data and is therefore included in the model of ethnic identity proposed in this book.

and a half tribes; see Judg 20:1), which, in a seemingly stunning reversal, now represents the "Israel" group, turn to him for help to address their immediate military needs in the conflict with the Ammonites (see Judges 10). Thus, for circumstantial reasons, the outsider (with *no* patrimonial currency) gains status as "the Gileadite" (11:40) and becomes a tribal "head" within "Israel" (Judg 11:8, 11; see Jair, Judg 10:3).

As he leads "Israel," Jephthah's identity seems no longer to be equivocal because he prosecutes a war that has the distinct characteristics of divine warfare with *ḥērem* elements (Judg 11:30; see Kamrada 2009). Competing territorial claims are reminiscent of the situation in Numbers 21 (see chap. 3). Whereas the situation dealt with Moab's claim to the *mishor* in Numbers 21, here the "sons of Ammon" enter the fray and stake a claim to the area for themselves. According to the Hebrew narrative (we do not have the Ammonite version), Ammon is caught in a classic case of diplomatic "spin" in its claim to the area (Judg 11:13). In Jephthah's reported speech, Jephthah makes the case that, unlike Moab (see Num 21:26), Ammon's historical connection to the *mishor* does not exist (perhaps alluding to the tradition that places the border of Ammon at the Jabbok/Wadi Zarqa; Num 21:24). I take Jephthah's reference to "Chemosh, your god," when addressing the Ammonite as a deliberate irony modeled after the initial taunt against Moab as recorded in the Song of Heshbon (see discussion in chap. 3). The points may be rephrased rhetorically as follows (Judg 11:24–26):

- Have you become the people of Chemosh, that you would claim this land for yourselves?
- Do you not remember a previous contender, Balak, who unsuccessfully attempted to take the land back from us?
- Do we not have an ancestral claim to this land, harking back 300 years?

In light of the documented encroachment of the region (Judg 3:13–14; 6:33), even during Jephthah's days (Judg 10:8), Jephthah's idealized version of the settlement history of the region (not unlike line 10 of the Mesha Inscription) plays into the strong ironic tone of his speech and should perhaps be viewed as *intentional* in order to provoke a military confrontation. To paraphrase again: "Every one knows the *mishor* is a hugely contested area, but it is ours and has been so for a very long time; so come and get it, if you can!" Whether the nuances proposed here are correct,[26] clearly Jephthah's provocation worked according to plan as the king of Ammon chose to pursue his policies through other means (i.e., war, Judg 11:28). Thus the speech may reflect another witness to the tribal record, in which competing territorial claims are answered with no small use of irony (see chap. 3).

The complexity of Jephthah's characterization deepens further in the incident with his daughter. The event (which became part of Israelite lore, Judg

---

26. For other viewpoints on Jephthah's speech, see Boling 1988: 52–53; Block 1998: 361–62; Butler 2009: 283–86; B. G. Webb 2012: 322–24.

11:39–40) creates a great sense of ambivalence over Jephthah's judgeship. Crucial details are noticeably absent, but it appears that Jephthah did sacrifice his daughter (Judg 11:34–40; Block 1999; Hackett 1987).[27] Accordingly, Jephthah's behavior is taken to reflect a localized expression of Yahwism that is more akin to Moabite practices in the sacrifice of Mesha's son ([as *ḥērem* dedication] see 2 Kgs 3:37; Kamrada 2009: 71–72; Hackett 1987).[28] Further accentuating the perception of distance in the Jephthah narrative is the nature of the internecine conflict with the Ephraimites in Judges 12. In no small part, the *casus belli* relates to the otherness of the Gileadites, underscored by dialectal differences (Judg 12:4, 6). Thus, as Butler puts it, "the east-west divide of Josh 22 is not completely settled" (Butler 2009: 293; see also Judg 8:6) and gives further credence to Transjordan's otherness within the larger Israel group.

The Status of Reuben Revisited

This perception of Transjordan provides an important backdrop for whether Reuben enjoyed a favored status early on in the tribal history of ancient Israel, as F. M. Cross claimed (see chap. 1). Key poems attributed to ABH, while acknowledging Reuben's primogeniture, offer a strikingly negative view of the firstborn son of Jacob. His social status as firstborn is consistently undermined (but see Gen 37:29–30). Thus, following a well-known theme in the Genesis narratives, primogeniture was no guarantee of social preeminence (Cain/Abel, Esau/Jacob, Joseph/his brothers; Manasseh/Ephraim). The tribal blessing of Genesis 49 (vv. 2–4) does not bode well for Reuben: "unstable as water, you shall not excel" (v. 4). Similarly, the Song of Moses underlines Reuben's weakness: even though he is the firstborn, his progeny "will be few" (Deut 33:6). As seen above, in the Song of Deborah, the Reubenite group is highlighted with "Gilead" for not joining the tribal coalition against a Canaanite group (in contrast to Machir, Judg 5:14). In fact, the poem makes a point of emphasizing Reuben's failure (Judg 5:15, 16; contra Cross 1988: 48). Thus, the Reubenites are perceived to have broken an ancestral pact of solidarity with their "brothers" (Num 32:6–15).

Thus, Cross's contention that Reuben's favored status among the tribes underwent a subsequent recasting appears to be overstated (Cross 1988: 57). Perhaps a more reasonable interpretation of the data is reflected by the Chronicler

---

27. Butler underscores the point: "[No] exegetical ingenuity finds an escape that condemns the daughter to perpetual virginity rather than death" (Butler 2009: 292).

28. As with every part of this narrative, opinions abound about why Jephthah's actions were not condemned in the narrative. Kamrada suggests a "*ḥērem*-as-dedication" backdrop to Jephthah's vow. In this interpretation, Jephthah was bound to fulfill his vow, lest he breach Yahweh's holy requirements and incur *ḥērem*. Kamrada highlights the *voluntary* disposition of Jephthah's daughter as a "woman of marriageable age" so that the notion of *self*-sacrifice, rather than *human* sacrifice (clearly proscribed in biblical law) seems to be projected by the narrative. Thus, according to this interpretation, Jephthah's daughter would be portrayed as a true heroine in the story (and remembered as such), who through her sacrificial death averted the consequences of her father's foolish vow (Kamrada 2009: 78–85).

who, while acknowledging Reuben's primogeniture, never assumes that Reuben's standing as firstborn resulted in social preeminence (1 Chr 5:1–3; Knoppers 2011: 177). In this perspective, the view that the Reuben group may have introduced the rest of the tribes to Yahwism (via Reubenite place-names in Judah) as a principal repository of the Mosaic legal traditions does not seem to find strong support in biblical sources (contra Cross 1988: 50–51).[29]

Primacy of Gad?

In contrast, the record seems to highlight Reuben's apparent subservience to Gad in ancestral tribal blessings: "Blessed be he who enlarges Gad" (Deut 33:20). Reuben's "blessing," however, in a patrimonial setting looks more like a curse: "Let his men be few" (Deut 33:6). Though not as bluntly put, in the formal land grant of Numbers 32, Gad is consistently fronted (Num 32:1, 2, 6, 25, 29, 31, 33; contrast Josh 1:12; 22:10; Deut 29:8, passim), which may be an indication of Gad's preferential status. Thus, the *r'wbny* as a tribal group may very well have faded into the shadows and, if still present, became incorporated into the designation "Gilead" (Judg 20:1). Supporting evidence based on presence/absence may also be construed to support the rise of Gad as the preeminent tribe in central Transjordan. In 1 Sam 13:7, Hebrew warriors fled before the Philistine "to the land of Gad and Gilead." By the time of David's census (2 Sam 24:5), the Reubenites have seemingly disappeared, in which case L. Geraty's (1993: 627) explanation that Reuben was absorbed into Gad would have some merit. This may explain why tribal-allotment texts sometimes avoid precise separations between Gad and Reuben, as if they were perceived as one group (Num 32:1, 2), along with some overlap in their territories (see Josh 13:15–17; Num 32:34–37; Deut 3:12). Hence, the part of Cross's argument for a Reubenite presence early in the region, followed by its subsequent disappearance, would be confirmed (Cross 1988; Herr 1999).

Such a Reubenite drawdown and Gadite surge may also find support from line 10 of the Mesha Inscription: the "men of Gad" had lived in Ataroth "from a long time ago" (see chap. 3). Following this reasoning, Weippert goes further and proposes that Mesha was a Gadite (hence, Gad was never really connected to the tribes of Israel; Weippert 1997: n. 32) and that his claim in line 10 was judicial in nature: he was bolstering his claim to land that was rightfully his in the first place (1997: 26). In this respect, the designation Dibon-Gad (Num 33:45–46) may provide support to this construct. Mesha may have viewed the men of Gad as his own.

According to the shifting-frontier model of tribal identity proposed here, there is no a priori reason to reject the idea that the "men of Gad," with ties to Israel—as the Israelite sources clearly affirm—might have shifted tribal identity, so that Mesha in effect conducted a war of liberation of a group he deemed his own, who lived in the "land of Ataroth" (MI line 10). However, there are

---

29. In fairness, Cross's connection of Reuben's demise with the fallout of the Mushites against the Aaronids does not hinge on the text's view of Transjordan per se.

problems with the Gad-Moab connection. The context of line 10 makes the correlation difficult to sustain. The point that Mesha appears to be making is that he is not a 'man of Gad' *'š gd* but a *dbny* (van der Steen and Smelik 2007). The fact that the men of Gad have settled the area for a long time, if we keep them in some way connected to Israel, would underscore the scope of Mesha's accomplishment. He has finally restored the land to Chemosh and has exacted revenge on an old enemy, *yśr'l* (MI, lines 10–11).

Furthermore, the above arguments for a *specifically* Reubenite drawdown remain open to question for the following reasons. The absence of the Reubenite designation cannot always be construed to mean absorption or assimilation, especially when "Gilead" is used to describe Transjordan as a whole, and the "Gad and Gilead" designation is used to describe the land bounded by the two rivers (Arnon/Mujib and Jabbok/Zarqa). In light of Transjordan's unique geographical status in the Hebrew sources, the Reubenites may have been included in David's census (a key event in Cross's hypothesis), especially since the itinerary is essentially geographical rather than a tribal description (2 Sam 24:5). The problem is compounded when one considers the Chronicler's sources related to the early Monarchy, which document Reubenite involvement (1 Chr 11:42; 12:37; 26:32; 27:16). Eliezer, son of Zichri, is recorded as chief officer in David's military divisions (1 Chr 27:16; see also 1 Chronicles 5).

Following the model proposed here, both Reuben and Gad experienced different periods of abatement (e.g., at the time of the war of Deborah) and intensification (e.g., perhaps in the Jephthah story and, more explicitly, in the Benjaminite war). Nevertheless, the emphasis on the designation "Gad" in both the Hebrew and the Moabite sources could be understood to suggest Gadite preeminence over Reuben in the region "between the two rivers" in the early phases of settlement. This would then fall in line with the tribal blessings of Israelite lore, which also point to Gadite expansion and Reubenite compression. However, these "snapshots" of abatement and intensification in the available literary landscape caution us against drawing the conclusion that one tribal group gained *lasting* preeminence. Groups that disappeared in the background could reemerge later. Such are tribal dynamics on the social shifting frontier (see chaps. 1 and 3). Finally, the contested highlands, cast in the *longue durée*, witnessed a well-documented drawdown—now for *all* the Israelite tribes in Transjordan, first with the Aramean imposition (2 Kgs 10:33) and, finally, with the decimating effects of Tiglath-pileser III's campaign in the 8th century B.C. (2 Kgs 15:29; 2 Chr 5:26).

Summary

Bentley's research (1987) has shown that individual practices have the potential to yield important background for understanding how ethnic identity was viewed at the group level in a particular sociohistorical context. Translated into a patrimonial social structure, individual expressions may also reflect the viewpoint of the larger group, especially when it pertains to religious identity (van der Toorn 1996: 3).

The examples reviewed here are interpreted as indicating that Yahwism was a primary ethnic marker in early Israel. However, any sort of pristine Yahwistic ethnicity appears to have been rapidly superseded by other competing identities (contra Dever 2005: 269). Judges 2–3 seem to confirm this viewpoint, so that Yahwism soon became only one among many competing social currents in early Israel. This fluid setting also formed the backdrop for newly found identities: members of traditionally hostile groups (Moab) or members of tribal groups standing at the periphery (Kenite) could undergo profound transformations of identity and become part of the supratribal entity called Israel in the days preceding the Monarchy.

While some of the inhabitants of Transjordan may have been connected to Yahwism and Israel, they probably maintained their local distinctiveness. Within a shifting social frontier, primordial ties with the larger Israelite group could easily be severed, and local expressions of tribal identity would have been common. However, these tribal groups could also reintegrate with the Yahwistic community and even gain circumstantial preeminence, signaled by ḥērem victories over tribal enemies. In this respect, the documentary sources seem to signal long-term patterns of intensification and abatement in tribal identities connected to the larger "covenantal Israel" group.

From a geographical standpoint, the usage of "Gilead" along with "Gad" as designations for the tribal groups in central Transjordan makes it difficult to plot the ebb and flow of Reuben. We could certainly assign to "Gad" a preferential status, but any claim to a permanent preeminent status seems highly unlikely according to the shifting social frontier model. Thus Cross's case for a substantial and permanent drawdown of Reuben during the course of the Iron I cannot be confirmed. As a group that was deemed an outsider (outside the heartland), the Reubenites could not have played a leading role in the development of Yahwism in early Israel. This preferred status is especially questioned when Reuben's ad hoc commitment to Yahwism is examined (that is, unwillingness to fight "Yahweh's war" [Judges 5]). It seems more likely that, during the formative period of settlement in the region, the banner of Yahwism was carried with more-diffuse patterns of circumstantial loyalty to the covenant by tribes that had a common eponymous ancestral identity. In this framework, the tribes of Israel in the land of Gilead found themselves on the periphery of Yahwism. Yet, as the structure of the book of Judges well attests, tribal leadership shifted in unexpected and unpredictable ways, so that even the least likely candidate from the frontier could find himself a tribal head during the days when "there was no king in Israel."

In chap. 5, I examine the material-cultural evidence from the Mādabā Plateau Region during the early Iron I to determine whether ethnic markers that point to tribal groups—Israelites, Moabites, or other more localized expressions—may be discerned in the social frontier setting of the Mādabā Plateau Region.

CHAPTER FIVE

The Mādabā Plateau Region during the Early Iron I

Part 1. The Mādabā Plateau Region as a Culturally Defined Zone

Introduction

In light of the dynamic ethnicity model presented in chap. 2, from a material-cultural perspective the central question addressed here in chap. 5 is the available archaeological evidence for the early Iron I. Specifically, do stylistic variations and/or other mediums of communication in the material record reflect ethnic identity during this formative phase in the history of Iron Age Transjordan?

As a baseline for discussion, chap. 5 outlines the settlement patterns of the Mādabā Plateau Region during the Late Bronze / Iron I and early Iron I, and then presents a description of Tall al-ʿUmayri, the type site for the region, the Iron I levels at Tall Mādabā, and related tomb assemblages. The second part of the chapter is devoted to a discussion of the available material indexes that might be used as ethnic markers during this transitional period.

Late Bronze / Iron I Continuity in the Central Highlands

N. Glueck's comprehensive reconnaissance survey of Transjordan in the early 1930s remains a useful reference for the available survey data in Transjordan. Glueck's findings were published in five volumes in the AASOR series (Glueck 1934; 1935; 1939; 1951a; 1951b). This landmark study laid the foundations for modern research in the region and for several recent or ongoing excavations in Jordan (such as Tall Jalul, Tall Jawa, Khirbat al-Mudayna Wadi ath-Thamad; see maps 3–4).

Volume 1 (1934) outlines the results of the first series of surveys in 1932 and 1933. The majority of the sites surveyed are concentrated in the region north of the Wadi al-Mujib. Particular attention is devoted to the MPR, including the area south and west of Mādabā. Volume 2 (1935) chronicles the results of the spring and summer of 1933 and 1934 and focuses on the regions south of the Wadi al-Mujib and north of the Hijaz, which in biblical geography represents Moab and Edom. Volume 3 (1939) deals with the survey results of the seasons conducted in 1936–38. This publication reviews the prior regions surveyed and provides a concluding report on the archaeology of southern and central Transjordan. In the highlands, the region between Amman and the Wadi Zarqah was especially well surveyed. A few sites were added in the region north of Mādabā and south of the Wadi Hisban: Mount Nebo, Khirbat al-Mukhayyat, Khirbat ʿAyn Musa (Glueck 1939: 19). Finally, vols. 4–5 concentrate on the East Jordan Valley and the regions between the Wadi Zarqa and the Wadi Yarmuk. This final publication (1951a–b) includes a separate volume that is composed of plates featuring the pottery from the region surveyed. Thus, to his credit, Glueck provides significant ceramic documentation for his analysis of the survey data, at least for the Jordan Valley and the northern highlands.

For the central highlands, therefore, vols. 1 and 3 provide the most information. The descriptive narrative of the reconnaissance survey, while an interesting read, resembles a travelogue rather than the content of a modern survey publication (see Finkelstein 1997). In his brief conclusions, however, Glueck notes the important site of Jalul and the presence of Late Bronze sherds on the mound, though he still maintains his hypothesis of a settlement gap during the Late Bronze Age (Glueck 1934: 5, 82; compare with 1939: 264–65; no plates provided). Another problem with Glueck's conclusions, equally well documented, is the collapse of Iron I and Iron IIA into one "early Iron Age I" period (= 1230–920 B.C.; Glueck 1939: xxiii). In the absence of Iron I plates (what is provided is clearly Iron II painted ware; see Glueck 1934: 14–22; observe pls. 20, 22–24; see also vol. 2.124–37, pl. 26A–29B), Glueck's survey data can only provide a preliminary understanding of the region during the transitional Late Bronze / Iron I phase in northern Moab. Nevertheless, even though no fine-tuned sequencing is provided, Glueck's concentration of sites on the wadi systems and along the King's Highway turns out to be essentially accurate for Iron Age central Transjordan (Glueck 1934: pl. 1), as I will show below. Likewise, his "Iron I" fortified phase has been supported by subsequent field research, although his decision to link this settlement intensification to the emergence of a Moabite "state" during the Iron I requires qualifications.

J. Sauer's reappraisal of Glueck's study achieved an important corrective concerning patterns of settlement during the Late Bronze / Iron I period (Sauer 1986). Outlining excavations and survey results up through the 1980s, Sauer essentially closed the Middle Bronze–Late Bronze gap that Glueck had originally proposed. Though Sauer's vision of Late Bronze "cities" in Transjordan seemed overstated at the time (Dearman 1992: 69), his analysis essentially has proven to be on target. Monumental architecture includes the Amman Airport temple (Hennessy 1966; Hankey 1974; Herr 1983) and the fortified settlement at Sahab (Ibrahim 1987; see also Sauer 1986: 8; Strange 2001; van der Steen 1999). Tomb C at Sahab has also yielded significant Late Bronze deposits (Dajani 1970). In the Baqʿah Valley, mortuary data have produced a wealth of Late Bronze ceramics and small objects (McGovern 1986). At Tall Jalul, the excavator has confirmed previous survey results with the discovery of Late Bronze pottery, although not yet associated with structures (Younker et al. 1996: 70). At 'Umayri, the regional type-site, ongoing excavations have uncovered a substantial LB II building (Stratum 14) and related LB II levels (Herr and Clark 2009: 76–81). The few LB I indexes are interpreted as a possible hiatus during the LB I, following the MB IIC rampart (Herr and Clark 2009: 75–76).

Excavation results in the MPR appear to support cultural continuity during the transitional Late Bronze / Iron I phase in central Transjordan (maps 3–4; Herr and Najjar 2001: 324). The site of Tall al-'Umayri confirms the picture initially produced by the data from Sahab Tomb C (Dajani 1970), Mādabā (Harding 1953), and the Baq'ah Valley (McGovern 1986; 1987; also Ibrahim 1987: 78). Architecture in the form of several buildings is present at the site (Herr and Clark 2009; 2004). Likewise Tall Mādabā suggests the presence of a substantial settlement at the end of the Late Bronze (Foran and Klassen 2013). Thus, if site density is taken into consideration, the Late Bronze Age may not represent a period of abandonment in the central highlands (map 1; see Bramlett 2008) but, rather, a period of active interregional connections, as is similarly found in the Jordan Valley (Pella, Dayr 'Alla, etc.), though still somewhat different from Cisjordan during this period (van der Steen 1999: 181; McGovern 1987: 267; Ji 1995: 122).

In summary, the available picture of settlement patterns indicates that Late Bronze sites were clustered in the Dayr 'Alla (Jordan Valley) and Amman areas (map 3). Sites were small, but larger buildings (public and/or religious) were not absent (Routledge 2004: 63, fig. 4:1; van der Steen 1999: 178). In the MPR, Late Bronze Age 'Umayri should be viewed as part of the Amman settlement cluster, whereas Mādabā and Jalul (site 2312001; see map 3) appear to form another cluster within the plain proper.

Early Iron I Settlement Patterns

The distributional patterns generated in this study are derived from the JADIS (Jordan Antiquities and Database Information System) database for Jordan (maps 1–6), as well as published materials. The wide range of survey projects involved in creating this database, the diverse collection methods used, and the varying degrees of intensity of coverage that each survey achieved have clearly affected the quality of the data assembled in JADIS. Nevertheless, broad patterns of settlement can be discerned that reinforce observations made in previous studies. What appears clear from the available *vue d'ensemble* is that, in the MPR, the shift from Late Bronze to early Iron I witnessed an increase in sedentary settlement (maps 1, 3). This intensification is reflected by a sharp increase in the number of sites, from 14 in the Late Bronze (map 1) to 97 in the Iron I (map 3).

The JADIS data also indicate that many Late Bronze sites were reoccupied during the Iron I (71%; see maps 3 and 4–5). In this regard, Tall al-ʿUmayri may reflect a broad trend of settlement continuity in the region (see below). A similar continuity may be ascribed to the situation at Mādabā (Foran and Klassen 2013). However, until we gain a better understanding of the Iron I ceramic sequence (including from Tall Hisban Stratum 21; Ray 2001; Sauer 1994: 233–38), whether this settlement increase continued throughout the Iron I period cannot be established.

The typical early Iron I settlement probably combined plow agriculture and livestock production (LaBianca and Younker 1995: 402). Domestic architecture included variations of the four-room configuration. These small farmsteads, some of which were fortified, may thus represent the bulk of the settlement increase (see Routledge 2004: table 4.2; Swinnen 2009: 33; Boling 1988: 35).

The picture reflected in the JADIS data confirms the findings of the Hesban Survey (Ibach 1987), which indicated a similar process of abatement in site numbers during the Late Bronze (6 sites, 4.1% of sited surveyed; Ibach 1987: 157), followed in the Iron I period by intensification (30 sites, 20% of sites surveyed; Ibach 1987: 160). Finkelstein has also noted this trend, relating it to the situation in the highlands of Cisjordan (Finkelstein 1998a: fig. 1).

As maps 4–5 illustrate, Iron I expansion occurred in the marginal zones of the plateau as well as along the bottoms of wadis (see Routledge 2004: 89, fig. 5:1; van der Steen 1999: 178; McGovern 1987: 268). This is true both for the Hisban, ʿUmayri, and Sahab/Amman regions and the region immediately north and south of the Wadi al-Mujib (map 3; see also Routledge 2004: fig. 5:2 and Glueck 1934: pl. 1). More specifically, a noticeable clustering occurs around Hisban (17 sites; 17.5%), ʿUmayri (26 sites; 27%) and especially around Sahab/Amman (39 sites; 40%). However, the numbers drop significantly in the center of the MPR. The Mādabā/Jalul area has produced only 9 sites (9%), while the Dhiban region has 6 (6%). This lack of settlement sites in the immediate vicinity of Mādabā has already been noted for earlier periods (Harrison 1997: fig. 6).

However, while sites in the geographical center of the MPR appeared to be on the fringe of this intensification process, we now know that the Mādabā area also participated in the early Iron I settlement process. The geomorphology of the region, characterized by active soil aggregation from slope erosion, may have contributed to this uneven picture of the archaeological landscape. It is possible that sites could have been covered by aggrading soils, as the terrain eroded from the hills that surround the (primarily northern) perimeter of the plateau.

In this context, it is important to remember that the MPR, broadly defined by the Wadi al-Mujib in the south and the so-called Ammonite foothills in the north (south of the Wadi Zarqa), represents a diverse and complex landscape, in terms of both topography and climate (Harrison 1997: 3–4). In reality, the region is composed of microecological zones that may or may not have been culturally related to one another. The Iron I site clusters (northeastern MPR; and along the wadi bottoms), therefore, may also be a reflection of this intra-regional fragmentation.

While site-density analysis remains elusive with the available data, it is still possible to project some trends. First, in light of the abandonment of Late Bronze monumental architecture for smaller Iron I agropastoral forti-fied settlements, the increase in the number of early Iron I sites may not necessarily have resulted in an increase in aggregate settled area. Second, the nucleated clusters evident during the Iron I may point to an incipient settle-ment hierarchy. If the site of ʿUmayri is taken into consideration (clearly an important site within its own cluster, as discussed below), the evidence may point forward to the emergence of a two-tiered settlement hierarchy within the MPR toward the end of the Iron I and early Iron IIA (as Harrison [2009] has proposed; see also Routledge 2004).

Thus, while it may be premature to interpret the Iron I period as mark-ing the beginnings of an urbanization process in the region, the available evidence appears to anticipate developments that emerged more visibly in the Iron II (map 6). Further rank-size analysis will help to refine these general observations (see Savage and Falconer 2003).

Late Bronze–Iron I Sequence from Tall al-ʿUmayri

Tall al-ʿUmayri is situated at the northern edge of the Mādabā Plateau and sits at the center of the Iron I settlement expansion. The ongoing excavations and a steady output of publications have provided the best evidence available to document the Late Bronze / Iron I transition and early Iron I period in central Transjordan.[1]

Late Bronze Age II (Stratum 14)

Since the 1998 season, the Late Bronze levels (LB II, Field B, Stratum 14) preceding the Iron I settlement in the western defense system have emerged and represent a significant period of settlement at the site. The description of the structure (approx. 16 × 12 m) has recently been published in some detail (Herr and Clark 2009: 77–81). The multichamber building contains a cult niche with five standing stones along with "plastered mudbrick presenta-tion altar" (Room 3, Bramlett 2009: 80). Supporting this religious function, Room 5 is interpreted as a favissa (vestry) for the storage of cultic artifacts. Rooms 1 and 2, on the other hand, yielded little evidence of the function of the building. Whether we should narrowly designate the building a "temple"

---

1. Ongoing publications of Tall Jawa (JADIS site 2314048), particularly the ceramic assemblage, will also provide an important comparative perspective (Daviau 2003; 2001). Tell Jawa during the Iron I (Field A, Stratum X, represented in walls and fill layers) is iden-tified by the excavator as an unwalled village (Daviau 2003: 29–43).

(Bramlett 2009: 80) or "palace" (Herr 2009: 81) remains contested. What is clear, however, is that the structure served a prominent function(s) including that of a sacred space.

The end of Stratum 14 in Field B is attributed to a single destruction event (Bramlett 2008: 188). This is vividly illustrated in Room 3 of the monumental building with thick destruction debris between 75 cm and 140 cm with the characteristic ash, burned inclusions, as well as charred beams. The pottery assigned to this destruction level has been dated to LB IIA and early LB IIB periods (2008: 188).

The LB II evidence from Field F (outside the Acropolis) has come from fill layers that seal a Middle Bronze destruction level. The Late Bronze fill was then sealed by a retaining wall dated to the Iron I (Low 1997: 191–95). There appears, therefore, to be stratified evidence of a Late Bronze–Iron I transitional phase that extended beyond the limits of the fortification wall of the Iron I settlement (Herr 1998: 253).

Late Bronze–Iron I

In Field B, excavators have identified a defensive system and related dwellings that are preserved in two subphases. The first phase, Stratum 13 (previously Field Phase B/11B), consists of ephemeral evidence from debris in the preexisting Middle Bronze rampart (Herr and Clark 2009: 70; Clark 1997: 55). The lack of levels connected to Stratum 13 is explained by an earthquake that ended the initial Late Bronze / Iron I settlement, which began ca. 1230 B.C. (Herr and Clark 2009: 70, 81). The site was (presumably) immediately resettled, and repairs to the damaged rampart were conducted using debris from Stratum 13. The second phase, Stratum 12 (previously Field Phase B/11A), is a destruction level with substantial remains inside the settlement. Apart from an increased frequency of LB II cooking pots, the pottery in the rampart layers and inside the compound are almost identical. In contrast to the pottery from the rampart phase, Stratum 12 cooking pots have a more upright stance and longer flange (Herr 2002b: 139; see also 1998: 255; 2000a: 187). Thus, it is on the basis of the presence of transitional materials in the rampart fill that excavators have concluded there was a first Late Bronze / Iron I phase (Stratum 13), which preceded the rebuilding of the rampart and wall system. The excavators assume that the inhabitants felt the need to rebuild the settlement with strong fortifications following the earthquake (Herr and Clark 2009: 81; Clark 2002: 51). Whether subphase 13 will be confirmed with architectural remains appears doubtful (Herr and Clark 2009: 81). Consequently, the substance of the Late Bronze / early Iron I cultural horizon at ʿUmayri comes from Stratum 12 inside the settlement.

Field B at ʿUmayri enjoys the benefit of a significant horizontal exposure and represents one of the best-preserved early Iron Age fortification systems in the southern Levant (Herr and Clark 2009; Herr 2002a: 11). According to the 1998 field season report (Herr et al. 2000: 34–35), the wall has been traced to a length of approximately 85 m, although not continuously. Its height reaches 2.5 m in places. Clearly this perimeter wall represents a substantial defensive system for the Iron I settlement. Earlier conclusions that indicated the possible presence of a gate (Herr and Clark 2004: 116–18) have now been dismissed (Herr and Clark 2009: 82). Inside the settlement, three houses have been uncovered—Buildings A, B, and C—parts of which are well preserved (A and B) with walls up to 2.5 m in height (see map 5). In typical Iron Age fortification technique (see Arad; Herzog 2002), the outer casemate wall functions as the extension wall of the back room of the houses. The inner casemate wall separates the back room from the front rooms. The assemblage assigned to Building A (completely excavated) includes collared pithoi found in Room A3, the perimeter room (about 10 pithoi in the northern half of the room). Room A2 has been tentatively assigned a cultic function on account of a standing stone and a counterpart stone found standing in proximity on a pavement (Lawlor 2002: 106–8; see figs. 3, 4, 5; Clark 2000: 76). Room A1, a kitchen, contained a storage bin, mortar, hand grinder, and a circular hearth (Clark 2000: 74–75). Building B, a four-room house that has been completely excavated and restored,[2] served also as a domestic facility (presence of grinding stones, hearths, and animals). It housed a substantial number of storage vessels (Herr and Clark 2009: 88). The main room (B3) had two parallel rows of closely spaced post bases. The southern end of this tripartite, trapezoid-shaped room (9.30 m [north wall]; 4.90 m [south wall]; 7.50 m [east wall]) was paved with flagstones. A concentration of collared pithoi, believed by the excavators to have been stored on the second floor, was found in B3 (Clark 2002: 97). Like Room A3, casemate broad room B4 served as storage. About 75 collared pithoi have been recovered. Some lined the walls of this room. The destruction debris (about 1.70 m thick) from the second floor contained the smashed remains of additional pithoi. Small finds from the second-story destruction layer included part of an alabaster vessel, a few weapons, and ballistic missiles. Cooking pots, painted biconical jugs, and large jugs with handles on the shoulders complete this early Iron I assemblage (Herr 1998: 255). Skeletal remains of four individuals were found in the southern half of B4. The individuals appear to have died on the second floor, since their remains were scattered in the debris from this upper floor (Clark 2002: 99).

Iron I pottery was also recovered from the so-called Ammonite Citadel in Field A. Here the assemblage was found in Iron I layers associated with the destruction of the western defense system (Herr 2002b: 138). Similarly, in Field F, evidence of Iron I levels were uncovered (Low 1997: 195–202, 237; 2000: 157–63). Above the destruction, a small storeroom produced late Iron I sherds, possibly indicating that a small settlement survived after the fortified Iron I phase (Herr et al. 2000: 35–36).

---

2. See fig. 1 below. For further discussion on the architecture of the so-called four-room house, see Holladay 1997a: 337–42; 1997b: 105–8.

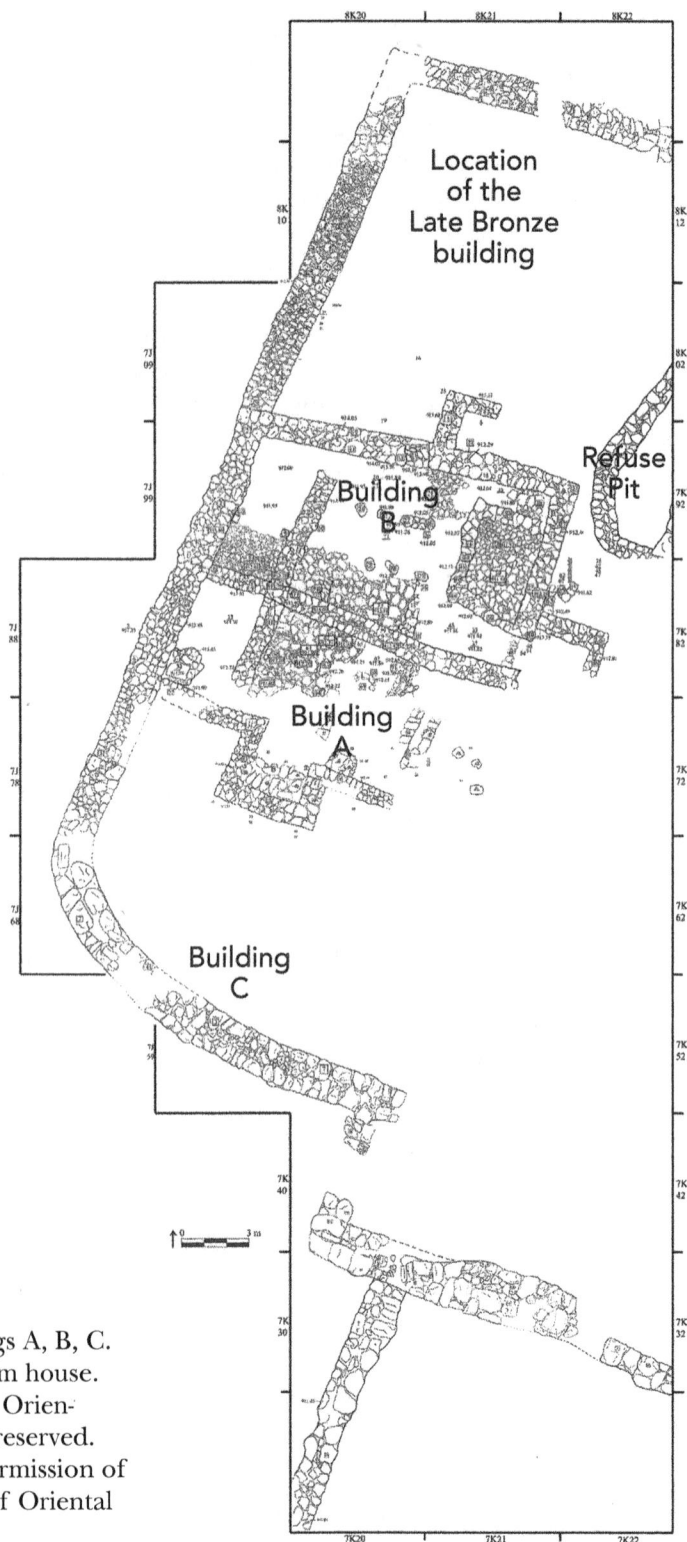

Fig. 1. ʿUmayri Buildings A, B, C. Building B is a four-room house. © American Schools of Oriental Research. All rights reserved. Republished here by permission of the American Schools of Oriental Research.

A large trash pit was discovered during the 1998 excavations east of Buildings A and B. Osteological analysis indicates the presence of mostly small mammals (sheep and goats), with a small percentage of cattle, gazelle, and pigs (4%). The faunal remains also include two lion bones and one bone of the Asian brown bear subspecies (Herr et al. 2000: 35; Clark and Bramlett 2002: 109).

Late Bronze / Iron I Tall Mādabā

Mādabā is one of the largest sites in Jordan, at approximately 13–16 ha. Over a century of excavations at Mādabā have focused primarily on the Late Byzantine era. However, survey (Harrison 1996b) and ongoing excavations on the southeastern slope of the lower tell (Harrison et al. 2000: 218–20) and on the western slope of the acropolis (Harrison et al. 2003; 2010; Foran and Klassen 2013) have yielded substantial results concerning the Iron Age settlement and lend support to the importance attributed to the site in textual sources (Num 21:30; Josh 13:9, 16; 1 Chr 19:7; Isa 15:2; Mesha Inscription, lines 7–9).

Field A

During the first field season, in 1996, a probe on the lower tell provided a sectional overview of some of the occupational history of the site. This 8-m vertical section uncovered levels from EB I/II (including architectural phases; Harrison et al. 2000: 218–19) and from an Iron IIB (paralleled to field phase 6 in Field B) midden. It is in these deposits that collared pithoi rims were found in secondary contexts (Harrison et al. 2000: 220; Petter 2005b: pl. 4).

Field B

Ongoing full-scale excavations on the western slope of the acropolis (Field B) have now reached LB II / Iron I levels.[3] Preliminary reports account for a substantial fortification wall already present during the EB I (5–7 m wide) that continued during the Iron Age (possibly connected to Mesha's building projects in the region [9th century B.C.; see Mesha Inscription, line 30; Isa 15:2; see Harrison 1996a: 1–6; 2009]). Middle Bronze and Late Bronze materials have been recovered in fill layers connected to the upper part of the wall. The latest preliminary report (Foran and Klassen 2013) describes clear evidence of settlement during the Late Bronze / Iron I linked to a partially excavated building situated against the inner face of the fortification wall. A Mycenean stirrup jar (Foran and Klassen 2013: fig. 2:5) and a painted biconical strainer jug (2013: fig. 2:6) were found on surfaces associated with the earliest levels of the building (in plaster-covered fills sealed against the wall; Harrison 2009: 38).

---

3. Exposed phases include Late Ottoman (FP 1), Late Byzantine/Early Islamic (FP 2), Early Roman/Nabatean (FP 3, FP 4), Late Hellenistic (FP 5, FP 6), Late Iron IIB (FP 7), Iron IIB (FP 8), Iron I/Iron IIA (FP 9), and Late Bronze / Iron IA (FP 10; Foran 2008).

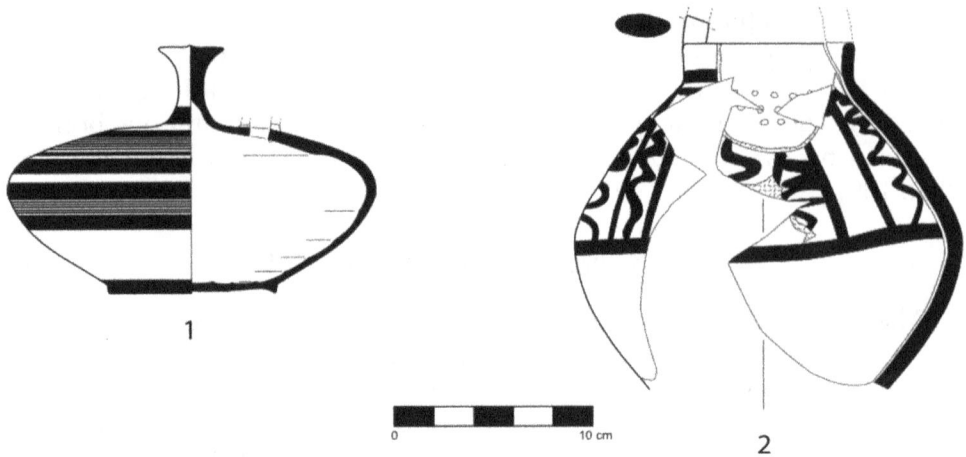

Fig. 2. Tall Mādabā Late Bronze / Iron I diagnostics (reproduced after Foran and Klassen 2013, by courtesy of the authors).

In addition, "numerous reconstructable" collared pithoi, mostly of the long-neck type (see discussion on chronology below) were recovered in the eastern section of the building (Foran and Klassen 2013). The excavators duly note parallels with the store-jars at ʿUmayri and unpublished materials at Tall Jawa. However, the Mādabā family of store-jars seems to emanate from a more homogeneous morphological tradition than at ʿUmayri, along with a unique form (Foran and Klassen 2013: fig. 5:5). Though we may surmise a storage function for the space where most of the jars were found, until more evidence is recovered we cannot comment further on the building floor plan. Bowls fitting within the regional matrix (see below) complete the emerging picture of the Tall Mādabā Late Bronze / Iron I horizon (Foran and Klassen 2013: figs. 2:8–12). Field Phase 9 points to a second occupational phase of the Late Bronze / Iron I structure. The assemblage contains diagnostics more at home in the Iron IIA, along with collared store-jars of the short-neck type (2013: figs. 2:8–12). Thus, Tall Mādabā also seems to fit within larger regional settlement trends during the early Iron II period (Harrison 2009: 33–34).

Tomb Assemblages in the Mādabā Plateau Region

Mādabā Tomb A

Tomb assemblages represent the other main source of data to document the nature of the early Iron I settlement in the MPR. A significant repertoire comes from a tomb in Mādabā excavated in 1947 (Harding 1953). The tomb, situated in a long-open, natural cave, was one among several east of the ancient tell on the land that then belonged to Mitri et-Twal. The cave was apparently robbed in antiquity. As a result, information about the stratigraphic sequence and osteological/dentition data is nonexistent. In addition, potential supplementary data from the adjacent caves were never collected. Since

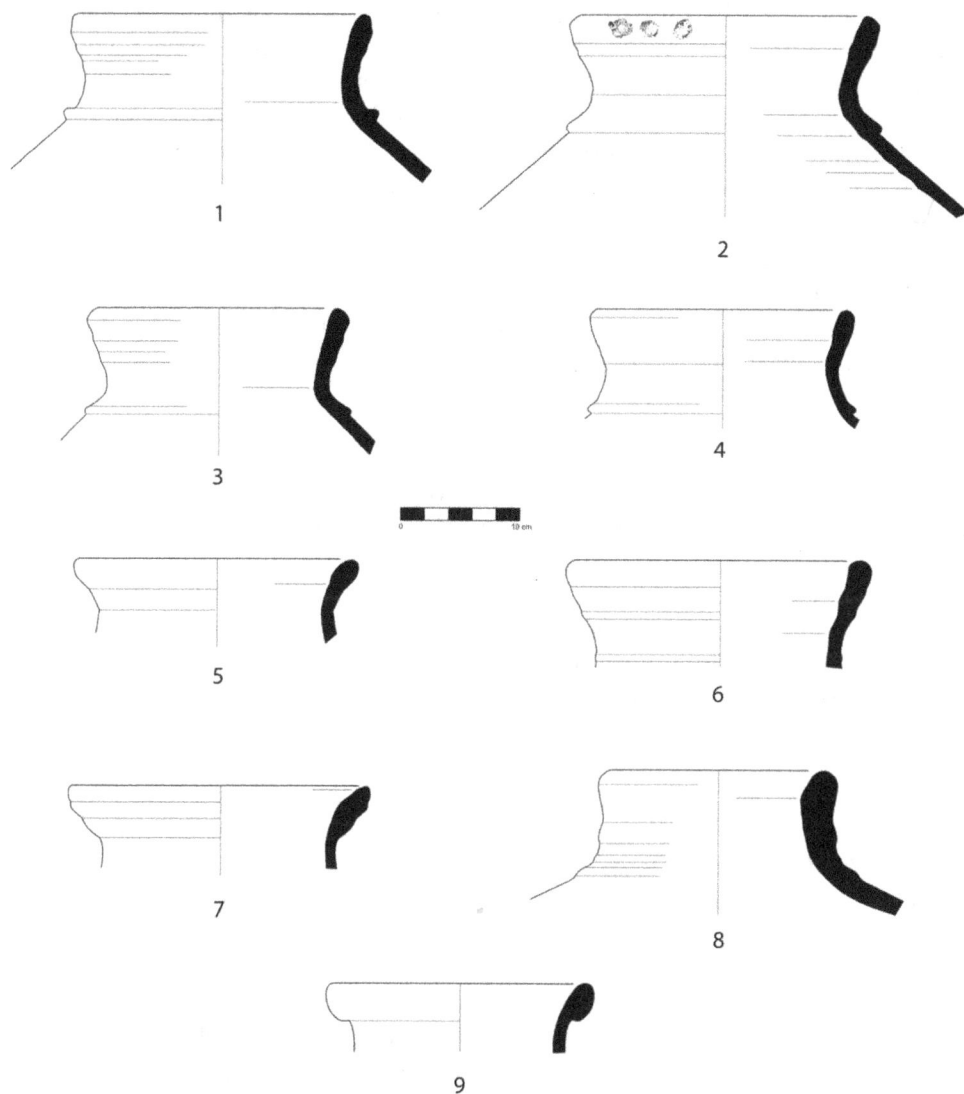

Fig. 3. Tall Mādabā Field B Collared Pithoi (reproduced after Foran and Klassen 2013, by courtesy of the authors).

the cave was filled to the ceiling with debris, however, it is unlikely that much postdepositional disturbance occurred.

In spite of the lack of context for the finds, the tomb is representative of the cave type common to the highlands of both Transjordan and Cisjordan during the Iron I (Bloch-Smith 2002: 120–21). The variety of vessels and small finds points to multiple burials (Bloch-Smith 1992: 170). On the basis of attested examples of undisturbed tombs, we may surmise that individuals were laid on their backs in the center of the cave, with personal objects surrounding them. To make room for new burials, bones and objects were swept aside to the periphery (Bloch-Smith 1992: 36–37). The presence of men, women, and children, as evidenced in the Baqʿah Valley, indicates that these caves were probably family tombs (1992: 36–37; see also McGovern 1986).

Artifacts recovered from the tomb also reflect the expected assemblage found in tombs of this period. Small finds include, in order of frequency: bronze earrings (over 60); bronze bracelets or anklets (over 40); beads (30); bronze toggle pins (about 10); bronze finger rings (8); 3 bronze daggers; a few iron bracelets/anklets, iron rings, silver earrings, and several other bronze objects (Harding 1953: 32–33). Four scarabs were recovered, 2 of which were identified as Ramesside (perhaps 19th Dynasty). One appeared to be of the Hyksos type (Harding 1953: 33).

Sahab Tomb C

Located south of Amman, Sahab Tomb C was excavated in the late 1960s (Dajani 1970). This large, rock-cut cave tomb (8.20 m long; 4.50 m wide; 1.80 m high) is characterized by a small shaft in the ceiling ("chimney-like"; Dajani 1970: 29) near the southeast corner opposite the stepped entrance (see Dajani 1970: pl. 1). Of note is the presence of rock-cut benches on the northern side (150 cm wide) and the southern side (50 cm wide). The tomb has a depositional sequence that began during the Late Bronze and continued into the Iron II. During the course of its use, several types of burials were adopted: primary bench burials (Late Bronze / Iron I), secondary wooden coffin burials, and jar burials for both adults and children (Bloch-Smith 1992: 166). Areas C and C–D represent the Late Bronze / Iron I repertoire.

Jabal Nuzha Tomb (Amman)

The Jabal Nuzha tomb in Amman is a small, circular, rock-cut tomb (approx. 3 m in diameter). Similarly to Sahab Tomb C, a rock-cut bench was located in a niche on the east side (approx. 1 m high, 3 m long, and 1.25 m wide). About 75% of the cave was filled with dust, which allowed the 160 vessels to remain virtually undisturbed. Unfortunately, no skeletal information was included in the report, despite the undisturbed nature of the discovery (Dajani 1966). No nonceramic artifacts are mentioned, although this may be explained as due to poor excavations/publications protocol.

Regional Trends

Until a full typology of the Mādabā assemblage is generated, we cannot draw overly precise conclusions; nevertheless, the emerging picture suggests the following trends. Almost half of the Mādabā Tomb A assemblage consists of bowls (42%): 31% have loop handles (either raised or horizontal), and 18% are carinated. Morphological parallels for carinated bowls are encountered at Tall Mādabā (Foran and Klassen 2013: fig. 2:9), ʿUmayri (*MPP* 3: fig. 4.27:14; *MPP* 4: fig. 4.31:18), Sahab Tomb C (Dajani 1970: pl. 5:20, 109, 124), and the Baqʿah Valley (Cave A4; McGovern 1986: fig. 50:13–17).

Regarding collared pithoi, both Mādabā and ʿUmayri[4] appear to reflect the diverse range of rim and collar morphological variations encountered for this vessel type. Foran and Klassen (forthcoming) do note a more homogeneous technology for the Mādabā pithoi. Typical variations at ʿUmayri include everted rounded or triangular rim (with groove or ribbing), upright rim, with or without waving on the neck (*MPP* 3: fig. 4.14:1; 4.16:1; 4.17:1; 4.18:1; 4.19:9–10; 4.20:1–5, 6, 7; *MPP* 5: fig. 4.10:7, 15; 4.14:1–2; 4.17–23; 4.24:1–8; 4.25:1–4; 4.26:1–10; 4.27:3–4). Herr also notes two parallels with the Amman Airport structure (*MPP* 5: 141; see Kafafi 1983: fig. 21:74, 76).

Pyxides, to date not attested on the tall at Mādabā, are of the low-carination type, with a flat bottom and vertical loop handles (Harding 1953: fig. 15:70–73; *MPP* 4: fig. 4.32:7–8). Their surface treatment includes widely spaced vertical lines in one register (*MPP* 4: fig. 4.32:7). Decor is reddish-brown, and the fabric is pink. Undecorated vessels from Mādabā Tomb A have pink fabric. Other parallels are found at Sahab Tomb C (Dajani 1970: pl. 5:117, 137, 161 [undecorated]) and farther north in Jordan at Saḥem (Fischer 1997: fig. 16:5 [undecorated]).

Lentoid flasks are the second-largest vessel type represented in Mādabā Tomb B (22%), of which 63% are decorated. Mādabā Tomb figs. 15–16:71–81, 84, 87, 88, 92, and 93 are part of the Amman Museum collection, while 82 and 90 are accessioned in the Mādabā Museum. Flasks from Mādabā Tomb A (Harding 1953: fig. 15:77, 83) have decoration (usually red) that includes pie-shaped designs, concentric circles, and spirals. The cross-shaped motif may have different spacing and may only cover the body partially. Many flasks are attested without surface treatment as well. It is possible that pie-shaped decoration reflects a local tradition indigenous to the MPR. Fabric color is gray-white or pink with gray core.

Parallels are found at ʿUmayri (see fig. 4 [*MPP* 3: fig. 4.28:2]; *MPP* 5: fig. 4.16:11); Jabal Nuzha (Dajani 1966: pl. 17:49, 51); Sahab Tomb C (Dajani 1970: pl. 11:177); and Saḥem Tomb (Fischer 1997: fig. 15:1–2).

Exterior and interior fabric color for the lamps is pink with a gray core (Mādabā Tomb A, Harding 1953: fig. 17:112). Carinated lamps are also representative of a trend that perhaps extends beyond the MPR (Baqʿah Valley Cave A4, McGovern 1997: fig. 55:60; cf. *MPP* 3: fig. 4.28:1).

Based on my personal examination of the existing Mādabā Tomb A vessels at both the Amman and Mādabā museums, the Mādabā fabric, characterized as "buff" by Tomb A excavators (Harding 1953), ranges in color from light pink to light brown.

As is typical of Iron I coarse ware, few vessels manifest surface treatment. There are, however, some vessels for which a white/light pink slip is apparent. Although we are hampered by the different levels of detail recorded in the reports, it appears that this pink/buff ware (also at ʿUmayri) extends to the Amman region (Jabal Nuzha; see Dajani 1966: 50–51). At Sahab and Baqʿah,

---

4. See *MPP* 3 and *MPP* 5 for the sample of collared pithoi available at ʿUmayri.

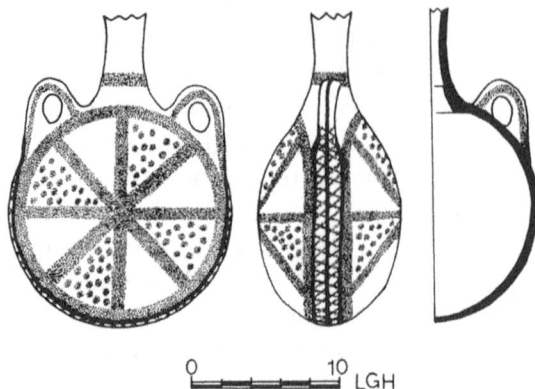

Fig. 4. Lentoid flask from Tall
al-ʿUmayri. Reproduced with
permission from *Madaba Plains
Project 3: The 1989 Season at Tell
el-Umeiri and Vicinity and Subsequent Studies* (ed. Larry G. Herr,
Lawrence T. Berrien Springs,
MI: Andrews University Press,
1997) 85, fig. 4.28:2.

the ware tends to be more red than buff (see Dajani 1970: 32–33; McGovern
1986: 150–58), though a white slip is not uncommon in the Baqʿah tomb
assemblage. Thus, this preliminary examination seems to confirm the MPR
as a culturally defined zone. But the morphological variety reflected in the
collared pithoi from Tall Mādabā and ʿUmayri may also point to localized diversity. A similar phenomenon seems to obtain at Tall Jawa (P. M. M. Daviau,
personal communication, 2005). These differences in ware could indicate distinct traditions in pottery production in the MPR. However, as settlement
patterns seem to suggest, this regional distribution may stretch beyond the
MPR. Carinated bowls are found in the mortuary assemblage of Cave A4 in
the Baqʿah Valley (see McGovern 1986: fig. 50:13–17) and at Sahab as well.
Other parallels include pyxides and lentoid flasks. This should not come as a
surprise since similar assemblages are encountered in Cisjordan and fit within
the broader southern Levantine horizon during the transitional Late Bronze /
Iron I period (Cooley and Pratico 1995).

Thus, in the MPR, the presence of collared pithoi at Tall Mādabā confirms
projections from earlier surveys and textual data of the presence of a permanent settlement during the early Iron I. Perhaps related to the substantive
size of the settlement, collared pithos sherds were also found in the lower tell
(Area A in secondary contexts) beside the acropolis (Area B).

The material-cultural relationship between ʿUmayri and Mādabā also
seems to be established. However, within this picture of general homogeneity,
microvariations, particularly with the collared pithos also indicate some level
of microdiversity in pottery production. Additional macroscopic and micro-
scopic analyses will undoudtedly refine these broad trends.

Chronological Considerations

In terms of absolute dates (typically 1200 B.C.), our current understanding of the Late Bronze / Iron I transition in Transjordan remains based on
typological arguments. Recent analyses have exposed some of the problems
inherent in typologically derived approaches in transitional periods, including

the Late Bronze / Iron I transition in Transjordan (Finkelstein 2011). This section reviews the combined available evidence from ʿUmayri and Mādabā, including collared pithoi morphology.

Egyptian chronology still represents a solid means of anchoring our ceramic sequences in the Levant (Shortland 2005; for Transjordan specifically, see Strange 2001; van der Steen 1999). However, a development in contemporary discussions is the increasing lack of attention devoted to these external chronological controls. This problem is perhaps best illustrated in the debate concerning the chronology of the state-formation process (e.g., the Iron I/ II transition) in ancient Israel. Specific sites that suit a particular argument are claimed to be anchor sites. Other sites, which clearly weaken the case presented, are ignored. I. Finkelstein, in his low chronology for the United Monarchy proposes linking the Megiddo VA–IVB assemblage to the Iron Age enclosure at Jezreel (Finkelstein 1996). Since the Jezreel sequence is usually dated to the period of the Omrides in the 9th century B.C. (Ussishkin 1997: 246), Finkelstein then assumes that Megiddo VA–IVB must also be a 9th-century B.C. assemblage. However, it is more reasonable to date Megiddo VA–IVB in the 10th century B.C. on account of Sheshonq's campaign of 925 B.C. (see Shortland 2005) attested at the site (a nonstratified fragment from his victory stele; see Stager 2003; Kitchen 1996). As several advocates of a 10th-century B.C. high chronology have argued (see Stager 2003; Master 2001), parallels with Megiddo VA–VIB are also encountered at Tanaach (Stratum IIB), a site within Megiddo's regional sphere. Thus, it appears that Tanaach IIB and Megiddo VA–IVB are both destruction levels that should be linked to 925 B.C. (Stager 2003: 66). The destruction of the Jezreel Iron Age enclosure occurred later in the 9th century B.C. However, and perhaps indicative of the extent of the impasse, not even calibrated dates in support of a 10th-century B.C. setting manage to persuade advocates of a low chronology (Finkelstein and Piasetzky 2003; Finkelstein 2005; see Mazar 2005).

Another problem related to a typology-driven chronology emerges if horizons from different ecological zones are compared. Again, the "10th-century debate" provides an apt illustration for the Late Bronze / Iron I transition in Transjordan. In his reappraisal of the Arad fortress stratigraphic sequence, Z. Herzog down-dates the building of the first Arad fortress (Stratum XI) from the 10th century B.C. (Aharoni's Solomonic fortress; see Herzog et al. 1984), to the 9th century B.C. The date of the first Arad fortress has been assigned to the 9th century B.C. (Mazar and Netzer 1986). The pottery assemblage clearly fits within a 9th-century B.C. horizon (Singer-Avitz 2002). Thus, Arad in the 10th century B.C. (Stratum XII) was a relatively small outpost and did not reflect a substantial settlement in the region during the Solomonic period.

However, to shore up support for a low chronology of the Monarchy, Herzog uses the data from Arad as evidence for the absence of monumental architecture during the 10th century B.C. *elsewhere* in ancient Israel. To claim that the settlement history of the Beer-sheba valley, a marginal zone, necessarily coincides chronologically with the situation farther north, in the highlands remains an unsubstantiated connection. In fact, it seems reasonable to assert that a monumental build-up would have first appeared in the heartland of the kingdom (Gezer, Hazor, and Megiddo in the 10th century B.C.) and then spread to the marginal zones (such as the Arad valley) in subsequent times.

The same caveat obtains in dating highland material culture in Transjordan (and Cisjordan). Ecological variations do exist within the general highland environmental landscape. In this regard, the MPR as a highland agropastoral plateau reflects some differences from the other highland regions on both sides of the Jordan River. When attempting to generate chronologically significant conclusions for Late Bronze / Iron I Transjordan, we should take variations between highland regions into consideration. In the presence of parallel material cultures, without precise chronological anchors, we cannot always determine whether these cultures precede, follow, or overlap with each other.

The Late Bronze / Iron I Transition at ʿUmayri

The cooking pot with triangular, slightly flanged rim is a significant piece with which to anchor the destruction of ʿUmayri Stratum 13 in the Late Bronze / Iron I (see Herr 1998: 255). In the Late Bronze Age, the rim is triangular with a short vertical or slightly everted rim, but in Iron I the rim gradually lengthens and becomes more inverted. In support of the two-phase hypothesis (Stratum 13 / Stratum 12), Herr notes that the triangular everted form is frequent in the earlier of the two Iron I phases (that is, data from the rampart) but rare inside the settlement. Thus, the emerging picture seems to support a pre-earthquake, Late Bronze / Iron I phase that preceded the fortified early nature of the Iron I assemblage of Stratum 13 at ʿUmayri (see Herr 1998). The ephemeral nature of Stratum 13 has led I. Finkelstein (2011: 116) to question the validity of this interpretation. In his view, the rampart fill layer does not necessitate a distinct stratigraphic phase, and he argues that we should instead view Stratum 12 as the first Iron I phase at ʿUmayri. In response—while the excavators have always qualified the tentative nature of Stratum 13, the presence of more Late Bronze / Iron I (with a larger proportion of LB II) forms in the rampart fill than inside the settlement requires an explanation that goes beyond the reason suggested by Finkelstein.

To arrive at a context in the late 13th century B.C. for ʿUmayri, Herr looks to the el Burnat/Mount Ebal site near Shechem and to other parallels in the highlands of Palestine (Herr 1999). Herr singles out common potters' marks and the so-called Manasseh Bowl at el Burnat/Mount Ebal as diagnostic (Herr 1999: 70; Hawkins 2012: 214–15). Besides cooking-pot morphology, important chronological markers that anchor el Burnat/Mount Ebal to the transitional Late Bronze/ Iron I sequence are Mycenean ceramics (Zertal 1986–87: 137; see Hawkins 2012) and two Egyptianized scarabs dated to the second half of the reign of Ramesses II. Accordingly, Stratum II spanned about 40 years, from 1240 to 1200 B.C. (Zertal 1986–87: 109, 115). However, in his contribution to the Baqʿah Valley final report, J. Weinstein cautions readers about the extent to which scarabs can be used to date an assemblage. Since seals often served as heirlooms, it is difficult to arrive at precise chronological conclusions on the basis of glyptic evidence *alone*. Seals have been found in stratigraphic contexts that are later than the period in which the object was manufactured (Weinstein 1986: 289; contra Münger 2003). Seemingly aware of the problem, A. Zertal was careful to place the *terminus ante quem* in the middle of the 12th century B.C. (Zertal 1986–87: 109) but admitted it could be later (Megiddo Stratum VI [11th century B.C.]; 1986–87: 144). Nevertheless, the combined evidence of Mycenean ceramic, cooking-pot morphology, and the supplementary glyptic data does seem to confirm the transitional Late Bronze / Iron I nature of the settlement at el Burnat/Mount Ebal, which provides a general framework for dating the materials at ʿUmayri. Thus, Finkelstein's recent effort to down-date ʿUmayri to the Iron IB (his "middle Iron I") is ultimately not persuasive (Finkelstein 2011: 116–17). His case weakens considerably when data from Mādabā (both tomb and tall materials) and Iron I collared-rim store-jar morphology are taken into consideration (see below).

Finkelstein's other point of contention concerns Herr's assumption that, since ʿUmayri closely antedated El Burnat/Mount Ebal, the sites should be seen as way points in a westward migratory pattern from the Jordan Valley up into the eastern highlands, with a final settlement process in the western hill country. This scheme, originally proposed by Zertal and promoted by Finkelstein in his earlier views (Zertal 1986–87; Finkelstein 1995) has now been largely abandoned (Stager 1998; Finkelstein 2011; but see Zevit 2001: 102–7; Hawkins 2012: 215). In light of the ecological differences and independent regional dynamics, teasing out overly precise chronological sequences in which ʿUmayri's chronology would antedate el Burnat/Mount Ebal becomes difficult. Whether a diffusionary model based on an east-to-west movement during the Late Bronze / Iron I transition can be retained will require support from other lines of evidence, including textual.

The Dating of Mādabā Tomb A and Tall Mādabā

The Mādabā tomb excavators dated the pottery assemblage and small finds on the available comparative data at the time—namely, at Tell Beit Mirsim, Tell Faraʿ (North), and Lachish Fosse Temple level III (Harding 1953: 27). Their identification of the assemblage as transitional Late Bronze / Iron I appears essentially correct on the basis of the currently emerging regional assemblage. On the one hand, the Baqʿah Valley horizon could be interpreted to confirm the early Iron I nature of the Mādabā bowls. In contrast to decorated LB II bowls, Iron I bowls have no surface treatment. Whereas LB II bowls have high base rings, Iron I bowl bases are flat or with low rings. On the other hand, the Mādabā tomb contains Late Bronze diagnostics, such as pyxides and pilgrim flasks. In the case of the flasks, strap handles are usually found at the end of the sequence (loop handles are more common earlier). In terms of surface treatment, flasks with concentric circles, well attested at the Mādabā tomb, are found in LB II levels in the Baqʿah Valley but not in the Iron I (McGovern 1986: 82). The Mādabā toggle pins are dated to the Iron I (see Harding 1953: 27); however, in the Baqʿah Valley, copper toggle pins were also in use during the Late Bronze Age (Harding 1953: 27). Thus, the tomb assemblage reflects a typical transitional Late Bronze / Iron I setting of the late 13th century.

Additional Late Bronze evidence in the Mādabā tomb also exists in the form of two 19th Dynasty scarabs. Their good state of preservation makes it difficult to determine whether they were recently acquired heirlooms or were contemporary with the assemblage. Thus, while the original excavators felt that these seals were heirlooms and, accordingly, dated the assemblage to the early Iron I (see Harding 1953: 27), there is nothing that precludes dating the glyptic data contemporaneously with the 19th Dynasty.

The emerging horizon from the tall in Field B at Mādabā (Field Phase 10) appears to confirm the Late Bronze / Iron I nature of the tomb, particularly with the presence of a Mycenean IIIB stirrup jar dated on typological grounds to the late 14th/early 13th century B.C. (Foran and Klassen 2013), and a decorated biconical strainer jug that finds a morphological parallel in the Iron I Baqʿah Valley (Foran and Klassen 2013; see McGovern 1986: fig. 53:41–42). Surface treatment (vertical waves lines bordered by dark red bands from the carination to the neck), however, suggests a vessel more at home in the Late Bronze tradition (McGovern 1986: fig. 53:41–42). Other distinctive forms include carinated bowls and collared pithoi of the long-neck type.

The Chronological Significance of the Long-Necked Pithoi
in the Mādabā Plateau Region

Highland sites in Transjordan confirm the long-neck style of the collared pithoi during the early Iron I (see appendix B). No collared pithoi with short necks are attested in the early Iron I levels at ʿUmayri. At Tall Mādabā, the emerging evidence seems to follow this trend. Short-neck jars, for example, appear in Iron IIA levels in Field B (Foran and Klassen 2013).

The *terminus ante quem* for the long-necked store-jar in Transjordan comes from the findings at Sahab (*not* tomb C). Though collared pithoi are poorly published, the assemblage is mixed and consists of both short-necked and long-necked collared pithoi (short-necked 5 cm; Ibrahim 1978: fig. 1; a photograph of short-necked and long-necked rim sherds, pl. 19). Although the excavator dates these pithoi to the late 13th century B.C. (Ibrahim 1978: 121), a similar pattern as the one encountered at Shiloh seems to occur at Sahab. Therefore, the presence of both subtypes may reflect a transitional Iron I/ Iron II period. Seal impressions at Sahab, common in Iron II, have been interpreted as a further indicator that these collared jars belonged to a later phase in Iron I (Herr 1999: 71). However, similar impressions are also present on the early Iron I collared pithoi at Mādabā (e.g., Tall Mādabā Field B Collared Pithoi, fig. 3 above [Foran and Klassen 2013]). This practice may in fact reflect localized traditions present throughout the Iron I.

Thus, these imposing jars (weighing around 80–120 kg, full) reflect a stable ceramic tradition. The standard Iron I form remained the long-necked type form (see appendix B) which underwent little chronologically significant changes for most of its use in the Iron I. It is only toward the end of the Iron I that the short-necked type begins to replace long-necked jars.

Summary on Chronology

In the absence of relevant calibrated dates (the dates from the Baqʿah Valley are too high to be helpful; see Strange 2001), the beginning of the Iron I in Transjordan in absolute terms cannot yet be determined. However, on the basis of relative sequences from ʿUmayri, and the Mādabā tomb assemblages (such as the presence of 19th Dynasty scarabs at Mādabā Tomb A), we may be able to date the Tall Mādabā assemblage early in the Iron I rather than later in the sequence, which would fit within the earlier sequence at ʿUmayri (Stratum 13/12). What cannot be determined is whether the sequence in Transjordan precedes, follows, or is concurrent with the sequence in Cisjordan during the Late Bronze–Iron I.

Part 2. Material Culture and Ethnicity

Tomb Assemblages and Ethnicity

In her discussion of ethnic identity from a functional perspective, D. Edelman leaves the door open for mortuary data as a possible ethnic marker (see chap. 2 above). A priori, this seems to represent a reasonable perspective, since tomb assemblages reflect deep-seated traditions concerning the identity of the departed and, perhaps more importantly, the identity of those who buried their dead (Gilmour 2002: 112). R. Gonen, for instance, has argued that the multiple interment cave burial type reflects practices indigenous to the region but that as many as eight types that were introduced in the course of the Late Bronze reflect foreign origins (Gonen 1992: 21–31).

However, in his study of Late Bronze mortuary data (Gezer Cave 1.10A, burial pits at Acco, and double-pithos burials at Tell es-Saʿidiyeh), G. Gilmour suggests that the presence of nonindigenous elements in tomb materials does not necessarily signal the deceased's ethnic status. The larnax (clay case with multihandled lid) burial at Gezer Cave 1.10A (LB IB) is clearly of Minoan design. Though it was produced locally, it is quite unique in the Gezer assemblage. To add to the special status of the tomb, it was found in an abandoned cistern transformed into a burial cave (Gilmour 2002: 113–14; see also Seger and Lance 1988: 52, 114, 152).

Before a Cretan label is attached to Gezer Cave 1.10A, however, other material-cultural indexes need to be examined. Gilmour notes that, apart from the Minoan larnax, there is no other evidence to single out this tomb as Aegean in origin (Gilmour 2002: 114). While there is no simple solution to the

question, perhaps the most reasonable way to interpret this process is to recognize the foreign origins of the inhabitants of Gezer associated with Gezer
Cave 1.10A.[5] Nevertheless, the local nature of the assemblage also signals
assimilation, so the larnax may serve as a manipulated primordial symbol of
origins rather than a contemporary socioethnic reflex (as in the discussion on
Uriah, "the Hittite," in chap. 3). Thus, for reasons that will probably remain
unknown to us (intense grief? [Gilmour 1992: 114]; trade? [Holladay 2001]),
in the burial of these two children (seven or eight years old), the localized
population chose to reconnect with their primordial roots.

Egyptian influence in Transjordan during the Late Bronze has been documented in Egyptian textual sources (Redford 1982b; Kitchen 1992) and perhaps also in the iconography of the Baluʿa Stele (Routledge and Routledge
2009: 76; Strange 2001: 300–302; Ward and Martin 1964). This cultural influence continued into the Iron I (Dornemann 1982: 136). In Egyptian mortuary
practices, seals were considered amulets designed to invoke good health and
security. For instance, as a standard funerary provision, the Eye of Horus was
a symbol of life and power and had the ability to conquer death (Bloch-Smith
1992: 84). Thus, it may be possible that Egyptian seals functioned in a similar
role in the burial practices of the highland populations of Transjordan (see
seal number 216 at Mādabā; Harding 1953: 33).[6]

However, the presence of foreign seals cannot be construed to draw firm
conclusions about the origins of the dead and/or bereaved. Their presence
in tomb assemblages does not represent a unique occurrence (in contrast to
the Minoan larnax at Gezer) but appears to be a widespread custom throughout the highland region, on both sides the Jordan (see Bloch-Smith 1992).
If anything, these nonindigenous elements in the tomb assemblage confirm
the view that the people buried in the MPR belonged to the highland culture
encountered both in Cis- and Transjordan, which during the Late Bronze and
the early Iron I came under a certain degree of Egyptian influence.

Finally, with respect to a possible correlation between tomb architecture
and ethnic identity, even if the bench burial cave subtype can be identified as
nonindigenous (Cyprus; see Gonen 1992: 23–24), the origins of the subtype
say very little about the population's current status. This is especially true in
the case of the Sahab tomb, since the ceramic assemblage represented in this
tomb does not markedly differ from the regional repertoire.

Cultic Installations and Ethnicity

According to the textual data reviewed in chap. 4, the most promising
ethnic marker appears to be religious ritual behavior. From the Song of Deb-

---

5. Perhaps as part of a diaspora (see Holladay 2001).
6. New Kindgom seals are also present at ʿUmayri (Eggler, Herr, and Root 2002:
248, passim).

orah, tribal identity as the "people of Yahweh" brought some cohesion among eclectic tribal groups both in Transjordan and Cisjordan (Judges 5). However, the situation in Transjordan represents a context considerably more fluid than in the heartland of Yahwism. Since Transjordan stands outside the boundaries of the "promised land," these groups living on the frontier may not have held identical religious traditions (e.g., Jephthah). To add to this complex picture, texts also allude to a fragmented nature of Yahwism during the time of the Judges. Some groups may have rallied together for exceptional circumstances such as armed conflict with the Canaanites. However, times of pan-tribal unity and unified Yahwism are exceptions. Instead, religious assimilation and resulting diversity of the varying groups in the region appears to have been the norm from the early history of Israelite settlement in the region (Judg 3:5–6).

In Cisjordan, successful efforts have been made to identify Yahwistic type features in the archaeological record during the Iron II (Zevit 2001; Taylor 1993: 30).[7] In this regard, Arad is a type-site that argues for a convergence of ethnic and religious identities with the material culture in a transitional zone. In the northwestern quadrant of the fortress, the Arad temple featured a tripartite configuration with a rectangular courtyard, a central hall ("the holy place"), and a square cultic niche ("the holy of holies," 1.2 m × 1.2 m). Pottery analysis and a recent reappraisal of the fortress's stratigraphy point to an 8th-century B.C. setting (Singer-Avitz 2002: 159–76; Herzog 2002).[8] The sanctuary was quite small and followed a local broad-room layout. The main altar (2.20 m × 2.40 m) was located in the courtyard. In its second phase, the altar was constructed with unhewn stones (see Exod 27:1). Excavators discovered several artifacts related to the cult, among which were an incense burner, priestly vessels, and a stele (*mṭbḥ*?; compare Exod 24:4)[9] inside a small niche. After two building phases, in what is interpreted as an intentional cancellation of the temple, two incense altars at the entrance of the niche / "holy of holies" were laid on their sides and covered with a protective earth layer. In the same niche, two standing-stones were found on the floor, lying on their flat sides. To complete the process, after the dismantling of the top of the walls, both the hall and the niche were also covered with a protective layer of earth (Herzog 2002: 39–40). Completing the picture, epigraphic evidence also suggests that Arad's temple officials were related to Jerusalem priestly families (Herzog et al. 1984: 32). In turn, this could point to the Yahwistic nature of this important shrine on Judah's southern border (e.g., Arad Letter 21, line 4, "May Yahweh reward [my] lord," Gogel 1998: 391).

---

7. In addition to epigraphic materials, the main diagnostic artifacts are figurines, altars, ceramic stands, decorated cult stands, and model shrines (Zevit 2001: 267).

8. M. Aharoni's conclusion that the temple was first built in the 10th century B.C. (Solomonic age) can no longer be accepted (Herzog et al. 1984).

9. J. Holladay suggests that these steles could have been inscribed with paint (as are the Dayr ʿAlla inscriptions; Holladay, private written communication, 2005).

This relatively neat convergence is difficult to recover in the available Iron I artifacts and installations that are recognized as unequivocally cultic[10] (Nakhai 2001: 170–76)—for example, "the Bull Site" (Mazar 1990b: 351–52), Khirbet et-Tell's "room 65," the household shrine at Tell el-Wawiyat, and perhaps el-Burnat/Mount Ebal (Zertal 1986–87; see discussion in Hawkins 2012 and in Mazar 1990b: 350). One would be hard-pressed to isolate specifically Yahwistic features in these. Consequently, the arguments for assigning Israelite religious practices tend to fall back on other criteria, including the geographical location of a particular installation (e.g., Khirbet et-Tell within the traditional territory of Israel; Dever 2005: 113). In other cases, however, the generic designation "Canaanite" remains the preferred designation, perhaps on account of antecedent religious traditions (e.g., "standing stones"; Dever 2005: 119; see Nakhai 2001: 91).

Published data from the excavations at Tall al-ʿUmayri illustrate some of the problems. In Field B, Building A (Rooms 1 and 3) has been interpreted as housing two cultic chambers (Rooms 2 and 4). The flagstone floor in Room 2 contained an upright, rectangular standing stone. The smooth surface appears to be natural. Facing this stone, another smooth rectangular stone was found on the floor. In Room 4, a similar symbolic value has been attached to the arrangement of eight small stones (similar in shape to the larger stones of Room 2; Lawlor 2002: 107). Other finds that could be interpreted as cultic include a platform and a chalice in the back room. However, no cultic implements (tools, etc.) or supporting iconographic data were found within the structure. In the absence of supporting epigraphic data, we would be premature in drawing any specific conclusions regarding the nature of the cult or the identity of its participants (see further discussion in Lawlor 2002: 106). This house shrine nevertheless represents a significant development in our otherwise lean picture of Iron I religion in central Transjordan and typically mirrors the general material-cultural religious landscape in the highlands of the southern Levant.[11]

Geographical Distribution and Ethnic Identity

Most recent covariance studies have also begun to embrace dynamic views of ethnic identity within a social context. Thus stylistic elements such as homogeneity (e.g., absence of style; see Faust 2006) may also signal social realities. This has led R. Miller to view the homogeneous distributional patterns of

10. R. K. Hawkins provides an excellent summary of the various criteria to identify a site as cultic (Hawkins 2012: 15–28).

11. Archaeological data on religious installations and artifacts in Moab (Iron II, but it could also include earlier levels; Dolan 2009: 130) are emerging from excavations on the Wadi Thamad (a Wadi Mujib tributary). Site WT-13 along with an installation interpreted as a Moabite *bmt* ('high place') have yielded multiple figurines (including female and anthropoid) as well as several model shrines (Dolan 2009: 130–31, 141).

Iron I material culture of highland Cisjordan as the presence of ethnic Israel in the region (R. D. Miller 2004: 55–68; see also Faust 2006).

As Z. Zevit's own argument for covariance in the Iron I material culture illustrates (Zevit 2001: 107), the disagreement with functional approaches (as discussed in chap. 2; e.g., Bloch-Smith 2003: 406–11) tends to revolve around differing hermeneutics. No one seems to question the continuities between the Late Bronze and Iron I material cultures (see Dever 1992). In the case of the collared pithos—although this store-jar tradition is linked to the Iron I population increase in the highlands, it is also found on the coast and seems to evolve from the Late Bronze Age store-jar. On the one hand, Zevit (and Faust, Dever, and Miller) interprets morphological evolutions of this sort as transmitters of ethnic variations. On the other hand, a more functional approach may see these traits as stylistic-technological evolutions for which ethnic motivations are not prerequisite. Likewise, the presence of the collared store-jar and four-room house type (with all its variations, see Faust 2006) outside Israelite traditional geographical boundaries can be interpreted as adaptation and usage by non-Israelites or can be interpreted from a more functional, ethnic-neutral viewpoint.

In the MPR and surrounding region, however, the emerging data at Tall Mādabā and the existing evidence at ʿUmayri suggest a Late Bronze–Iron I continuity already represented at the Mādabā Tomb and farther north, in the Baqʿah Valley (see McGovern 1997).[12] Thus, from a strictly regional standpoint, it is difficult to imagine a change of order that would signal ethnic change during the Late Bronze–Iron I period. At ʿUmayri, although Stratum 14 ends in destruction, there is no settlement hiatus between LB II (Stratum 14) and Late Bronze / Iron I (Stratum 13/12; Herr and Clark 2009: 70, 81).

While the geographical argument still holds sway for some interpreters in Cisjordan, the transitional nature of the MPR makes covariance there an especially delicate task. Even if one were to assume that collared pithoi and the four-room architecture were encoded with Israelite ethnicity in central Transjordan (and that Khirbat al-Mudayna al-ʿAliya's [Routledge 2000a] inhabitants borrowed the architecture from their northern neighbors), the regional dynamics, as argued in this book, cast serious doubts on deeming a particular period the property of a certain tribal group. The most reasonable explanation is that the cultural assemblage is shared by a variety of groups for functional reasons.

Nevertheless, in light of the proposed model of ethnic identity, which acknowledges the possibility that pottery technology may convey a socioethnic message, microvariations present at the regional level will need further examination (see chap. 2, p. 22 above). Wavy ridging on the collared pithoi (and potter's marks), though less frequent at Mādabā, are rarely found in Cisjordan

---

12. A similar continuity is also documented at the Western Cemetery of Tell Dothan, a highland site situated in the traditional territory of Israel (Cooley and Pratico 1995; see Master 2008).

(perhaps at Shiloh; see Finkelstein 1993: fig. 6:58). These are potentially significant differences for ʿUmayri, Sahab, and Mādabā. A clearer diagnostic,
the pie-shaped decoration on lentoid flasks, seems to be isolated in the MPR.
Therefore, the many varieties of rim profiles on the collared pithos and the
emerging picture of technological diversity potentially point to an overall
context of microdiversity in the MPR. Perhaps these technological variations
encoded localized social signals, differentiating microcultural zones within the
region.

The textual evidence signaling that religious identity was the predominant
ethnic marker among Iron I tribal groups in the MPR may find support in
the ʿUmayri house shrine. The data, however, do not indicate whether Yahwism (or a regional adaptation of Yahwism) provided the impetus for this
religious installation. In light of this background, while F. M. Cross's historical instincts were right in situating a shrine within the MPR (he proposed a
site near Mount Nebo as a possible location), the evidence (both textual and
archaeological) is too ambiguous to confirm his suggestion that it was Reubenite (Cross 1988: 51). The cluster of settlements at the northern edge of the
traditional Reubenite territory (the *mishor*; see Josh 13:15–21) in traditional
Ammonite territory (the foothills north of ʿUmayri; see Josh 13:25) raises
the question whether the currently available picture of settlement patterns
provides sufficient evidence to support the case for singling out Reubenites in
the MPR. The impression left by the survey data confirms the textual records,
which seem to attribute shared significance to the Gadites within the regional
sphere broadly defined by the two rivers (Mujib/Arnon and Zarqa/Jabbok; see
discussion in chap. 4).

Complicating matters further, the historical picture offered in the available documentary sources suggests some *va et vient* by Amorite, Moabite, and
Ammonite interlopers (see chaps. 3–4). Thus, when we superimpose the textual evidence on the archaeological landscape, we have a general sense of the
identity of the inhabitants of the MPR during the Iron Age I, but we lack the
historical controls to ascertain who the precise occupiers of ʿUmayri were at
the time of ʿUmayri Stratum 12 (and Stratum 14) or Mādabā Field Phase 10.

CHAPTER SIX

Prospects for Historical Dynamics

Summary

The shifting social frontier theoretical construct appears particularly well adapted to the southern Levantine highland culture. In Transjordan, however, the prevailing model of settlement, the "Reubenite Hypothesis," follows a narrow culture-historical trajectory. The primary catalyst for the emergence of Israel and Yahwism in Canaan during the Late Bronze / Iron I transition is linked to the Reuben tribal group. In its movement from the southern regions, it first occupied the MPR (including Tall al-ʿUmayri) and then spread to the highlands west of the Jordan. Accordingly, the primacy of Reuben found in some genealogical records (Genesis 49) reflects a genuine tradition of tribal headship in early Israel.

Unilateral approaches to ethnic theory, which lean heavily on a particular line of evidence at the expense of others, appear to be inadequate. To rely exclusively on archaeological evidence is to mute the value of ancient texts as informants of a past culture's self-awareness. Similarly, textual perspectives that overlook material-cultural data can only provide a limited view of what was undoubtedly a complex and dynamic process, particularly in tribal societies. As a baseline definition, tribal ethnicity should be cast as a social process that encompassed both primordial and instrumental characteristics; the primordial anchors (in the case of Israel, ancestry and religion) could be manipulated according to shifting loyalties among the varying groups.

When the notion of a shifting social frontier is applied to northern Moab in premonarchic times, several texts illustrate a contested history between competing groups in this region. As tribal groups vied for control, it appears that the region north of the Arnon (Wadi Mujib) changed hands repeatedly. According to my proposed analyses of the Song of Heshbon (Num 21:27–30), the surrounding narrative text in Numbers 21, and the Mesha Inscription, limiting these tribal conflicts to the time of Mesha's military campaigns (9th century B.C.) unnecessarily compresses the deep historical memories that appear to be embedded in these texts.

The textual data are also interpreted to suggest that the dictates of primordial ethnicity based on a common ancestry served only to situate specific groups' origins. Within the fluid context inherent to the highland social frontier, one's origin did not necessarily signal current ethnic identity. From the perspective of biblical sources, the most discernible trait during the formative Iron I was adherence to Yahweh, by the "people of Yahweh" (see Judges 5). Thus, as the examples of Jael the Kenite and Ruth attest, members of competing groups could be joined to "Yahweh's family" (*mšpḥh*).

Conversely, within a fluid tribal setting, this identity as people of Yahweh could easily be manipulated to take on different circumstantial traits. Perhaps the Deuteronomic evaluation of Judg 3:6 ("they took their daughters as wives . . . their own daughters they gave to their sons . . . they worshiped their gods"), framed in Yahwistic covenantal terms, supplies an additional socio-ethnic backdrop to the situation.

The context in Transjordan reflects similar instrumental impulses where any perceived pan-tribal ethnic loyalties gave way to localized expressions of tribal identities. The general viewpoint in biblical texts is that the "land east of the river" stood outside the bounds of the Israelite homeland. In this regard, the record on Jephthah, the "Gileadite," leaves a distinct impression of "otherness" by highlighting Jephthah's circumstantial promotion to preeminence in Israel and the aberrant incident with his daughter (Judges 11). It appears that the fluctuating loyalties of the Transjordanian tribal groups located between the Mujib/Arnon and the Zarqa/Jabbok rivers made it especially difficult to plot one particular tribe's preeminence within the pantribal entity. Therefore, the case for Reuben as *primus inter pares* seems overly specific. The Israelite tribal records, while acknowledging Reuben's primogeniture, seems to reflect a more dynamic approach to blood-tied ancestry. Reuben's primordial status was no guarantee of circumstantial preeminence within the larger Israel group. Instead, not only is Reuben characterized negatively in historical memory, it is precisely his lack of social standing that is perceived negatively.[1] This lack of favor, however, does not negate the possibility that Reuben might have played an ad hoc preeminent role at some point in the history of the region. Along with Gad (Mesha Inscription, line 10; see McDonald 2000: fig. 9), both tribal groups had claims to the land "between the two rivers." In the vicissitudes of frontier life, tribal groups may have appeared and disappeared on the historical scene, following the patterns of abatement and intensification that were indelibly etched in the *longue durée* history of the region (see Judges 3, 5, 10; 1 Chr 5:9).

Turning to the material-cultural landscape of the MPR, settlement-pattern analysis reveals a settlement increase at the beginning of the Iron I period, with clusterings to the northern edge of the MPR, into the foothills. Agropastoral settlements became commonplace. However, at the northern edge of the MPR, the site of Tall al-ʿUmayri sits at the center of this settlement increase and represents our most important window to date into the Late Bronze /Iron I material culture. As a stratigraphic anchor, the ʿUmayri as-

---

1. In contrast, other examples of negative evaluations by biblical writers do not necessarily imply a lack of sociopolitical status. In the case of Omri, the Deuteronomic assessment carefully underlines Omri's political preeminence (2 Kgs 16:25, 27).

semblage supplies rich comparative data for the existing local tomb assemblages and the early Iron I horizon at Tall Mādabā. The ongoing excavations at Mādabā, perhaps the true regional center in the MPR, are confirming the major role this strongly fortified settlement seems to have played during this formative period.

Narrowly defined cultural approaches have yielded uneven results in plotting the relationship between style (and technology) and ethnic identity in the highland culture of the southern Levant. While there are times when a covariant relationship appears to exist (Philistine material culture as ethnic signal), covariance cannot be assumed in transitional cultural zones. Thus, the distributional data and documented continuities with the Late Bronze assemblage seem to favor a functional interpretation of the data. We cannot rule out, however, the possibility of some form of *adopted* covariance for the highlands material culture, especially in zones traditionally assigned to Israel. In this process of adaptation, Iron I highland populations perhaps infused socioethnic signals into these material-cultural forms. What cannot be ascertained with certainty is *when* these generic functional forms may have come to be "owned" by the population along with the distinctive "Israel" label. In the end, if ethnic labels must be applied, it appears that in light of the textual data pointing to cultural dilution during the period of the Judges, the case for "Israel" labels on the material culture of the time is much harder to sustain than "Canaanite."

Turning to Transjordan, a true frontier environment, the ambiguity dissipates so that a functional model appears better suited to interpreting the available data. Perceptions of otherness and the fluid setting of Israel groups in "Gilead" may have prevented these groups from attaching pantribal "Israel" labels to their regional material culture. In this respect, the available cultic and mortuary data do not appear to supply distinctive social signals from which the ethnic identities of the region's inhabitants can be identified.

Tribal Frontier Historical Dynamics

In view of the documented difficulties in isolating ethnically defined religious traditions during the Iron I (from a material-cultural standpoint), plotting archaeologically the spread of Yahwism from Transjordan to Palestine during the Late Bronze / Iron I appears not to be a productive avenue to pursue. This negative assessment, however, does not spell the end of the quest for the origins of Yahwism and of Israel. At the risk of recounting the obvious, biblical sources, while viewing Transjordan as a frontier and/ or refuge (see Gen 19:30–38), never deny the existence of early groups tied to Israel and plot the progression of the people of Yahweh from the south (see Numbers 21; Deut 2:4; Hab 3:3; and passim) and across the Jordan River along a westward arch. However, documentary sources also offer a textured and complex picture of tribal movements occurring along the traditional trade routes, including the "King's Highway," the several trunk roads across the Jordan Valley, and routes linking northern points to the southern Levant. Such diversity is well attested in the documents describing Israelite origins and multilayered relationships with Canaan, Aram (e.g., Rainey 2007), and Egypt (e.g., Hoffmeier 1997). Texts also underscore the "tented" culture of tribal Israel (e.g., "to your tents, O Israel," 1 Kgs 12:16; see Homan 2002), which would presumably reflect an inconsistent material-cultural imprint on the archaeological landscape. Furthering this perception is the notion of borrowed material culture described in some of the available textual traditions (e.g., "cisterns that you did not dig," Deut 6:11). Nevertheless, the Merneptah Stele anchors the existence of a demographic constituency named "Israel" in Canaan in the late 13th century B.C. What still eludes us from the standpoint of the Merneptah excerpt, however, is when and how "Israel" came to be in the region. Observed Late Bronze / Iron I material-cultural continuities, along with other factors (not least of which are Israel's own tribal eponymous traditions in Transjordan, e.g., Gen 32:28) may cause some to reach further across what the late Brian Peckham used to call the "red line" of 1200 B.C. in order to find Israel's ethnogenesis (van der Veen, Theis, and Görg 2010).

Ethnohistorical research in the historiography (Shryock 1997), subsistence strategies (Ji 2002), and migrations (Levy and Holl 2001) of modern tribal societies have already contributed significantly to our understanding of the social dynamics present in ancient tribal societies. Tribal martial interactions in which manipulated ethnic identities (from shared ancestry)[2] and shifting territorial claims occurred also provide insights into some of the historical problems related to Israel's earliest presence in Canaan. Shifting settlement patterns among tribal societies (see Boling 1988), the nature of a "city" in transitional frontier areas as nonpermanent settlements, the king as tribal sheikh (Glueck 1959: 114), and the common use of hyperpole in the "conquest" literary genre (see Younger 1990)—all deserve a fresh examination in historical reconstructions of Israelite origins in both Transjordan and Canaan.

That some assumptions need to be questioned is made particularly clear in view of the developments in the Mādabā Plains Region. Tall al-ʿUmayri Stratum 12 (LB/Iron I) and Stratum 14 (LB II) were well-fortified strongholds that ended in violent conflagration. While the identities of both inhabitants and attackers remain unknown (although we can expect some of the usual suspects discussed in this study), in plotting the history of this type-site, a peaceful infiltration approach clearly will not do. Likewise, in the heart of the MPR, Tall Mādabā is beginning to tell its own story. From the preliminary findings of the ongoing excavations, Mādabā was a significant settlement early in the Iron I period with a substantial fortification system. On the basis of the documented Late Bronze / Iron I continuity evident at Mādabā Tomb A and the *tall*, it may be that, as at ʿUmayri, Late Bronze levels could be encountered

---

2. In his recent history of Oceanic people groups, N. Thomas notes that "tribes with common ancestors would come to see each other as ethnically different peoples" (Thomas 2011: 11).

in the future. As the original quest for Heshbon demonstrates (Merling and Geraty 1994), specific historical-geographical identifications can be surprisingly elusive in the shifting frontier zone of the Mādabā Plateau Region (e.g., we do not know what biblical settlement can be identified with Tall al-ʿUmayri).[3] However, when criteria suited to transitional zones are applied, a more definite picture emerges of a region inhabited by variegated groups, who each claimed the area for themselves, some more successfully than others. These fluxes are well documented both in the history of the Judges and in the *longue durée* perspective. As available records also suggest, only a strong tribal leader would have been able to unify the warring tribes and give them a pantribal identity. David and Mesha (who shared Moabite primordial ancestries) fulfilled this role for their respective tribes, as did kings such as Shaka Zulu (Laband 1997) and Kamehameha I (Daws 1974) in other times and places in tribal historical memories.

---

3. McDonald tentatively suggests Abel-keramim (Judg 11:33; McDonald 2000: 166).

Appendix A

Gazeteer of Iron I Sites in Central and Northern Transjordan

Site Name	Site No.	Easting	Northing	Size	Topo Zone	Elevation
RASHIDIYYEH WEST	2014024	35.62207	31.88176		Hillside terrace	−248
NIMRIN	2014027	35.6274	31.90194		Alluvial plain	−185
GHRUBBAH EAST	2014030	35.58932	31.90471		Unknown	−270
DAMIEH	2016001	35.54929	32.10517		Alluvial plain	−335
DEIR ALLA	2017001	35.62388	32.19779	4	Hilltop	−202
UMM HAMAD EL-	2017007	35.59663	32.15291	2	Alluvial plain	−277
SAMRA	2017008	35.56746	32.1636		Plateau	−290
MEIDAN	2017015	35.62594	32.16962		Unknown	−230
ZAKARI	2017016	35.60445	32.16339		Unknown	−260
ARQADAT	2017038	35.58733	32.17654		Valley bottom	−260
QATARET ES-SAMRA I	2017039	35.56959	32.16013		Unknown	−310
BASHIR	2017045	35.607	32.171		Valley bottom	−260
REMEILEH	2017048	35.60991	32.16895		Unknown	−265
RABIʿ	2017063	35.59632	32.19448		Unknown	−254
SAIDIYEH	2018001	35.57902	32.26905		Alluvial plain	−232
MAZAR	2018002	35.60881	32.22344	2	Alluvial plain	−223
AMMATA	2018003	35.62129	32.24059		Hillside terrace	−185
QOS	2018008	35.62272	32.24606		Hilltop	−195
NN / AKS SITE 061	2018013	35.62224	32.29954		Unknown	120
GHAZALA	2018034	35.61201	32.22762		Hilltop	−239
KERAYMEH (NORTH)	2018045	35.60529	32.27095		Unknown	−200
BUWEIB	2018051	35.59318	32.24063		Unknown	−257
KHARABEH	2018055	35.59323	32.23522		Hilltop	−260
KURAYMAH	2018059	35.59951	32.27314		Unknown	−197
QELAYA	2018060	35.59943	32.27008		Unknown	−205
ABU HABIL SOUTH	2019004	35.58168	32.36657	0.7	Alluvial plain	−216
MAHRUQAT	2019012	35.59516	32.39208	4.5	Wadi terrace	−190
RAS HAMID	2019018	35.62652	32.3743	2	U. Slope	200
SOFARA	2019022	35.62271	32.31576	2	Unknown	100

Site Name	Site No.	Easting	Northing	Size	Topo Zone	Elevation
ABU EL-HILAN	2019023	35.60728	32.37019		Wadi terrace	−40
HEJEIJEH	2019073	35.61197	32.34096		Hilltop	10
HENEIDEH	2019074	35.61148	32.33872		Hilltop	100
ABU DAHNUN	2019077	35.59768	32.31673		Hilltop	−162
ABU ES-SUS	2019080	35.56278	32.37471		Unknown	−245
PELLA	2020002	35.61708	32.45204	25	Hilltop	−40
MEQBEREH	2020005	35.5933	32.4014	0.7	Alluvial plain	−190
ABU EL-KHARAZ	2020006	35.59977	32.40091	8.05	Hilltop	−116
ABU ALUBAH	2020016	35.5993	32.42536		Hilltop	−120
ABU ES-SALIH	2020018	35.63044	32.39946	2.7	Hilltop	220
MAʿAJAJEH	2020023	35.56648	32.40412		Hilltop	−267
ARBAʿIN	2021001	35.59373	32.52033		Alluvial plain	−200
QESEIBEH	2021015	35.61444	32.55588		Unknown	−100
SHEIKH MOHAMMAD	2021017	35.5867	32.49802		Alluvial plain	−255
REFEIF	2021035	35.61971	32.50609		Unknown	−98
SHUNAH ESH-SHEMALI	2022002	35.61101	32.60997		Alluvial plain	−200
ABU QAMEL	2022021	35.58198	32.58956		Unknown	−250
SAKHINEH	2022025	35.61601	32.59156		Unknown	−130
JISR EL-MAJAMIʿ	2022028	35.57439	32.62587		Unknown	−250
UMM LAHWAD	2111006	35.70154	31.60172		Unknown	700
IKTANU	2113001	35.67331	31.81883		Low spur	−140
RAMA	2113004	35.64703	31.82687	0	Alluvial plain	−205
UMM EL-QUTTEIN	2113006	35.69341	31.83095	0	Unknown	−50
SHAGHUR	2113035	35.65274	31.83072	0	Unknown	−198
JAZZIR	2115017	35.7254	32.02053	0.015	Unknown	650
NN / IRAQ EL-AMIR	2115033	35.7184	31.94589	0	Hilltop	490
DHAHAB EL-	2117003	35.68895	32.18542	0	Hilltop	−10
MUGHANNI WEST	2117005	35.65856	32.19779	0	Hilltop	−10
SABHA & ZIQHAN CAVES	2117007	35.65085	32.18803	0	Unknown	−200
UMM EL-IDHAM	2117014	35.67997	32.16848	0	Unknown	390
DHAHAB EL-	2117016	35.69004	32.1863	0	Hilltop	−25
NN / GYPSUM MINE	2117017	35.70588	32.18416	0	Unknown	−50
HAJJAJ	2117018	35.68474	32.15035	0	Hilltop	500
HEMMEH EAST	2117026	35.64942	32.19356	0	Hilltop	−195
RUWAISEH	2117027	35.71812	32.20374	0	U. Slope	360
KHARABE	2118003	35.68007	32.24423	0	Hillside terrace	200
DEBBET KANAS	2118012	35.7155	32.29396	0	Unknown	700
AMRIYE	2118014	35.71548	32.29306	0	Unknown	730
AQDE	2118015	35.68004	32.27939	0	Unknown	420
NIMR	2118017	35.65888	32.28164	0	Unknown	160

Site Name	Site No.	Easting	Northing	Size	Topo Zone	Elevation
UMM ZAYTUNA	2118020	35.63924	32.26312	0	Unknown	174
KHAMMAM	2118032	35.6806	32.29832	0	Unknown	410
MRABBA	2118033	35.67964	32.30194	0	Slope	380
HARABA	2118034	35.70605	32.26171	0	Unknown	742
HASHIMIYYA / FARA	2119002	35.66027	32.36547	0	Ridge	560
HALAWA	2119003	35.6651	32.38521	3	Saddle	450
AUSARA	2119004	35.69481	32.38368	0	Ridge	460
SAFIT	2119029	35.71697	32.30746	0	Hillside terrace	600
BUSTAN	2119031	35.72535	32.30367	0	Unknown	705
RUWEIS	2119032	35.72766	32.30993	0	Unknown	660
KEDADI	2119033	35.74056	32.24473	0	Unknown	680
JUBB	2119047	35.70273	32.3285	0	Unknown	670
MANSURA	2119048	35.69569	32.30611	0	Unknown	418
NN / AKS SITE 023	2119052	35.71055	32.30579	0	Unknown	535
NN / AKS SITE 038	2119059	35.67158	32.31654	0	Unknown	760
NN / AKS SITE 042	2119061	35.69047	32.30893	0	Unknown	457
MUSHEIRIFA	2119068	35.6958	32.30972	0	Hillside terrace	558
SUWWAN	2119073	35.71698	32.34353	3	Hilltop	886
MAQLUB	2120013	35.68475	32.40283	5	Hilltop	360
SAQAH	2120018	35.63472	32.40028	1	Hilltop	240
KUFR ABIL	2120029	35.67139	32.41844	0	Hilltop	430
KELEBAN	2120034	35.72389	32.39658	0.375	Wadi terrace	520
ZQEQ (SOUTH)	2120040	35.63883	32.39568	2	L. Slope	120
MIRYAMIN	2120043	35.6376	32.42636	6	Hilltop	350
DEIR QEQUB	2120054	35.65385	32.47291	0.1	Hillside terrace	260
ASHRAFIYYA	2120055	35.70583	32.4682	0	Unknown	530
SIR	2120064	35.68377	32.44162	0	Unknown	500
UMM HAMDE	2120068	35.73775	32.43325	0	Unknown	800
HUSSA	2120069	35.74243	32.44757	0.42	Unknown	740
ZUBIYA	2120070	35.65568	32.46295	0	Unknown	270
MENWEH	2120102	35.67522	32.47607	0	Hilltop	400
NN / WADI ZIQLAB	2121018	35.67895	32.53009	1.57	Unknown	305
NN / WADI ZIQLAB	2121019	35.68115	32.53275	0.07	Unknown	318
DEIR ABU SAʿID	2121065	35.68753	32.49654	0	Unknown	325
HUSSEIN	2121079	35.73622	32.48828	0	Hilltop	400
BOND	2122034	35.66837	32.60425	1.5	High spur	80
UMM EL-GHOZLAN	2122076	35.71076	32.59703	0	Plateau	180
EDʿAN	2122090	35.73984	32.64239	0	Hilltop	342
DHIBAN	2210002	35.7766	31.50363	0	Hilltop	690
LIBB	2211011	35.76388	31.6076	0	Hilltop	711

Site Name	Site No.	Easting	Northing	Size	Topo Zone	Elevation
MAKHAYYAT	2212003	35.7459	31.74867	0	Hilltop	740
HESBAN	2213001	35.81187	31.80133	3.75	Hilltop	895
NN / HESBAN REGION	2213008	35.82927	31.81808	0	Plateau	900
AL	2213009	35.83038	31.81986	12.56	Hilltop	930
UMM EL-QANAFID	2213055	35.82887	31.83973	0	Hilltop	860
NN / HESBAN REGION	2213061	35.80032	31.83856	0	Gulley	730
NN / HESBAN REGION	2213062	35.81821	31.83636	0	Unknown	770
RAWDA	2213066	35.82471	31.84162	0	Hilltop	886
ABU SILAN / HESBAN	2213067	35.82107	31.82638	0	Hilltop	885
HESBAN	2213070	35.8309	31.83698	0	Valley bottom	825
NN / HESBAN REGION	2213072	35.81007	31.84646	0	Hilltop	860
UMM ES-SARAB	2213077	35.83818	31.83321	0	Hilltop	894
BEDDIH / HESBAN	2213088	35.84073	31.84758	0	Hilltop	905
MUSHAQQAR /	2213101	35.78946	31.79371	7.065	Hilltop	810
NN / HESBAN REGION	2213103	35.81462	31.78774	0	Ridge	835
AYOUN MUSA	2213104	35.74256	31.7785	0	Unknown	520
IRAQ EL-AMIR	2214002	35.75827	31.91991	0	High spur	480
NN / HESBAN REGION	2214013	35.81936	31.8742	0	Slope	902
NA'UR	2214025	35.83109	31.87755	0	Unknown	770
HAJJAR	2214026	35.83133	31.91993	0	Unknown	825
MUWEINA	2214051	35.757	31.87377	6	High spur	550
KHANDAQ	2215027	35.76112	32.01164	0	Unknown	640
SAFUT	2216001	35.83498	32.03887	1.773	Hilltop	927
HAWAYAH	2216005	35.82818	32.09312	0	Hilltop	690
HAWAYAH	2216006	35.82807	32.08952	0	Unknown	630
UMM ED–DANANIR	2216009	35.81846	32.08703	2.5	Unknown	665
KHABYEH	2216013	35.78305	32.10675	0	Hilltop	682
ABU THAWWAB	2217001	35.84839	32.1639	6	Wadi terrace	490
GHREIMUN	2217002	35.74517	32.18602	0	Unknown	70
MSHATTA	2217003	35.75693	32.15421	0	Unknown	460
ABU TRAB	2217039	35.84337	32.17303	0	U. Slope	400
SAKHNE	2218001	35.74296	32.2537	0	Unknown	610
UMM JOZE	2218010	35.79971	32.27048	0	Unknown	930
REMUN	2218012	35.82874	32.28246	0	Unknown	825
UMM JALUD	2218025	35.792	32.2959	0	Unknown	1002
ILLIYET QARQOSH	2218036	35.79456	32.24084	0	Hilltop	1020
MEHNA	2219005	35.75261	32.36259	1	Valley bottom	820
UMM EL-HEDAMUS	2219007	35.74733	32.36361	4	Hilltop	950
SUF	2219029	35.84033	32.31376	0	Unknown	955
DHAHR EL-KHIRBEH	2219039	35.80481	32.33259	8	Hilltop	1130

Site Name	Site No.	Easting	Northing	Size	Topo Zone	Elevation
MUZABAL	2219040	35.77665	32.34944	1	High spur	1000
NN / AKS SITE 041	2219042	35.76499	32.31543	0	Unknown	880
HAMID	2219043	35.76697	32.31088	0	Slope	1000
BEIDA / WY 1	2220018	35.7497	32.40684	1.1	Ridge	780
MAHRAMA	2220021	35.78827	32.41681	4.7	Slope	980
MUSLIMANI	2220023	35.76424	32.3957	0	L. Slope	850
FARA	2220031	35.833	32.41942	0	Unknown	1016
DEIR BURAK	2220032	35.84715	32.42992	0	Unknown	964
IRBID	2221002	35.84911	32.55971	20	Plateau	578
RAʿAN	2221003	35.82056	32.56576	0	Unknown	495
JEBATON / WZS 70	2221004	35.74688	32.48895	0.88	Unknown	580
ESRIN	2221031	35.7593	32.54729	0	Hilltop	380
SOM	2222014	35.799	32.59149	0	High spur	380
ZAFARAN	2222038	35.84469	32.62202	0	Unknown	565
DABULYA	2222042	35.83547	32.59969	0.7	Hillside terrace	450
SRIS	2222043	35.83616	32.58795	0	Unknown	480
SAMOQA	2222044	35.81617	32.59562	0.75	Plateau	430
TUQBUL	2222045	35.81432	32.60467	0	Unknown	430
FOʿARAH	2222046	35.76891	32.6174	0	Unknown	365
QUSEIR FUARA	2222047	35.77748	32.61902	1.08	Hillside terrace	355
ISARA	2222050	35.75324	32.62767	0	Unknown	330
ABU EL-HUSSEIN	2222051	35.75997	32.60408	0	Unknown	322
HAUWAR	2222052	35.76849	32.60389	0	Unknown	365
JIJJIN	2222053	35.77216	32.58487	0	Unknown	390
YUBLA	2223009	35.82547	32.68827	0	Unknown	430
SAMAR	2223012	35.78888	32.67737	0	Unknown	470
BIYAD	2223026	35.81952	32.66857	0	Hilltop	503
RUMEIL	2310002	35.87671	31.57626	0.0283	Hilltop	510
ALIYAN	2310003	35.88485	31.53279	0	Hillside terrace	690
ALAYA	2310004	35.86275	31.56755	0	Unknown	671
KAUM	2310007	35.85182	31.55427	0	Unknown	660
ZAʿFARAN	2311001	35.87372	31.616	0	Unknown	719
ZAʿFERAN II	2311007	35.87378	31.6178	0	Unknown	700
MEDEINEH (ON WADI	2311014	35.91052	31.58983	0.65	Hilltop	629
JALUL	2312001	35.85902	31.72093	7.2	Hilltop	820
MANJA	2312003	35.85663	31.74623	0	Hilltop	809
NN / HESBAN REGION	2313013	35.86579	31.80374	0	Ridge	932
UMM EL-ʿAMAD	2313014	35.90435	31.78753	12.56	Hilltop	823
UMM EL-HANAFISH	2313015	35.8769	31.82152	0	Hilltop	822
NN / HESBAN REGION	2313023	35.87868	31.84492	0	Hilltop	890

Site Name	Site No.	Easting	Northing	Size	Topo Zone	Elevation
NN / MĀDABĀ PLAINS	2313029	35.93029	31.84014	0	Slope	850
NN / MĀDABĀ PLAINS	2313043	35.87254	31.85137	0	Ridge	880
ABU JABER VILLAGE	2313044	35.91468	31.84771	0	Hilltop	860
MUQABLEIN	2314001	35.91125	31.9064	0	High spur	936
NN / HESBAN REGION	2314006	35.85065	31.86088	0.1	Hillside terrace	910
NN / HESBAN REGION	2314012	35.86354	31.86781	0	Hilltop	944
FAHUD	2314015	35.91816	31.85755	0	Hilltop	878
FAHUD	2314016	35.92147	31.86198	0.675	Hilltop	914
UMEIRI	2314018	35.89108	31.86989	6.4	Hilltop	920
UMEIRI	2314019	35.89533	31.87069	0	Hilltop	900
NN / MĀDABĀ PLAINS	2314026	35.8868	31.86818	0	Hilltop	940
NN / MĀDABĀ PLAINS	2314028	35.88788	31.86906	0	Unknown	910
NN / MĀDABĀ PLAINS	2314032	35.90757	31.89025	0	Hilltop	910
NN / MĀDABĀ PLAINS	2314040	35.91014	31.87126	0	Slope	881
NN / MĀDABĀ PLAINS	2314042	35.90817	31.87581	0	Hilltop	895
NN / MĀDABĀ PLAINS	2314044	35.86972	31.89652	0	Hilltop	950
NN / MĀDABĀ PLAINS	2314047	35.87917	31.89451	0	Hilltop	927
JAWA	2314048	35.94451	32.21941	0	Hilltop	928
NN / MĀDABĀ PLAINS	2314049	35.8808	31.87914	0	Hilltop	921
NN / MĀDABĀ PLAINS	2314053	35.90503	31.87678	0	L. Slope	888
BUNEIYAT SOUTH /	2314055	35.89053	31.88613	0	Hilltop	899
NN / MĀDABĀ PLAINS	2314059	35.91265	31.88382	0	Unknown	869
ARQUB ABU MSALTI	2314066	35.90861	31.85596	0	Hilltop	880
JAZOUᶜA	2314123	35.90441	31.85696	25	Hilltop	850
AMMAN / FORUM-	2315001	35.94231	31.95257	0	Valley bottom	750
AMMAN / CITADEL	2315002	35.93709	31.95449	20	Hilltop	839
UMM ER-RUJM	2315009	35.92735	32.01423	0	Hilltop	889
JERANIN (SOUTH)	2315045	35.93309	31.97839	4.5	Hilltop	879
AMMAN / UM	2315165	35.87416	31.97126	0	Unknown	975
KOM YAJUZ	2316006	35.91329	32.038	0	Hilltop	875
ASARET MERJ IBN SANAᶜ	2316007	35.86134	32.03557	0	U. Slope	1062
HERBEJ	2316010	35.88806	32.07734	0	Unknown	925
SUWWARI	2317001	35.86245	32.20686	0.33	Hilltop	238
UDHMA	2317013	35.88232	32.13067	0	Unknown	838
MASARRAH	2317021	35.93639	32.16459	0	Wadi terrace	590
JENABAH / JERASH	2317024	35.94141	32.18882	3	Valley bottom	320
GHUWEIRIN	2317038	35.89333	32.21067	0	Unknown	420
JERASH	2318002	35.89343	32.281	300	Plateau	580
KWEIM	2318046	35.85633	32.24848	1.6	Hilltop	450
AMAME	2318050	35.87825	32.23716	0	Unknown	460

Site Name	Site No.	Easting	Northing	Size	Topo Zone	Elevation
BEREIRIDH	2318063	35.91636	32.23448	0	Hilltop	484
QAFQAFA	2319004	35.9424	32.35109	0	Hilltop	980
ASFOUR	2319007	35.88523	32.32356	0	Hilltop	880
DEIR MERWAN	2319022	35.88405	32.35334	0	Unknown	950
HATTIN	2319023	35.88067	32.34711	0	Unknown	970
SAKHRA	2319025	35.85051	32.36763	3	Unknown	1100
ABU EL-ASAFIR	2319032	35.87302	32.30671	0	Unknown	860
HUTE	2319039	35.92099	32.31282	4	Wadi terrace	890
UMM EL-ABAR EL-	2320013	35.95175	32.4753	0	Unknown	610
UMM EL-ABAR ESH-	2320014	35.95594	32.47339	0	Unknown	600
HUSN	2321001	35.88313	32.49131	0.2	Hilltop	666
SAL	2321002	35.91329	32.56906	0	Unknown	585
BAYADA	2321003	35.9164	32.56628	1.5	Unknown	555
MUGHAYIR	2322002	35.93587	32.6082	0.16	Valley bottom	510
MAGID	2322005	35.94284	32.65853	1	Plateau	420
MUA'LLAQA	2322007	35.92723	32.6048	0.5	Plateau	490
KOM	2322015	35.91131	32.63943	0	Hilltop	460
QUWEILBEH	2323003	35.8722	32.68271	32	Hilltop	455
QURS	2323009	35.86189	32.72712	1.26	Hilltop	180
ADASIYE	2323011	35.93603	32.71098	0.75	Unknown	410
NN / SAHAB SURVEY	2413011	35.98969	31.84777	6	Hilltop	850
NN / SAHAB SURVEY	2413021	35.98766	31.85053	1.26	Ridge	840
NN / SAHAB SURVEY	2413023	36.00033	31.85023	2	Slope	810
SAHAB SW	2414007	35.99877	31.86739	1.7663	Unknown	830
MABRAK	2414052	35.98611	31.93351	0	High spur	930
AMMAN / MARKA	2415002	35.98528	31.97321	0.0416	Plateau	765
HAMIR	2415071	35.97703	31.97971	0.0156	Unknown	730
MRAMEH	2417006	35.98023	32.14373	0	Unknown	600
SAKHARA	2417018	35.95907	32.17759	0	Slope	520
QNEYE SOUTH	2418022	35.99786	32.22897	0.1	Hillside terrace	500
MGHEYIR ESH-	2422003	35.95845	32.61489	0	Unknown	480
FUKHAR	2422007	35.95949	32.58799	1.6	Hilltop	439
NN / SAHAB SURVEY	2413001	36.01312	31.83511	0.2	Slope	780
NN / SAHAB SURVEY	2413003	36.01312	31.83511	12	Low spur	770
SHAMI	2413027	36.01312	31.83511	1.5	Ridge	800
SAHAB	2414002	36.00756	31.87645	0.06	Plateau	875
NN / SAHAB SURVEY	2414010	36.00066	31.86096	0.785	Ridge	850
HUWETAN ABU SNESLE	2414011	36.0331	31.93656	0	Alluvial fan	770
NN / SAHAB SURVEY	2414014	36.02597	31.86246	0	Unknown	820
IRMEDAN	2414028	36.04359	31.90615	12	Unknown	820

Site Name	Site No.	Easting	Northing	Size	Topo Zone	Elevation
NN / SAHAB SURVEY	2414029	36.04405	31.89174	0.33	Unknown	820
BANAT	2414037	36.04395	31.9278	0	Hilltop	840
MUSHERFE ER-RAQQAD	2414041	36.00451	31.90524	0	Slope	890
NN / SAHAB SURVEY	2414045	36.05589	31.91816	0	Hilltop	829
NN / SAHAB SURVEY	2414046	36.03627	31.93664	16	L. Slope	780
NN / SAHAB SURVEY	2414047	36.03721	31.94027	0	Valley bottom	780
NN / SAHAB SURVEY	2414048	36.03721	31.94027	0.8	L. Slope	770
MARBAT	2414049	36.03227	31.92933	1.5	L. Slope	780
NN / SAHAB SURVEY	2415063	35.99776	31.95016	0.06	Slope	900
NN / SAHAB SURVEY	2415064	36.04657	31.94499	0	Hilltop	843
NN / SAHAB SURVEY	2415065	36.04754	31.94772	0	Slope	790
JAMUS	2417007	36.04806	32.13266	0.65	L. Slope	545
RUMEITH	2421001	36.01703	32.49429	0.4	Plateau	579
NN / SAHAB SURVEY	2513004	36.0747	31.82482	0	Unknown	820
NN / SAHAB SURVEY	2513005	36.08303	31.82862	0.5024	Ridge	820
NN / SAHAB SURVEY	2513006	36.07981	31.83035	0	Hilltop	820
MADUNA	2514004	36.09723	31.9146	0	Unknown	880
NN / SAHAB SURVEY	2514005	36.08823	31.86481	0.087	Hilltop	960
ABU EL-HAYYAT	2514008	36.07485	31.9204	0	Ridge	856
AYFE	2514014	36.0978	31.89658	0	Hilltop	866
NN / SAHAB SURVEY	2514015	36.06691	31.93735	0	Ridge	860
DA'JA	2514017	36.07608	31.88166	7	Ridge	870
NN / SAHAB SURVEY	2514018	36.06697	31.86882	0.21	Slope	905
HORANI	2514020	36.09819	31.88397	0.84	Ridge	930
NN / SAHAB SURVEY	2514022	36.06283	31.93275	0.8	Unknown	860
NN / SAHAB SURVEY	2514023	36.10069	31.93903	0.0558	Hilltop	810
SUKHNEH	2517002	36.06517	32.13441	0.6	Wadi terrace	495
RIHAB	2519001	36.09585	32.32573	0	Unknown	885
FEDEIN	2619001	36.20549	32.34471	7.5	Plateau	708
MAFRAQ	2619002	36.21105	32.34366	0	Unknown	698
HAWSHIYAN	3019002	36.64087	32.31727	0	Unknown	978
UMM EL-QUTTEIN /	3019009	36.6345	32.31715	0	Plateau	975
NN / SGNAS SITE 050	1800010	35.39789	30.67699	0.04	Slope	40
NN / SGNAS SITE 028	1800018	35.39469	30.67434	0	Unknown	20
FIDAN / KING SURVEY	1800034	35.39864	30.66525	0	Hilltop	60
BARQA EL-HETIYE	1800035	35.3846	30.60327	70	Unknown	100
TELAH	1802019	35.4132	30.83094	0	Unknown	–120
NN / SGNAS SITE 162	1802020	35.41686	30.81013	0	Unknown	–90
NN / SGNAS SITE 187	1802022	35.41588	30.81285	0.004	Unknown	–90
FEINAN	1900001	35.49681	30.62822	7.8	Hilltop	300

Site Name	Site No.	Easting	Northing	Size	Topo Zone	Elevation
GHWEIBEH	1901001	35.46821	30.69281	0	Unknown	140
NUHAS	1901002	35.4387	30.68164	0	Unknown	80
NN / SGNAS SITE 160	1901004	35.45244	30.6886	0.12	Unknown	−100
JARIEH	1901005	35.48939	30.70503	0	Unknown	300
NN / SGNAS SITE 191	1902004	35.46238	30.79213	1.2	Unknown	30
KHANAZIR	1903001	35.43948	30.87825	0	Hilltop	−175
NN / SGNAS SITE 139	1903010	35.47767	30.89917	0	Plateau	−200
NN / SGNAS SITE 237	1903013	35.45689	30.94557	0	High spur	−305
NN / SGNAS SITE 134	1903018	35.48619	30.90532	0.004	Plateau	−190
NN / SGNAS SITE 126	1903045	35.49651	30.9403	0	Unknown	−190
FEIFA-WESTERN	1903058	35.45679	30.94196	0	Ridge	−302
UMM JUFNA	1903060	35.49668	30.94661	0	Wadi terrace	−180
NN / SGNAS SITE 003	1904028	35.48388	31.01811	0	Unknown	−280
PETRA	1997001	35.44242	30.32979	300	Valley bottom	935
TAWILAN	1997002	35.48702	30.32968	2.45	Hillside terrace	1400
SHEMMAKH	1998003	35.51616	30.48895	0	Hilltop	1440
IRAQ EL-JANUBIEH	1998017	35.51785	30.47358	0	Hilltop	1520
RAWWAFA	2001014	35.62861	30.71943	0	Unknown	280
AISARAH / WHS 9	2003003	35.62812	30.8935	4	Plateau	1180
UMM ER-RIH / WHS 10	2003004	35.62187	30.89453	4.375	Hilltop	1182
JUMMAH / WHS 16	2003010	35.62013	30.90719	0.39	Slope	1189
HARDHOUN / WHS 18	2003012	35.62139	30.91528	0.935	Unknown	1200
ADDANIN / WHS 173	2003017	35.5882	30.92587	1.5625	Hilltop	920
MOMAN / WHS 174	2003018	35.58606	30.92411	0.675	L. Slope	860
RIHAB / WHS 178	2003022	35.57928	30.94409	2	Unknown	940
UMM SUWWANEH /	2003023	35.57928	30.94409	0.54	Slope	890
MLEIH / WHS 182	2003026	35.5614	30.94084	0.54	High spur	840
MAQHAZ / WHS 187	2003031	35.58835	30.8925	3.225	Low spur	745
HIBLAN SALIM / WHS 190	2003032	35.6117	30.94344	1.2	Unknown	880
QUSAH EL-HAMRAH	2003038	35.54766	30.89601	0.189	Unknown	300
NN / ASKP SITE 177	2006002	35.63091	31.18565	1.5	High spur	850
MEIDAN SE	2006009	35.6117	31.13554	0	High spur	1127
MEIDAN	2006011	35.60966	31.13738	0	Hilltop	1100
IʿSAL	2006104	35.53655	31.18754	0	Unknown	−380
DHRAʿ	2007034	35.56673	31.25639	0	Hilltop	−140
UDRUH	2097002	35.5984	30.3304	0	Unknown	1310
DUWAR	2099019	35.61439	30.57901	0	Hilltop	1050
NN / WHS 28	2102003	35.63445	30.8573	1.6	High spur	1230
MAJADIL / WHS 6	2103006	35.64348	30.88146	4	High spur	1157
NAUKHA / WHS 20	2103007	35.64291	30.86073	1.45	Hilltop	1220

Site Name	Site No.	Easting	Northing	Size	Topo Zone	Elevation
MASHMIL / WHS 23	2103010	35.66356	30.88917	6	Plateau	1155
KARAKA / WHS 24	2103011	35.67117	30.89983	0.04	Plateau	1148
NN / WHS 29	2103014	35.65136	30.90205	0.0036	Unknown	1140
KARAKA / WHS 31	2103016	35.66508	30.90627	0.32	Hilltop	1117
JERADIN / WHS 39	2103024	35.67745	30.89971	0.5775	Hilltop	1095
UMM QREQARAH / WHS	2103027	35.68482	30.93923	4.8	Plateau	735
UMM QERBEH / WHS 47	2103032	35.6551	30.92361	0.125	Unknown	740
ORAN / WHS 55	2103040	35.65176	30.91647	0.3422	Unknown	800
NN / WHS 106	2103076	35.68032	30.9276	0.045	Unknown	865
NN / WHS 192	2103111	35.65378	30.87584	0.25	Hilltop	1175
NN / WHS 200	2103117	35.63448	30.93486	0.0025	High spur	860
BUREIS / WHS 211	2103122	35.64539	30.87511	2.7	Slope	1145
ABU BANNA / WHS 212	2103123	35.6799	30.8753	1.225	Unknown	1172
NN / WHS 242	2103126	35.69414	30.89846	0.002	Wadi terrace	925
MUHAWISH / WHS 248	2103132	35.67965	30.86629	0.25	Plateau	1198
NN / WHS 255	2103135	35.7112	30.90982	0.72	Unknown	730
NN / WHS 270	2103150	35.71678	30.92233	0.04	Slope	625
MDHAYNEIT / WHS 283	2103163	35.69958	30.86858	0.45	Ridge	1100
ABU USBA / WHS 284	2103164	35.70182	30.87395	0.15	Ridge	1120
DEIR / WHS 367	2103185	35.69957	30.90556	2	High spur	769
DAHS SOUTH / WHS 86	2104011	35.65311	30.96514	0.09	Hilltop	600
AIN EL-GHUZLAN /	2104035	35.67288	30.96113	3	Slope	635
SHORABAT / WHS 147	2104037	35.68367	30.97263	0.25	Wadi terrace	315
NN / WHS 168	2104045	35.66314	30.98748	0.0245	Wadi terrace	245
MUAFA / WHS 169	2104046	35.64322	30.98609	0.9	Low spur	180
NN / WHS 223	2104061	35.68994	30.9725	0.027	Unknown	310
ARD EL-HAUREH /	2104063	35.69326	30.97874	0.09	Unknown	305
NN / WHS 239	2104077	35.72857	30.96898	0.075	Wadi terrace	350
DUBAB	2104098	35.63624	31.03673	2.419	Hilltop	1220
MAJRA	2104106	35.68516	31.02581	0	Wadi terrace	1289
AKUZEH	2104112	35.72102	30.998	0	Hilltop	1010
MIHNA	2105002	35.69523	31.12299	0	Slope	1183
NN / ASKP SITE 293	2105018	35.64291	31.08891	0	Unknown	830
ZABDAH	2105020	35.66202	31.09753	0	Plateau	1225
BAQR	2105025	35.67094	31.07931	0	Unknown	1208
MAUTA	2105029	35.7011	31.21937	0	Unknown	1150
NN / ASKP SITE 309	2105034	35.70767	31.08125	0	Slope	1205
MIDDIN	2105041	35.73394	31.12038	0	Hilltop	1120
UMM SUWWANAH	2105046	35.66894	31.04508	0	Ridge	1279
SUL	2105056	35.73435	31.06175	0	Slope	1180

Site Name	Site No.	Easting	Northing	Size	Topo Zone	Elevation
NN / ASKP SITE 413	2105059	35.69518	31.04724	0	Unknown	1270
AWSAJ	2105060	35.70037	31.04533	0.56	Unknown	1274
KERAK CASTLE	2106001	35.70422	31.18143	2.15	Hilltop	1050
SARAH	2106003	35.69942	31.19686	0	Ridge	705
IZRA	2106021	35.69936	31.15808	0	Unknown	1095
NEQQAZ	2106022	35.70662	31.15522	0.54	Hilltop	1110
NN / ASKP SITE 208	2106023	35.70913	31.1696	0.65	Ridge	1055
QARYATEIN	2106025	35.71337	31.17131	1.6	Ridge	1070
THANIYYAH	2106026	35.7248	31.16746	0	Hilltop	1035
NN / ASKP SITE 168	2106030	35.69696	31.22126	0.019	Hilltop	1060
SAKKA	2106034	35.65992	31.21031	0.06	Wadi terrace	709
DWEIBIE	2106039	35.63416	31.15131	0	Hilltop	550
ALAQAN	2106041	35.65073	31.14376	0.4375	Unknown	910
NN / ASKP SITE 258	2106042	35.65709	31.14633	0.024	Slope	940
AINUN	2106045	35.68666	31.15384	0	High spur	1000
TALISAH	2106047	35.70021	31.15085	0	Ridge	1128
LABUN	2106048	35.69282	31.1492	0	Unknown	1053
NN / ASKP SITE 268	2106049	35.69384	31.14828	0	Hilltop	1170
HAWIYYAH	2106051	35.70836	31.14256	0.975	Unknown	950
BIRJES	2107008	35.7084	31.25439	1.4275	Unknown	950
NN / ASKP SITE 155	2107010	35.64088	31.24226	0	High spur	455
UMM NAJIL	2107015	35.70878	31.23093	0	Unknown	1045
RAKIN	2107016	35.70863	31.22552	0	Plateau	1060
BEIT LAJJAH	2107038	35.72787	31.31079	1.92	Hilltop	936
DEIR	2107042	35.68312	31.25131	2.475	Hilltop	991
HARAZIYA / NWAKS	2107045	35.69878	31.28525	0.375	High spur	700
QABU	2107055	35.69594	31.25916	0.021	Ridge	985
UMM QAL'A	2107059	35.65186	31.29705	0.06	Wadi terrace	420
YARUT	2107061	35.72336	31.30006	0	Wadi terrace	905
IMRA'	2108008	35.6891	31.35128	0	Unknown	955
MAJDALEIN	2108009	35.71912	31.33532	8	Wadi terrace	905
HIMMEH	2108011	35.68017	31.33253	0	Unknown	912
SHAHTAR	2108012	35.71054	31.32919	0.066	Unknown	865
TADUN	2108014	35.72931	31.32428	7	Plateau	916
TADUN III / NWAKS SITE	2108031	35.72613	31.32345	1.5	Unknown	870
WADI FAWWAR	2108035	35.68593	31.31348	0.04	Hilltop	510
MEDEINEH (ON WADI	2109006	35.73554	31.43056	0.36	Plateau	750
SMARRAH	2109007	35.73059	31.44149	0	Hilltop	280
FARIDIYYEH / WHS 362	2203030	35.75191	30.90716	0.5	Hillside terrace	740
MABRA / WHS 604	2203180	35.80844	30.90865	2	Slope	725

Site Name	Site No.	Easting	Northing	Size	Topo Zone	Elevation
DHAT RAS	2204036	35.76522	31.00608	0	Plateau	1168
UMM HAMAT	2204039	35.76618	31.03943	0	Unknown	1122
SHQEIRAH	2204044	35.78858	30.98123	1.5625	Plateau	1110
BATRA	2205020	35.79357	31.11639	0	Hilltop	1022
NASER	2205021	35.80161	31.10449	0.075	Hilltop	1020
NASIR	2205023	35.80349	31.09724	0	Hilltop	1048
UMM ALANDA	2205031	35.54997	31.25763	7.5	Slope	1095
ADER	2206001	35.76366	31.20541	0	Plateau	945
ABU ER-RUZ	2206024	35.73681	31.22042	1.5125	Ridge	1009
MREIGHA	2206049	35.8089	31.1386	0.8	Hilltop	962
SMAKIEH	2207001	35.80657	31.30819	0	Plateau	840
RABBAH	2207002	35.74144	31.27172	0	Plateau	965
MISDAH	2207017	35.74663	31.30588	0.81	Unknown	933
HMEIMAT (SW)	2207018	35.76673	31.31086	3.45	Low spur	873
HMEIMAT (SE)	2207020	35.77172	31.30173	4	Unknown	880
MISNA	2207033	35.76274	31.28209	0	Unknown	908
MUHARAKAT NORTH	2207040	35.83504	31.2769	0	Ridge	975
MUHARAKAT SOUTH	2207041	35.75543	31.24707	1.5	Ridge	960
ZARRAAH	2207042	35.76783	31.24049	0.42	Unknown	986
HEJFEH	2207046	35.78429	31.22932	1.6875	Slope	971
BALUᶜ (NORTH)	2208001	35.78305	31.36551	0	Plateau	830
BALUᶜ (SOUTH)	2208002	35.78289	31.36011	1.8	Plateau	830
NN / ASKP SITE 40	2208011	35.79719	31.34627	2.25	Unknown	810
NASIB	2208012	35.76338	31.33979	0	Unknown	873
SAADUNI	2208013	35.75414	31.3472	3.5	Unknown	870
ABU ZARUAH	2208025	35.77989	31.32951	0.01	Hillside terrace	855
QASR	2208032	35.75114	31.3166	0	Unknown	916
UMM EL-HABAJ	2208033	35.77015	31.3198	4.5	Hilltop	872
HMEIMAT (NW)	2208034	35.76579	31.31449	0	Unknown	885
NN / ASKP SITE 120	2208036	35.84282	31.32633	0	Slope	721
SHIHAN	2208039	35.74043	31.38176	0	Hilltop	1066
MISAR	2209011	35.75574	31.40218	0	Hilltop	870
NN / WHS 732	2302095	35.89752	30.84537	0.04	Alluvial plain	825
NN / WHS 1015	2303228	35.84354	30.92863	0.18	Slope	622
NN / WHNBS SITE 106	2303274	35.93596	30.88571	0.1256	Ridge	860
NN / WHNBS SITE 142:B	2303314	35.93573	30.88842	0	Hillside terrace	810
NN / WHNBS SITE 216:A	2303391	35.91947	30.90033	0	Unknown	810
NN / WHNBS SITE 216:B	2303392	35.91947	30.90033	0.075	Unknown	810
NN / WHNBS SITE 330	2303514	35.88851	30.90031	0.0004	Unknown	770
NN / WHNBS SITE 335	2303519	35.8883	30.90365	0	Unknown	820

Site Name	Site No.	Easting	Northing	Size	Topo Zone	Elevation
NN / WHNBS SITE 344	2303532	35.87772	30.89955	0	Slope	760
NN / WHNBS SITE 347	2303535	35.87433	30.89828	0.0176	Saddle	800
NN / WHNBS SITE 350:B	2303543	35.87482	30.87951	0	Ridge	760
NN / WHNBS SITE 396	2303598	35.86821	30.90707	0	Unknown	750
NN / WHNBS SITE 398	2303600	35.86704	30.90628	0.0036	Unknown	895
NN / WHNBS SITE 427	2303636	35.87794	30.91398	0.5	Unknown	880
NN / WHNBS SITE 430	2303639	35.87747	30.91218	0.56	Alluvial plain	908
NN / WHNBS SITE 440	2303665	35.87293	30.90372	0	Unknown	770
NN / WHNBS SITE 443	2303670	35.86578	30.90613	0.0016	Unknown	760
NN / WHNBS SITE 453:A	2303680	35.85744	30.90686	0	Unknown	700
NN / WHNBS SITE 463	2303693	35.85415	30.91243	0.0012	Ridge	790
NN / WHNBS SITE 474	2303704	35.87097	30.91873	0.0012	Ridge	970
NN / WHNBS SITE 480	2303712	35.86881	30.90967	0.6	Slope	880
NN / WHNBS SITE 493	2303725	35.86669	30.91206	0.24	Unknown	850
NN / WHNBS SITE 499	2303731	35.86347	30.91286	0.0084	High spur	860
NN / WHNBS SITE 505	2303739	35.84766	30.91916	0.45	Unknown	680
NN / WHNBS SITE 506	2303740	35.84926	30.91696	0.023	Slope	960
NN / WHNBS SITE 523	2303760	35.85002	30.92145	0	Ridge	800
NN / WHNBS SITE 524	2303761	35.85083	30.92053	0	Ridge	840
NN / WHNBS SITE 525:A	2303762	35.85154	30.9197	0.035	Ridge	860
NN / WHNBS SITE 527	2303765	35.85447	30.91964	1.5	Ridge	870
NN / WHNBS SITE 529:A	2303767	35.85752	30.91678	0.16	Ridge	860
MHAY	2304005	35.86424	30.9913	0	Hilltop	1044
KHASHM ES-SIRAH	2305026	35.85072	31.06464	0.0736	Hilltop	1025
NN / ASKP SITE 375	2305033	35.87031	31.12372	0	Hilltop	994
NN / LIMES ARABICUS	2306019	35.91102	31.18683	0.04	Plateau	834
MEDEINEH (SOUTH ON)	2307077	35.87405	31.28235	3.025	High spur	700
MEDEINEH (NORTH ON)	2308061	35.86584	31.32311	2.5	Hilltop	700
SALIYEH	2309002	35.92035	31.45534	0.048	Ridge	810
JUMAIYIL	2309007	35.90445	31.48546	0.04	Hilltop	760
JUMEIL	2310010	35.8952	31.49288	0	Unknown	730
NN / WHNBS SITE 253	2403012	35.9579	30.8816	0	Plateau	880
NN / LIMES ARABICUS	2407038	35.97433	31.23228	0	Alluvial fan	830
AL	2408016	35.94549	31.35107	0.408	Hilltop	845
MUSEITBEH	2409001	35.98348	31.48905	0	Unknown	740
LEHUN	2309001	35.85954	31.45805	66	Ridge	748
NN / LIMES ARABICUS	2508013	36.06127	31.37997	0.075	Slope	740
NN / LIMES ARABICUS	2407022	36.03268	31.28501	0.0517	Hillside terrace	830
NN / LIMES ARABICUS	2407026	36.00148	31.2614	0.007	Hilltop	859
NN / LIMES ARABICUS	2408013	36.00247	31.35876	0.01	Slope	770

Site Name	Site No.	Easting	Northing	Size	Topo Zone	Eleva-tion
NN / LIMES ARABICUS	2408028	36.00149	31.39395	0	Wadi terrace	660
NN / LIMES ARABICUS	2409005	35.9997	31.40391	0.0064	Plateau	730
NN / LIMES ARABICUS	2405001	36.04952	31.1164	0.0576	Ridge	900
NN / LIMES ARABICUS	2406020	36.01853	31.20225	0.0359	Slope	820
NN / LIMES ARABICUS	2406023	36.04282	31.12977	0.0324	Valley bottom	860
QATRANA	2407025	36.04243	31.24338	2.25	Plateau	770
NN / LIMES ARABICUS	2408010	36.01725	31.34289	0.0044	Ridge	820
NN / LIMES ARABICUS	2408011	36.02136	31.34569	0.6	Valley bottom	790
NN / LIMES ARABICUS	2408023	36.02471	31.37282	0.0025	Hilltop	780
NN / LIMES ARABICUS	2408026	36.01049	31.39052	0	Wadi terrace	600
NN / LIMES ARABICUS	2409006	36.00415	31.42464	0	Hilltop	770
NN / LIMES ARABICUS	2505004	36.05782	31.11929	0.0225	Ridge	900
NN / LIMES ARABICUS	2505005	36.05997	31.11754	0.0225	Ridge	900
NN / LIMES ARABICUS	2505007	36.07769	31.08638	0.0512	Plateau	900
NN / LIMES ARABICUS	2505011	36.12786	31.12538	0	Unknown	860
NN / LIMES ARABICUS	2505016	36.14187	31.0779	0.075	Gulley	860
NN / LIMES ARABICUS	2505018	36.13752	31.08322	0	Wadi terrace	860
NN / LIMES ARABICUS	2505019	36.13867	31.07963	0	Valley bottom	860
NN / LIMES ARABICUS	2505022	36.13942	31.08957	0.03	Slope	850
NN / LIMES ARABICUS	2505024	36.13899	31.10399	0.8	Slope	840
NN / LIMES ARABICUS	2505030	36.11736	31.12605	0.15	Gulley	900
NN / LIMES ARABICUS	2505034	36.11474	31.10886	0.25	Ridge	880
MANQASH	2506013	36.05275	31.1814	0.1224	Unknown	840
NN / LIMES ARABICUS	2506030	36.13321	31.1219	0	Wadi terrace	850
NN / LIMES ARABICUS	2509005	36.06625	31.42247	0	Slope	770
JAWA	3319010	37.00474	32.33619	16	Hilltop	1045

APPENDIX B

The Collared Pithos as a Chronological Marker

Origins of the Collared Pithos

The earliest evidence for the emergence of the collared pithos comes from Late Bronze levels at Aphek (Stratum X12; LB II "Egyptian Residence," Beck and Kochavi 1985). Stratum X12 is a sealed destruction level, dated to 1230 B.C. (Egyptian low chronology) on the basis of a letter from Ugarit found in the northwestern corner of hall 1721 (part of the Egyptian residency). It was in this context that a collared pithos was found (Beck and Kochavi 1985: fig. 5:1). Although the jar was broken off at the collar level, the presence of the collar and its size are clear markers of the type. On the basis of the projected angle turn immediately above the collar, this pithos appears to be of the long-necked type. Other attested collared pithoi on the coast were used as burial jars at East Nami and in domestic contexts (unpublished) at Tel Nami on the Sharon plain (Artzy 1994: 136; see also 1993). These Late Bronze / Iron I contexts outside the typical distributional limits of the vessel are significant. The everted-rim profile of these early coastal examples clearly links the collared pithoi to Late Bronze store-jars and confirms the well-documented ceramic continuity characterizing the Late Bronze / Iron I (for example, cooking-pot typology). While we cannot create absolutes dates for the highland context on the basis of the Nami findings, a general *terminus post quem* in the late 13th century B.C. remains a helpful point of departure.

Morphological Variations: The Long-Necked and Short-Necked Subtypes

In his analysis of the collared pithos at Taanach, W. Rast divided the collared pithos into subtypes based on the two periods at Taanach (IA = 1200–1150 B.C., and IB = 1150–1125 B.C.). He isolated an early form, which consistently had a long neck (with thickened everted rim) and a later form with a short neck, which resulted from placing the diagnostic ridge (collar) closer to the rim (Rast 1978: 9).

On close examination of a sample of the available (published) data in the highlands of Cisjordan and Transjordan, I found that variations with respect to rim thickness and eversion appear to be random. However, Rast's long/

short-neck seriation proves to be essentially accurate. Early Iron I sites in both Cisjordan (Giloh and el Burnat/Mount Ebal) and Transjordan ('Umayri) indicate that no (or few; see Herr 2001) short-necked jars are attested in these levels. In contrast, short-necked jars are found in later Iron I sites (Shiloh) or transitional Iron I/II sites (Khirbet ed-Dawwara).

Giloh

In dating the Giloh assemblage (southwest suburb of Jerusalem),[1] the type-site of the highlands in Cisjordan during the Iron I, A. Mazar relied on his cooking-pots type A (early) and B for his Late Bronze / early Iron I sequence (Mazar 1981: 21–23). Mazar characterized the architecture of Building 8 in field C as an early four-room house, because rough stones were used as pillars, whereas, in his opinion, later in the Iron I, sites with four-room dwellings used wood pillars (1981: 10). The pottery assemblage consists predominantly of collared pithoi (33.7%) and, because it is a one-period site with perhaps two building phases reflected in Building 8, the pithos assemblage is stratigraphically secure. Any observation of typological variation is limited by the published materials (1981: fig. 9) but, if the plate statistically reflects the morphological repertoire (which it does, according to the excavator; Mazar 1981: 27), all forms but one (1981: fig. 9:6) qualify as long-necked pithoi (note beveled rim; see 1981: fig. 9:12).

In the second report on Iron I Giloh, published collared-pithoi fragments from building 105 (interpreted as a freestanding tower; Mazar 1990a: 82), a complete vessel from Area F (inside Building 80; see Mazar 1990a: fig. 5; 1981: fig. 5), and rim sherds confirm the predominance of long-necked pithoi. Presumably no short-necked occurrences were found (1990a: fig. 3:9–15). Thus, Rast's chronological typology reflects a trend at Giloh. Other morphological variations such as rim thickness and degree of eversion are too random to point to a chronological evolution (Mazar 1990a: fig. 3:10; 1981: 9:12). The importance of minor variations will be discussed below.

El Burnat/Mount Ebal

In contrast to Giloh, the settlement at el Burnat/Mount Ebal reflects two clear architectural phases (Strata II and I, the main phase), both dated to the Iron I. Cooking pots are not as abundant as at Giloh (this phenomenon is attributed by Zertal to the functional role of the site as a cultic center), but the pots that have been published do show the typical Late Bronze / Early Iron I triangular and flanged rim (Zertal 1986–87; see Hawkins 2012).

The collared pithoi proportions at Ebal in both strata (28.5% in Stratum II; 30% in Stratum I, Zertal 1986–87, table 1) are comparable to Giloh's. It is

---

1. Iron I sites mentioned here are only a sample that serves to illustrate the issue. There are, of course, other Iron I sites that could be cited (see Mazar 1990b: 334–38).

important to note that, as at Giloh, there are no short-necked pithoi at Ebal (Zertal 1986–87, figs. 16, 12). The pithoi that is described as short-necked by Zertal still fits within the category of the long-necked jar, according to our metrical typology (approx. 7.5 cm; Zertal 1986–87, fig. 13:1).[2] Thus, on the basis of neck typology alone, we may deduce that Ebal's strata reflect the early form of the collared pithos. Finally, the fact that both rounded and long rims occur in Stratum II and Stratum IB confirms the data from Giloh, which indicate that rim morphological variations fluctuate widely.[3]

Khirbet ed-Dawwara

Data from this small site in the central highlands north of Jerusalem yielded useful results. Here, the collared pithos plays an important role in identifying transitional Iron I/Iron II contexts. According to the excavator (Finkelstein 1990), it is a one-period site dated to the Iron I but probably was abandoned early in the Iron II. Although the remains are poorly preserved, there is evidence of what can be characterized as a typical hill-country defense system, with corresponding dwellings of the four-room type. In this configuration, the inner wall (although poorly preserved, the wall is up to 3.1 m wide) forms the back wall of the broad room of what appears to be three four-room dwellings (Buildings 131, 103, and 118 in Area A). With the fragmentary outer wall (only the inner face was uncovered beneath a later wall, probably Late Roman–Byzantine; Finkelstein 1990: 168), the whole system can be understood as the casemate-like defense/dwelling system encountered at other highland sites (1990: 168–69, 172).

Architectural phasing has not been detected, so relative chronology must be based on pottery alone. Although the assemblage at Dawwara appears to be Iron I (triangular flanged rim on cooking pots; Finkelstein 1990: fig. 16:3), early forms are rare, and the appearance of Red Slip Hand Burnish (1990: fig. 13:2) along with bowls that the excavator calls "forerunners" of Samaria ware (1990: 180; fig. 14:1) place this site in a transitional Iron I/Iron IIA period. But more importantly, this later phase seems also to be reflected in the collared-pithos assemblage which, besides the typical long-necked type (1990: figs. 13:10–11; 16:7, 8, 9), now also includes short-necked pithoi (1990: fig. 16:6, 9). A neckless variant is another significant development in the collared pithoi present at Dawwara (Finkelstein 1990: fig. 16:11–12). In light of the transitional nature of the site, this form probably represents the final

---

2. The metric criterion adopted here is the distance from the base of the neck to the rim. Jars with necks measuring 5 cm or greater are considered long-necked jars.

3. At ʿIzbet Sarta, Finkelstein concluded that rim thickness and eversion were chronological markers for his data: in Stratum III (12th century B.C.), the thick folded rim represents 62.5% of the corpus, whereas the thinner, less profiled lip represents 37.5%. In Stratum I (early 10th century B.C.), at 80%, the thinner rim clearly predominates (Finkelstein 1988: 277–78). While this may be true at this site, this trend appears to be a local phenomenon.

stage of the Iron I collared pithos and functions as the forerunner of the Iron II short-necked collared pithos (1990: 190; see Edom and Moab collared pithos, Finkelstein 1995: fig. 10:2).

As an additional illustration of this morphological transition in the collared pithoi, Shiloh should be mentioned briefly. Area C at Shiloh is the main source of data for the Iron I (Stratum V, Finkelstein 1993: 33). The assemblage is characterized by features found at sites dated to the 12th century B.C., including cooking pots with everted rims as well as the "Canaanite jar." But these early diagnostics occurred in smaller proportions at Shiloh than at other Iron I sites (Finkelstein 1995: 162). This later Iron I context is also reflected in the collared-pithos assemblage. Both long-necked and short-necked pithoi are attested (Finkelstein 1993: figs. 6:48–49 [long-necked]; 6:51:4, 6 [short-necked]).

Bibliography

Ackerman, S.

1998 *Warrior, Dancer, Seductress, Queen: Women in Judges and Biblical Israel.* ABRL. New York: Doubleday.

Adams, R. Mc

1974 The Mesopotamian Social Landscape: A View from the Frontier. Pp. 1–12 in *Reconstructing Complex Societies; An Archaeological Colloquium,* ed. C. B. Moore. Cambridge, MA: American Schools of Oriental Research.

1981 *Heartland of Cities.* Chicago: University of Chicago Press.

Ahlström, G. W.

1986 *Who Were the Israelites?* Winona Lake, IN: Eisenbrauns.

Albertz, R.

1994 *A History of Israelite Religion in the Old Testament Period.* 2 vols. Louisville: Westminster/John Knox.

Albright, W. F.

1924 *Excavations and Results at Tell el-Ful (Gibeah of Saul).* New Haven, CT: Yale University Press.

1939 The Israelite Conquest of Canaan in the Light of Archaeology. *BASOR* 74: 11–23.

1940 Review of *Megiddo I: Notes on the Megiddo Pottery,* by Lamon and Shipton. *AJA* 44: 546–50.

1942 *Archaeology and the Religion of Israel.* Baltimore: Johns Hopkins University Press.

1963 *The Biblical Period from Abraham to Ezra.* New York: Harper & Row.

2006 *Archaeology and the Religion of Israel.* Reprint. OTL. Louisville: Westminster/John Knox.

Alt, A.

1968 *Essays on Old Testament History and Religion.* Garden City, NY: Doubleday.

Alter, R.

1981 *The Art of Biblical Narrative.* San Francisco: Harper.

1999 *The David Story.* New York: Norton.

Andersen, T. D.

2000 The Evolution of the Hebrew Verbal System. *ZAH* 13: 1–65.

Anderson, B. W.

1998 *Understanding the Old Testament.* Abridged 4th ed. Upper Saddle River, NJ: Prentice Hall.

Artzy, M.

1993 Nami, Tel. Pp. 1095–98 in vol. 3 of *NEAEHL.* Ed. E. Stern. New York: Simon & Schuster.

1994 Incense, Camels and Collared Rim Jars: Desert Trade Routes and Maritime Outlets in the Second Millennium. *OJA* 13: 121–47.

Ashley, T. R.
1993   *The Book of Numbers*. Grand Rapids, MI: Eerdmans.

Bahn, P., and Renfrew, C.
1996   *Archaeology: Theories Methods and Practice*. 2nd ed. New York: Thames & Hudson.

Banks, M.
1996   *Ethnicity: Anthropological Constructions*. New York: Routledge.

Barth, F.
1969   *Ethnic Groups and Boundaries*. Boston: Little, Brown.
1994   Enduring and Emerging Issues in the Analysis of Ethnicity. Pp. 11–32 in *The Anthropology of Ethnicity: Beyond "Ethnic Groups and Boundaries."* Ed. H. Vermeulen and C. Govers. Amsterdam: Spinhuis.

Bartlett, J. R.
1968   The Historical Reference in Numbers XXI. 27–30. *PEQ* 101: 94–100.
1969   Sihon and Og, Kings of the Amorites. *VT* 20: 257–77.
1978   The Conquest of Sihon's Kingdom: A Literary Re-examination. *JBL* 97: 347–51.

Battenfield, J. R., and L. G. Herr
1989   Field C: The Northern Suburb. Pp. 258–81 in *Madaba Plains Project 1: The 1984 Season at Tell el-ʿUmeiri and Vicinity and Subsequent Studies*. Ed. L. T. Geraty et al. Berrien Springs, MI: Andrews University Press.
1991   Field C: The Northern Suburb. Pp. 74–86 in *Madaba Plains Project 2: The 1987 Season at Tell el-ʿUmeiri and Vicinity and Subsequent Studies*. Ed. L. T. Geraty et al. Berrien Springs, MI: Andrews University Press.

Beck, P., and M. Kochavi
1985   A Dated Assemblage of the Late 13th Century B.C.E. from the Egyptian Residency at Aphek. *IEJ* 12: 29–42.

Bell, G.
1907   *The Desert and the Sown*. New York: Dutton's.

Bennett, C.-M.
1983   Neo-Assyrian Influence in Transjordan. Pp. 181–87 in *SHAJ*, vol. 1. Ed. A. Hadidi. Amman: Department of Antiquities.

Bentley, G. C.
1987   Ethnicity and Practice. *JCSSH* 29: 24–55.

Bienkowski, P.
2000   Review of *Ancient Ammon*, ed. B. MacDonald and R. Younker. *BASOR* 320: 96–98.
2009   'Tribalism' and 'Segmentary Society' in Iron Age Transjordan. Pp. 7–26 in *Studies on Iron Age Moab and Neighbouring Areas in Honour of Michèle Daviau*. Ed. P. Bienkowski. Leuven: Peeters.

Bienkowski, P., and E. van der Steen
2001   Tribes, Trades, and Towns: A New Framework for the Late Iron Age in Southern Jordan and the Negeb. *BASOR* 323: 21–47.

Biran, A.
1989   The Collared-Rim Jars and the Settlement of the Tribe of Dan. Pp. 71–96 in *Recent Excavations in Israel: Studies in Iron Age Archaeology*. Ed. S. Gitin and W. Dever. AASOR 49.Winona Lake, IN: Eisenbrauns.

Biran, A., and J. Naveh
  1993   An Aramaic Stele Fragment from Tel Dan. *IEJ* 43: 81–93.
Blenkinsopp, J.
  2008   The Midianite Hypothesis Revisited and the Origins of Judah. *Journal for the Study of the Old Testament* 33/2: 131–53.
Bloch, Y.
  2009   The Prefixed Perfective and the Dating of Early Hebrew Poetry: A Re-evaluation. *VT* 59: 34–70.
  2012   The Third-Person Masculine Plural Suffixed Pronoun *-mw* and Its implications for the Dating of Biblical Hebrew Poetry. Pp. 147–70 in *Diachrony in Biblical Hebrew*. Ed. C. L. Miller-Naudé and Z. Zevit. Linguistic Studies in Ancient West Semitic 8. Winona Lake, IN: Eisenbrauns.
Bloch-Smith, E.
  1992   *Judahite Burial Practices and Beliefs about the Dead*. Sheffield: Sheffield Academic Press.
  2002a Death in the Life of Israel. Pp. 139–43 in *Sacred Time, Sacred Space: Archaeology and the Religion of Israel*. Ed. B. M. Gittlen. Winona Lake, IN: Eisenbrauns.
  2002b Life in Judah from the Perspective of the Dead. *NEA* 65: 120–30.
  2003   Israelite Ethnicity in Iron I: Archaeology Preserves What Is Remembered and What Is Forgotten in Israel's History. *JBL* 122: 401–25.
Bloch-Smith, E., and B. A. Nakhai
  1999   A Landscape Comes to Life: The Iron Age I. *NEA* 62: 62–92, 101–27.
Block, D. I.
  1999   *Judges–Ruth*. Nashville: Broadman & Holman.
  1997   *The Book of Ezekiel: Chapters 25–48*. Grand Rapids, MI: Eerdmans.
Boling, R. G.
  1988   *The Early Biblical Community in Transjordan*. Sheffield: Almond.
Boling, R. G., and G. E. Wright
  1982   *Joshua*. Anchor Bible 6. Garden City, NY: Doubleday.
Bourdieu, P.
  1977   *Outline of a Theory of Practice*. Cambridge: Cambridge University Press.
Bramlett, K.
  2004   A Late Bronze Age Cultic Installation at Tall al-ʿUmayri, Jordan. *NEA* 67: 50–51.
  2008   *Eastern Front: The Transjordanian Highlands in Late Bronze Age Hegemonic Contest*. Ph.D. dissertation. University of Toronto.
Bright, J.
  2000   *A History of Israel*. 4th ed. Louisville: Westminster John Knox.
Bunimowitz, S.
  1995   On the Edge of Empires: Late Bronze Age (1500–1200 BCE). Pp. 320–31 in *The Archaeology of Society in the Holy Land*. Ed. T. E. Levy. New York: Facts on File.
Bunimowitz, S., and A. Faust
  2010   Re-constructing Biblical Archaeology: Toward an Integration of Archaeology and the Bible. Pp. 43–54 in *Historical Biblical Archaeology and the Future: The New Pragmatism*. Ed. T. E. Levy. London: Equinox.
Butler, T. C.
  2009   *Judges*. Nashville: Thomas Nelson.

Callaway, J. A.
1995 The Settlement in Canaan: The Period of the Judges. Pp. 53–84 in *Ancient Israel*. Ed. H. Shanks. Englewood Cliffs, NJ: Prentice-Hall.

Caminos, R.
1958 *The Chronicle of Prince Osorkon*. AnOr 37. Rome: Pontifical Biblical Institute.

Cassuto, U.
1975 The Israelite Epic. Pp. 69–109 in *Biblical and Oriental Studies*, vol. 2. Trans. I. Abrahams. Jerusalem: Magnes.

Clark, D. R.
1997 Field B: The Western Defensive System. Pp. 53–98 in *Madaba Plains Project 3*. Ed. L. G. Herr et al. Berrien Springs, MI: Andrews University Press.
2000 Field B: The Western Defense System. Pp. 59–94 in *'Umayri*, vol. 4. Ed. L. G. Herr et al. Berrien Springs, MI: Andrews University Press.
2002 Field B: The Western Defense System. Pp. 48–116 in *'Umayri*, vol. 5. Ed. L. G. Herr et al. Berrien Springs, MI: Andrews University Press.

Clark, D. R., and K. V. Bramlett
2002 Field B: The Late Bronze Age Public Building and Later Structures. *AUSS* 40: 108–10.

Cohen, R.
1978 Ethnicity: Problem and Focus in Anthropology. *ARA* 7: 379–403.

Conroy, C.
1980 Hebrew Epic: Historical Notes and Critical Reflections. *Bib* 61: 1-30.

Cooley, R. E., and G. D. Pratico
1995 *Tell Dothan: The Western Cemetery, with Comments on Joseph Free's Excavations, 1953-1964*. AASOR 52. Boston: American Schools of Oriental Research.

Cornell, S.
1996 The Variable Ties That Bind: Content and Circumstance in Ethnic Processes. *Ethnic and Racial Studies* 19: 265–89.

Cross, F. M., Jr.
1973 *Canaanite Myth and Hebrew Epic*. Cambridge: Harvard University Press.
1988 Reuben, First-Born of Jacob: Sacral Traditions and Early Israelite History. *ZAW* 100: 46–65.
1998 *From Epic to Canon: History and Literature in Ancient Israel*. Baltimore: Johns Hopkins University Press.

Cross, F. M., Jr., and D. N. Freedman
1952 *Early Hebrew Orthography*. AOS 36. New Haven, CT: American Oriental Society.
1997 *Studies in Ancient Yahwistic Poetry*. Grand Rapids, MI: Eerdmans.

Dajani, R. W.
1966 Jabal Nuzha Tomb at Amman. *ADAJ* 11:1–52
1970 A Late Bronze–Iron Age Tomb Excavated at Sahab, 1968. *ADAJ* 15: 29–34.

Daviau, P. M. M.
2001 *Excavations at Tall Jawa*. Leiden: Brill.
2003 *Excavations at Tell Jawa, Jordan*, vol. 1. Leiden: Brill.

David, N., and C. Kramer
2001 *Ethnoarchaeology in Action*. Cambridge: Cambridge University Press.

Daws, G.
  1989 *Shoals of Time: A History of the Hawaiian Islands.* Honolulu: University of Hawaii Press.
Dearman, J. A.
  1989 The Levitical Cities of Reuben and Moabite Toponomy. *BASOR* 276: 55–66.
  1989 *Studies in the Mesha Inscriptions and Moab.* Atlanta: Scholars Press.
  1992 Settlement Patterns and the Beginning of the Iron Age in Moab. Pp. 65–75 in *Early Edom and Moab: The Beginning of the Iron Age in Southern Jordan.* Ed. P. Bienkowski. Sheffield: Collis.
Derks, T.
  2009 Ethnic Identity in the Roman Frontier: The Epigraphy of Batavi and Other Lower Rhine Tribes. Pp. 239–82 in *Ethnic Constructs in Antiquity: The Role of Power and Tradition.* Ed. T. Derks and N. Roymans. Amsterdam: Amsterdam University Press.
Derks, T., and N. Roymans
  2009 Introduction. Pp. 1–9 in *Ethnic Constructs in Antiquity: The Role of Power and Tradition.* Ed. T. Derks and N. Roymans. Amsterdam: Amsterdam University Press.
Dever, W. G.
  1980 New Vistas on the EB IV ("MB I") Horizon in Syria–Palestine. *BASOR* 237: 35–64.
  1992 The Late Bronze–Early Iron I Horizon in Syria–Palestine: Egyptians, Canaanites, "Sea-Peoples," and Proto-Israelites. Pp. 99–110 in *The Crisis Years: The 12th Century B.C. from beyond the Danube to the Tigris.* Ed. W. A. Ward and M. S. Joukowski. Dubuque, IA: Kendall/Hunt.
  1995 Ceramics, Ethnicity, and the Question of Israel's Origins. *BA* 58: 200–213.
  1998 Israelite Origins and the 'Nomadic Ideal': Can Archaeology Separate Fact from Fiction? Pp. 197–237 in *Mediterranean Peoples in Transition: Thirteenth to Early Tenth Centuries BCE.* Ed. S. Gitin, A. Mazar, and E. Stern. Jerusalem: Israel Exploration Society.
  2001 *What Did the Biblical Writers Know and When Did They Know It?* Grand Rapids, MI: Eerdmans.
  2003 *Who Were the Israelites and Where Did They Come From?* Grand Rapids, MI: Eerdmans.
  2007 Ethnicity and the Archeological Record. Pp. 49–66 in *The Archaeology of Difference: Gender, Ethnicity, Class and the "Other" in Antiquity.* Ed. Douglas R. Edwards and C. Thomas Mccollough. Boston: American Schools of Oriental Research.
  2009 Merenptah's "Israel," the Bible's, and Ours. Pp. 89–96 in *Exploring the Longue Durée: Essays in Honor of Lawrence E. Stager.* Ed. J. D. Schloen. Winona Lake, IN: Eisenbrauns.
Dion, P.-E.
  1997 *Les Araméens à l'Âge du Fer: Histoire Politique et Structures Sociales.* Paris: Gabalda.
Dolan, A.
  2009 Defining Sacred Space in Ancient Moab. Pp. 129–44 in *Studies on Iron Age Moab and Neighbouring Areas in Honour of Michèle Daviau.* Ed. P. Bienkowski. Leuven: Peeters.

Dornemann, R. H.
  1982 The Beginning of the Iron Age in Transjordan. Pp. 135–40 in *SHAJ*, vol. 1. Ed. A. Hadidi. Amman: Department of Antiquities.
  1983 *The Archaeology of the Transjordan in the Bronze and Iron Ages.* Milwaukee: Milwaukee Public Museum.
Dresher, B. E.
  2012 Methodological Issues in the Dating of Linguistic Forms. Considerations from the Perspective of Contemporary Linguistic Theory. Pp. 19–38 in *Diachrony in Biblical Hebrew.* Ed. C. L. Miller-Naudé and Z. Zevit. Linguistic Studies in Ancient West Semitic 8. Winona Lake, IN: Eisenbrauns.
Drews, R.
  1995 *The End of the Bronze Age: Changes in Warfare and the Catastrophe ca. 1200 B.C.* Princeton: Princeton University Press.
Driver, S. R.
  1956 *An Introduction to the Literature of the Old Testament.* New York: Meridian.
Eberling, G.
  1997 Ethnicity in Complex Societies: Archaeological Perspectives. *JAR* 5: 301–4.
Edelman, D.
  1996 Ethnicity and Early Israel. Pp. 42–47 in *Ethnicity and the Bible.* Ed. M. G. Brett. Leiden: Brill.
  2006 Review of *Chieftains of the Highland Clans: A History of Israel in the Twelfth and Eleventh Centuries B.C.* by Robert D. Miller II. *RBL* 1. http://www.bookreviews.org/.
Eggler, J., L. G. Herr, and R. Root
  2002 Seals and Seal Impressions from Excavation Seasons 1984–2000. Pp. 234–304 in *ʿUmayri*, vol. 5. Ed. L. G. Herr et al. Berrien Springs, MI: Andrews University Press.
Eichrodt, W.
  1961 *Theology of the Old Testament.* 2 vols. Trans. J. A. Baker. Philadelphia: Westminster.
Eller, J., and R. Coughlin
  1993 The Poverty of Primordialism: The Demystification of Ethnic Attachments. *Ethnic and Racial Studies* 16: 183–202.
Emerton, J. A.
  2002 The Value of the Moabite Stone as an Historical Source. *VT* 52: 483–92.
Epstein, A. L.
  1978 *Ethnos and Identity: Three Studies in Ethnicity.* Chicago: Aldine.
Esse, D. L.
  1991 *Subsistence, Trade, and Social Change in Early Bronze Age Palestine.* Chicago: Oriental Institute.
  1992 The Collared Pithos at Megiddo: Ceramic Distribution and Ethnicity. *JNES* 51: 81–103.
Faust, A.
  2006 *Israel's Ethnogenesis: Settlement, Interaction, Expansion and Resistance.* London: Equinox.
  2010 Future Directions in the Study of Ethnicity in Ancient Israel. Pp. 55–68 in *Historical Biblical Archaeology and the Future: The New Pragmatism.* Ed. T. E. Levy. London: Equinox.

Fawcett, L.
  2000 *Religion, Ethnicity and Social Change*. New York: St. Martin.
Fenton, S.
  2003 *Ethnicity*. Oxford: Blackwell.
Finkelstein, I.
  1986 *'Izbet Sartah*. Oxford: British Archaeological Reports.
  1988 *The Archaeology of the Israelite Settlement*. Jerusalem: Israel Exploration Society.
  1988–89 The Land of Ephraim Survey 1980–1987: Preliminary Report. *TA* 15–16: 117–83.
  1990 Excavations at Khirbet ed-Dawwara: An Iron Age Site Northeast of Jerusalem. *TA* 17: 163–208.
  1993 *Shiloh: The Archaeology of a Biblical Site*. Tel Aviv: Tel Aviv University Press.
  1994 The Emergence of Israel: A Phase in the Cyclic History of Canaan in the Third and Second Millennia BCE. Pp. 150–78 in *From Nomadism to Monarchy: Archaeological and Historical Aspects of Early Israel*. Ed. I. Finkelstein and N. Naʾaman. Jerusalem: Yad Ben-Zvi and Israel Exploration Society / Washington, DC: Biblical Archaeology Society.
  1995 The Great Transformation: The "Conquest" of the Highlands Frontiers and the Rise of the Territorial States. Pp. 350–65 in *The Archaeology of Society in the Holy Land*. Ed. T. E. Levy. New York: Facts on File.
  1996 Ethnicity and Origin of the Iron I Settlers in the Highlands of Canaan: Can the Real Israel Stand Up? *BA* 59: 198–212.
  1997 *Highlands of Many Cultures: The Southern Samaria Survey. The Sites*, vol. 2. Tel Aviv: Tel Aviv University Press.
  1998a From Sherds to History: Review Article. *IEJ* 48: 120–31.
  1998b Notes on the Stratigraphy and Chronology of Iron Age Taʿanach. *TA* 25: 208–18.
  2005 A Low Chronology Update: Archaeology, History and Bible. Pp. 31–32 in *The Bible and Radiocarbon Dating*. Ed. T. E. Levy and T. Higham. London: Equinox.
  2011 Tall al-ʿUmayri in the Iron Age I: Facts and Fiction with an Appendix on the History of the Collared Rim Pithoi. Pp. 113–28 in *The Signal Fires of Lachish: Studies in the Archaeology and History of Israel in the Late Bronze Age, Iron Age, and Persian Period in Honor of David Ussishkin*. Ed. I. Finkelstein and N. Naʾaman. Winona Lake, IN: Eisenbrauns.
Finkelstein, I., and A. Fantalkin
  2012 Khirbet Qeiyafa: An Unsensational Archaelogical and Historical Interpretation. *TA* 39: 38–63.
Finkelstein, I., and A. Mazar
  2007 *The Quest for the Historical Isreal: Debating Archaeology and the History of Early Israel*. Atlanta: Society of Biblical Literature.
Finkelstein, I., and E. Piasetzky
  2003 Recent Radiocarbon Results and King Solomon. *Antiquity* 771–79.
  2006 The Iron I–IIA in the Highlands and Beyond: ^{14}C Anchors, Pottery Phases and the Shoshenq I Campaign. *Levant* 38: 45–61.
Finkelstein, I., and N. A. Silberman
  2001 *The Bible Unearthed: Archaeology's New Vision of Ancient Israel and the Origins of Its Sacred Texts*. New York: Free Press.

Fischer, P. M.
1997 *A Late Bronze to Early Iron Age Tomb at Saḥem, Jordan.* Wiesbaden: Harrassowitz.

Fishbane, M. A.
1988 *Biblical Interpretation in Ancient Israel.* Oxford: Clarendon.

Foran, D.
2008 Preliminary Report: 2008 Field Season. *Tall Mādabā Archaeological Project.* http://www.utoronto.ca/tmap/prelim_2008.

Foran, D., T. P. Harrison, A. Graham, C. Barlow, and N. J. Johnson
2004 The Tall Mādabā Archaeological Project: Preliminary Report of the 2002 Field Season. *ADAJ* 48: 79–96.

Foran, D., and S. Klassen
2013 *Mādabā before Mesha: The Earliest Settlements on the City's West Acropolis.* SHAJ 11: 211–19. Amman: Department of Antiquities of Jordan.

Freedman, D. N.
1960 Archaic Forms in Early Hebrew Poetry. *ZAW* 72: 101–7.

Friedman, R. E.
1987 *Who Wrote the Bible?* San Francisco: Harper.

Fritz, V.
1994 *Das Buch Josua.* Tübingen: Mohr (Siebeck).
1999 Kinnereth: Excavations at Tell el-Oreimeh (Tel Kinrot). Preliminary Report on the 1994–1997 Seasons. *TA* 26: 92–115.

Gal, Z.
1992 *Lower Galilee during the Iron Age.* Winona Lake, IN: Eisenbrauns.

Garfinkel, Y., and Ganor, S.
2009 *Khirbet Qeiyafa,* vol. 1: *Excavation Report 2007–2008.* Jerusalem: Israel Exploration Society.

Garr, R. W.
1985 *Dialect Geography of Syria–Palestine, 1000–586 B.C.E.* Philadelphia: University of Pennsylvania Press. [Reprinted Winona Lake, IN: Eisenbrauns, 2004.]

Geertz, C.
1963 The Integrative Revolution. Pp. 105–57 in *Old Societies and New States.* Ed. C. Geertz. New York: Free Press.

Genz, H.
2002 *Die frühbronzezeitliche Keramik von Hirbet ez-Zeraqon: Mit Studien zur Chronoligie und funktionalen Deutung frühbronzezeitlicher Keramik in de südlichen Levante.* Wiesbaden: Harrassowitz.

Geraty, L. T.
1993 Heshbon. Pp. 626–30 in vol. 2 of *NEAEHL.* Ed. E. Stern. New York: Simon & Schuster.

Gibson, J. C. L.
1971 *Textbook of Syrian Semitic Inscriptions,* vol. 1: *Hebrew and Moabite Inscriptions.* Oxford: Clarendon.

Gilmour, G.
2002 Foreign Burials in Late Bronze Age Palestine. *NEA* 65: 112–19.

Glazer, N., and D. P. Moynihan
1970 *Beyond the Melting Pot: The Negroes, Puerto Ricans, Jews, Italians, and Irish of New York City.* 2nd ed. Cambridge, MA: M.I.T. Press.

Glueck, N.
    1934   *Explorations in Eastern Palestine, I.* AASOR 14. Ed. M. Burrows and E. A.
           Speiser. Philadelphia: American Schools of Oriental Research.
    1935   *Explorations in Eastern Palestine, II.* AASOR 15. New Haven, CT: American
           Schools of Oriental Research.
    1939   *Explorations in Eastern Palestine, III.* AASOR 18–19. New Haven, CT: Ameri-
           can Schools of Oriental Research.
    1951a *Explorations in Eastern Palestine, IV.* AASOR 25–28. New Haven, CT: American
           Schools of Oriental Research.
    1951b *Explorations in Eastern Palestine, IV. Plates.* AASOR 25–28. New Haven, CT:
           American Schools of Oriental Research.
    1959   *Rivers in the Desert: A History of the Negeb.* New York: Farrar, Straus & Cudahy.
    1970   *The Other Side of the Jordan.* Cambridge, MA: American Schools of Oriental
           Research.
Gogel, S. L.
    1998   *A Grammar of Epigraphic Hebrew.* Atlanta: Scholars Press.
Goldberg, J.
    1999   Two Assyrian Campaigns against Hezekiah and Later Eighth Century Biblical
           Chronology. *Bib* 80: 360–90.
Gonen, R.
    1992   *Burial Patterns and Cultural Diversity in Late Bronze Age Canaan.* Winona Lake,
           IN: Eisenbrauns.
Goody, J.
    1987   *The Interface between the Written and the Oral.* Cambridge: Cambridge Univer-
           sity Press.
Gosselain, O. P.
    1998   Social and Technical Identity in a Clay Ball. Pp. 78–106 in *The Archaeology of
           Social Boundaries.* Ed. M. T. Stark. Washington, DC: Smithsonian Institution
           Press.
Gottwald, N.
    1985   *The Tribes of Yahweh.* Philadelphia: Fortress.
Gray, G. B. A.
    1903   *A Critical and Exegetical Commentary on Numbers.* Edinburgh: T. & T. Clark.
Grenfell, M.
    2008   *Pierre Bourdieu: Key Concepts.* Durham: Acumen.
Gressman, H.
    1913   *Mose und Seine Zeit.* Göttingen: Vandenhoeck & Ruprecht.
Grosby, S.
    2002   *Biblical Ideas of Nationality Ancient and Modern.* Winona Lake, IN: Eisenbrauns.
Hackett, J. A.
    1980   *The Balaam Text from Deir ʿAllā.* HSM 31. Chico, CA: Scholars Press.
    1987   Religious Traditions in Israelite Transjordan. Pp. 125–36 in *Ancient Israel-
           ite Religion.* Ed. P. D. Miller, P. D. Hanson, and S. D. McBride. Philadelphia:
           Fortress.
    1998   There Was No King in Israel: The Era of the Judges. Pp. 177–218 in *The
           Oxford History of the Biblical World.* Ed. M. D. Coogan. New York: Oxford Uni-
           versity Press.

Hall, J.
1997 *Ethnic Identity in Greek Antiquity*. Cambridge: Cambridge University Press.
Halpern, B.
1983 *The Emergence of Israel in Canaan*. SBLMS 29. Chico, CA: Scholars Press.
1988 *The First Historians: The Hebrew Bible and History*. San Francisco: Harper.
1992 Kenites. Pp. 17–22 in vol. 4 of *ABD*. Ed. D. N. Freedman. New York: Doubleday.
Hankey, V.
1974 A Late Bronze Age Temple at Amman: I. The Aegean Pottery; II. Vases and Objects Made of Stones. *Levant* 6: 131–79.
Hanson, P. D.
1968 The Song of Heshbon and David's NîR. *HTR* 61: 297–320.
Harding, G. L.
1953 An Early Iron Age Tomb at Madeba. *PEFA* 6: 27–41.
Harrison, T. P.
1995 *Life on the Edge: Human Adaptation and Resilience in the Semi-Arid Highlands of Central Jordan during the Early Bronze Age*. Ph.D. dissertation, University of Chicago.
1996a History of Madaba. Pp. 1–18 in *Madaba: Cultural Heritage*. Ed. P. M. Bikai and T. A. Dailey. Amman: American Center of Oriental Research.
1996b Surface Survey. Pp. 19–24 in *Madaba: Cultural Heritage*. Ed. P. M. Bikai and T. A. Dailey. Amman: American Center of Oriental Research.
1997 Shifting Patterns of Settlement in the Highlands of Central Jordan during the Early Bronze Age. *BASOR* 306: 1–37.
2004 *Megiddo III: Final Report of the Stratum VI Excavations*. Chicago: University of Chicago Press.
2009 'The Land of Medeba' and Early Iron Age Transjordan. Pp. 27–45 in *Studies on Iron Age Moab and Neighbouring Areas in Honour of Michèle Daviau*. Ed. Piotr Bienkowski. Leuven: Peeters.
Harrison, T. P., and C. Barlow
2005 Mesha, the Mishor, and the Chronology of Iron Age Mādabā. Pp. 179–90 in *The Bible and Radiocarbon Dating: Archaeology, Text and Science*. Ed. Thomas E. Levy and Thomas Higham. London: Equinox.
Harrison, T. P., D. Foran, A. Graham, T. Griffith, C. Barlow, and J. Ferguson
2003 The Tall Mādabā Archaeological Project: Preliminary Report of the 1998–2000 Field Seasons. *ADAJ* 47: 129–48.
Harrison, T. P., B. Hesse, S. H. Savage, and D. W. Schnurrenberger
2000 Urban Life in the Highlands of Central Jordan: A Preliminary Report of the 1996 Tall Madaba Excavations. *ADAJ* 44: 211–29.
Hasel, M. G.
1994 *Israel* in the Merneptah Stela. *BASOR* 296: 45–61.
Hawk, L. D.
1999 *Joshua*. Collegeville, MN: Michael Grazier.
Hawkins, R. K.
2012 *The Iron Age I Structure on Mt. Ebal*. BBRSup 6. Winona Lake, IN: Eisenbrauns.
Hennessy, J. B.
1966 Excavation of a Late Bronze Age Temple at Amman. *PEQ* 98: 155–63.

Herr, L. G.
1983 Stratigraphy. Pp. 11–31 in *The Amman Airport Excavations, 1976*. Ed. L. G. Herr. AASOR 48. Cambridge, MA: American Schools of Oriental Research.

1998 Tell el ʿUmeiri and the Madaba Plains Region during the Late Bronze–Iron Age I Transition. Pp. 252–64 in *Mediterranean Peoples in Transition: Thirteenth to Early Tenth Centuries BCE*. Ed. S. Gitin, A. Mazar, and E. Stern. Jerusalem: Israel Exploration Society.

1999 Tall al-ʿUmayri and the Reubenite Hypothesis. *ErIsr* 26 (Cross Volume): 64*–77.*

2000a The Pottery. Pp. 185–203 in *ʿUmayri*, vol. 4. Ed. L. G. Herr et al. Berrien Springs, MI: Andrews University Press. [= *MPP* 4]

2000b The Settlement and Fortification of Tell al-ʿUmayri in Jordan during the LB/Iron I Transition. Pp. 167–79 in *The Archaeology of Jordan and Beyond: Essays in Memory of James A. Sauer*. Ed. L. E. Stager, J. A. Greene, and M. D. Coogan. Studies in the Archaeology and History of the Levant 1. Winona Lake, IN: Eisenbrauns.

2001 The History of the Collared Pithos at Tell el-ʿUmeiri, Jordan. Pp. 237–50 in *Studies in the Archaeology of Israel and Neighboring Lands in Memory of Douglas L. Esse*. Ed. S. R. Wolff. Chicago: The Oriental Institute / Atlanta: The American Schools of Oriental Research.

2002a Excavation and Cumulative Results. Pp. 8–22 in *ʿUmayri*, vol. 5. Ed. L. G. Herr et al. Berrien Springs, MI: Andrews University Press. [= *MPP* 5]

2002b The Pottery. Pp. 135–55 in *ʿUmayri*, vol. 5. Ed. L. G. Herr et al. Berrien Springs, MI: Andrews University Press.

2009 The House of the Father at Iron I Tall al-ʿUmayri, Jordan. Pp. 191–98 in *Exploring the Longue Durée: Essays in Honor of Lawrence E. Stager*. Ed. J. D. Schloen. Winona Lake, IN: Eisenbrauns.

Herr, L. G., and D. R. Clark
2004 Madaba Plains Project: Tall al ʿUmayri, 2002. *AUSS* 42: 113–27.

2009 From the Stone Age to the Middle Ages in Jordan: Digging up Tall al-ʿUmayri. *NEA* 72/2: 68–97.

Herr, L. G., D. R. Clark, and W. C. Trenchard
2002 Madaba Plains Project: Tall al ʿUmayri, 2000. *AUSS* 40: 105–23.

Herr, L. G., D. R. Clark, L. T. Gerrary, and Ø. S. LaBianca
2000 Madaba Plains Project: Tall al-ʿUmayri, 1998. *AUSS* 38: 29–58.

Herr, L. G., and M. Najjar
2001 The Iron Age. Pp. 323–45 in *The Archaeology of Jordan*. Ed. B. MacDonald, R. Adams, and P. Bienkowski. Sheffield: Sheffield Academic Press.

Herzog, Z.
2002 The Fortress Mound at Tel Arad: An Interim Report. *TA* 29: 3–109.

Herzog, Z., M. Aharoni, A. F. Rainey, S. Moshkovitz
1984 The Israelite Fortress at Arad. *BASOR* 254: 1–34.

Hess, R. S.
1994 Asking Historical Questions of Joshua 13–19: Recent Discussion Concerning the Date of the Boundary Lists. Pp. 191–205 in *Faith, Tradition, and History: Old Testament Historiography in Its Near Eastern Context*. Ed. A. Millard, J. K. Hoffmeier, and D. W. Baker. Winona Lake, IN: Eisenbrauns.

1996   *Joshua: An Introduction and Commentary.* Leicester: Inter-Varsity Press.

2007   *Israelite Religions.* Grand Rapids, MI: Baker.

Hess, R. S., G. A. Klingbeil, and P. J. Ray Jr.

2008   *Critical Issues in Early Israelite History.* BBRSup 3. Winona Lake, IN: Eisenbrauns.

Hesse, B.

1995   Husbandry, Dietary Taboos and the Bones of the Ancient Near East: Zooarchaeology in the Post-Processual World. Pp. 196–232 in *Methods in the Mediterranean.* Ed. D. B. Small. Leiden: Brill.

Hesse, B., and P. Wapnish

1998   Pig Use and Abuse in the Ancient Levant: Ethno-Religious Boundary-Building with Swine. Pp. 123–35 in *Ancestors for the Pigs: Pigs in Prehistory.* Ed. S. Nelson. Philadelphia: University of Pennsylvania Museum of Archaeology and Anthropology.

Hodder, I.

1982   *Symbols in Action.* Cambridge: Cambridge University Press.

Hoerth, A. J.

1998   *Archaeology and the Old Testament.* Grand Rapids, MI: Baker.

Hoffmeier, J. K.

1997   *Israel in Egypt: The Evidence for the Authenticity of the Exodus Tradition.* New York: Oxford University Press.

Hoftijzer, J., and G. van der Kooij, eds.

1990   *The Balaam Text from Deir ʿAlla Re-evaluated: Proceedings of the International Symposium Held at Leiden, 21–24 August 1989.* Leiden: Brill.

Holmstedt, R. D.

2012   Historical Linguistics and Biblical Hebrew. Pp. 97–124 in *Diachrony in Biblical Hebrew.* Ed. C. L. Miller-Naudé and Z. Zevit. Winona Lake, IN: Eisenbrauns.

Holladay, J. S., Jr.

1987   Religion in Ancient Israel under the Monarchy: An Explicitly Archaeological Approach. Pp. 249–99 in *Ancient Israelite Religion: Essays in Honor of Frank Moore Cross.* Ed. P. D. Miller, W. E. Lemke, and S. D. McBride. Philadelphia: Fortress.

1995   The Kingdoms of Israel and Judah: Political and Economic Centralization in the Iron IIA–B (*ca.* 1000–750 BCE). Pp. 368–98 in *The Archaeology of Society in the Holy Land.* Ed. T. E. Levy. New York: Facts on File.

1997a   Four-Room House. Pp. 337–42 in vol. 2 of *OEANE.* Ed. E. M. Meyers. New York: Oxford University Press.

1997b   House: Syro-Palestinian Houses. Pp. 94–114 in vol. 3 of *OEANE.* Ed. E. M. Meyers. New York: Oxford University Press.

2001   Toward a New Paradigmatic Understanding of Long-Distance Trade in the Ancient Near East: From the Middle Bronze II to Early Iron II—A Sketch. Pp. 136–98 in *The World of the Arameans,* vol. 2: *Studies in History and Archaeology in Honour of Paul-Eugène Dion.* Ed. P. M. Michèle Daviau, J. W. Wevers, and M. Weigl. Sheffield: Sheffield Academic Press.

Homan, M. M.

2002   *To Your Tents, O Israel! The Terminology, Function, Form, and Symbolism of Tents in the Hebrew Bible and the Ancient Near East.* Leiden: Brill.

Homès Fredericq, D.
  2000 Excavating the First Pillar House at Lehun (Jordan). Pp. 180–95 in *The Archae-
        ology of Jordan and Beyond: Essays in Honor of James A. Sauer.* Ed. J. A. Greene,
        M. D. Coogan, and L. E. Stager. Studies in the Archaeology and History of
        the Levant 1. Winona Lake, IN: Eisenbrauns.
Huehnergard, J.
  1990 Remarks on the Classification of the Northwest Semitic Languages. Pp. 282–
        93 in *The Balaam Text from Deir ʿAlla Re-evaluated: Proceedings of the International
        Symposium Held at Leiden, 21–24 August 1989.* Ed. J. Hoftijzer, and G. van der
        Kooij. Leiden: Brill.
Humbert, J. B.
  1993 Tell Keisan. Pp. 862–67 in vol. 3 of *NEAEHL.* Ed. E. Stern. New York: Simon
        & Schuster.
Hurvitz, A.
  1997 The Historical Quest for "Ancient Israel" and the Linguistic Evidence of the
        Hebrew Bible: Some Methodological Observations. *VT* 47: 301–15.
Hutchinson, J., and A. D. Smith, eds.
  1996 *Ethnicity.* Oxford: Oxford University Press.
Ibach, R. D.
  1987 *Archaeological Survey of the Hesban Region: Catalogue of Sites and Characteriza-
        tions of Periods.* Hesban 5. Berrien Springs, MI: Andrews University Press.
Ibrahim, M.
  1972 Archaeological Excavations at Sahab, 1972. *ADAJ* 17: 23–36.
  1975 Archaeological Excavations at Sahab, 1975. *ADAJ* 20: 69–82.
  1978 The Collared-Rim Jar of the Early Iron Age. Pp. 116–26 in *Archaeology of the
        Levant: Essays for Kathleen Kenyon.* Ed. R. Moorey and P. Parr.
  1987 Sahab and Its Foreign Relations. Pp. 73–81 in *SHAJ,* vol. 3. Ed. A. Hadidi.
        Amman: Department of Antiquities.
Jenkins, R.
  2002 *Pierre Bourdieu.* London: Routledge.
Ji, C.-H. C.
  1995 Iron Age I in Central and Northern Transjordan: An Interim Summary of
        Archaeological Data. *PEQ* 127: 122–40.
  1997a A Note on the Iron Age Four-Room House in Palestine. *Orientalia* 66:
        387–413.
  1997b The East Jordan Valley during the Iron Age I. *PEQ* 129: 20–37.
  2002 Tribes and Sedentarization in the Madaba Plains and Central Jordan during
        the Iron I and Ottoman Periods. Pp. 348–57 in *ʿUmayri,* vol. 5. Ed. L. G. Herr
        et al. Berrien Springs, MI: Andrews University Press.
Joffe, A.
  2001 Book Review of *The Archaeology of Ethnicity* by S. Jones. *JNES* 60: 211–14.
Jones, S.
  1997 *The Archaeology of Ethnicity.* London: Routledge.
Kafafi, Z.
  1983 The Local Pottery. Pp. 33–45 in *The Amman Airport Excavations, 1976.* Ed.
        L. G. Herr. Winona Lake, IN: American Schools of Oriental Research.

Kallai, Z.
1982   Conquest and Settlement of Trans-Jordan: A Historiographical Study. *ZDPV* 99: 110–18.

Kamrada, D. G.
2009   The Sacrifice of Jephthah's Daughter and the Notion of HEREM: A Problematic Narrative against Its Biblical Background. Pp. 57–86 in *With Wisdom as a Robe: Qumran and Other Jewish Studies in Honour of Ida Fröhlich*. Ed. K. D. Dobos and M. Kőszeghy. Sheffield: Sheffield Phoenix.

Kang, Sa-Moon
1989   *Divine War in the Old Testament and in the Ancient Near East*. New York: de Gruyter.

Kenyon, K. M.
1966   *Amorites and Canaanites*. Oxford: Oxford University Press.

Kessler, J.
2002   *The Book of Haggai: Prophecy and Society in Early Persian Yehud*. Leiden: Brill.

Keyes, C. F.
1978   *Ethnic Adaptation: The Karen on the Thai Frontier with Burma*. Philadelphia: Institute for the Study of Human Issues.
1981   The Dialectics of Ethnic Change. Pp. 3–30 in *Ethnic Change*. Ed. C. F. Keyes. Seattle: University of Washington Press.

Khoury, P. S., and J. Kostiner, eds.
1990   *Tribes and State Formation in the Middle East*. Berkeley: University of California Press.

Killebrew, A. E.
2001   The Collared Pithos in Context: A Typological, Technological, and Functional Reassessment. Pp. 377–98 in *Studies in the Archaeology of Israel and Neighboring Lands in Memory of Douglas L. Esse*. Ed. S. R. Wolff. Chicago: The Oriental Institute / Atlanta: The American Schools of Oriental Research.
2005   *Biblical Peoples and Ethnicity: An Archaeological Study of Egyptians, Canaanites, Philistines, and Early Israel 1300–1100 B.C.E.* Atlanta: Society of Biblical Literature.

Kitchen, K. A.
1992   The Egyptian Evidence on Ancient Jordan. Pp. 21–34 in *Early Edom and Moab: The Beginning of the Iron Age in Southern Jordan*. Ed. P. Bienkowski. Sheffield: Collins and National Museums and Galleries on Merseyside.
1996   *The Third Intermediate Period in Egypt (1100–650 BC)*. 2nd ed. Warminster: Aris & Phillips.

Kletter, R.
2006   Can a Proto-Isrealite Please Stand Up? Pp. 573–612 in *"I Will Speak the Riddles of Ancient Times": Archaeological and Historical Studies in Honor of Amihai Mazar on the Occasion of His Sixtieth Birthday*, vol. 2. Ed. A. Maeir and P. de Miroschedji. Winona Lake, IN: Eisenbrauns.

Knoppers, G. N.
2011   "Married into Moab": The Exogamy Practiced by Judah and His Descendents in the Judahite Lineages. Pp. 170–91 in *Mixed Marriages: Intermarriage and Group Identity in the Second Temple Period*. Ed. C. Frevel. New York: T. & T. Clark.

Kramer, C.
  1977   Pots and Peoples. Pp. 91–112 in *Mountains and Lowlands: Essays in the Archaeology of Greater Mesopotamia.* Ed. L. D. Levine and T. C. Young Jr. Malibu, CA: Undena.

KTU   Dietrich, M., O. Loretz, and J. Sanmartín, eds.
  1995   *Die Keilalphabetischen Texte aus Ugarit.* Alter Orient und Altes Testament 24. Kevelaer: Butzon & Bercker / Neukirchen-Vluyn: Neukirchener Verlag, 1976. 2nd ed.: M. Dietrich, O. Loretz, and J. Sanmartín, eds. *The Cuneiform Alphabetic Texts from Ugarit, Ras Ibn Hani, and Other Places.* Münster: Ugarit-Verlag.

Laband, J.
  1998   *The Rise and Fall of the Zulu Nation.* London: Arms & Armour.

LaBianca, Ø. S.
  1999   Salient Features in Iron Age Tribal Kingdoms. Pp. 19–23 in *Ancient Ammon.* Ed. B. MacDonald and R. W. Younker. Studies in the History and Culture of the Ancient Near East 17. Boston: Brill.

LaBianca, Ø. S., and R. W. Younker
  1995   The Kingdoms of Ammon, Moab and Edom: The Archaeology of Society in Late Bronze/Iron Age Transjordan (ca. 1400–500 BCE). Pp. 399–415 in *The Archaeology of Society in the Holy Land.* Ed. T. E. Levy. New York: Facts on File.

Lapidus, I.
  1990   Tribes and State Formation in Islamic History. Pp. 25–47 in *Tribes and State Formation in the Middle East.* Ed. P. S. Khoury and J. Kostiner. Berkeley: University of California Press.

Lattimore, O.
  1962   *Inner Asian Frontiers in China.* Boston: Beacon.

Lawlor, J. I.
  2002   Field A: A House-Shrine from the Time of the Judges. *AUSS* 40: 106–8.

Lee, B. P. Y.
  2003   *Reading Law and Narrative: The Method and Function of Abstraction.* Ph.D. Dissertation. University of Saint Michael's College in the University of Toronto.

Lemarchand. R.
  2003   Burundi: Ethnic Conflict and Genocide. Pp. 208–18 in *Race and Ethnicity: Comparative and Theoretical Approaches.* Ed. J. Stone and R. Dennis. Malden, MA: Blackwell.

Lemonnier, P.
  1986   The Study of Material Culture Today: Toward an Anthropology of Technical Systems. *JAA* 5: 147–86.

Lentz, C.
  1995   'Tribalism' and Ethnicity in Africa: A Review of Four Decades of Anglophone Research. Trans. P. Selwyn. *Cah. Sci. Hum.* 32: 303–28.

Levine, B.
  2000   *Numbers 21–36.* AB 4A. New York: Doubleday.

Levy, T.
  2010   The New Pragmatism: Integrating Anthropological, Digital, and Historical Biblical Archaeologies. Pp. 3–42 in *Historical Biblical Archaeology and the Future: The New Pragmatism.* Ed. Thomas E. Levy. London: Equinox.

Levy, T., and T. Higham
  2005 *The Bible and Radiocarbon Dating: Archaeology, Text and Science.* Oakville, CT: Equinox.
Levy, T., and A. F. C. Holl
  2002 Migrations, Ethnogenesis, and Settlement Dynamics: Israelites in Iron Age Canaan and Shuwa-Arabs in the Chad Basin. *JAA* 21: 83–118.
London, G.
  1989 A Comparison of Two Contemporaneous Lifestyles of the Late Second Millennium B.C. *BASOR* 273: 37–55.
Longman, T., III, and D. G. Reid
  1995 *God Is a Warrior.* Grand Rapids, MI: Zondervan.
Lord, A. B.
  1960 *The Singer of Tales.* Cambridge: Harvard University Press.
Low, R. D.
  1997 Field F: The Eastern Shelf. Pp. 188–221 in *MPP*, vol. 3. Ed. L. G. Herr et al. Berrien Springs, MI: Andrews University Press.
  2000 Field F: The Eastern Shelf. Pp. 155–83 in *ʿUmayri*, vol. 4. Ed. L. G. Herr et al. Berrien Springs, MI: Andrews University Press.
Lyons, W. L.
  2010 *A History of Modern Scholarship on the Biblical Word ḥerem.* Lewiston, NY: Edwin Mellen.
MacDonald, B.
  1988 *The Wadi el-Ḥasā Archaeological Survey, 1979–1983: West-Central Jordan.* Waterloo, ON: Wilfrid Laurier University Press.
  2000 *"East of the Jordan": Territories and Sites of the Hebrew Scriptures.* Boston: American Schools of Oriental Research.
MacDonald, B., and R. W. Younker, eds.
  1999 *Ancient Ammon.* Leiden: Brill.
MacEachern, S.
  1998 Scale, Style, and Cultural Variation: Technological Traditions in the Northern Mandara Mountains. Pp. 107–31 in *The Archaeology of Social Boundaries*, Ed. M. T. Stark. Washington, DC: Smithsonian Institution Press.
Macumber, P. G.
  2001 Evolving Landscape and Environment in Jordan. Pp. 1–30 in *The Archaeology of Jordan*. Ed. B. MacDonald, R. Adams, and P. Bienkowski. Sheffield: Sheffield Academic Press.
Malkin, I.
  2001 Introduction. Pp. 1–28 in *Ancient Perceptions of Greek Ethnicity*. Ed. I. Malkin Cambridge: Harvard University Press.
Mallowan, M. E. L.
  1956 *Twenty-Five Years of Mesopotamian Discovery.* London: The British School of Archaeology in Iraq.
Marfoe, L.
  1979 The Integrative Transformation: Patterns of Sociopolitical Organization in Southern Syria. *BASOR* 234: 1–42.
Master, D.
  2001 State Formation Theory and the Kingdom of Ancient Israel. *JNES* 60: 117–30.

2008 Israelite Settlement at the Margins of the Northern Hill Country: Connections to Joshua and Judges from Tell Dothan. Pp. 181–89 in *Critical Issues in Early Israelite History*. Ed. R. S. Hess, G. A. Klingbeil, and P. J. Ray Jr. Winona Lake, IN: Eisenbrauns.

Mazar, A.
1981 Giloh: An Early Israelite Settlement Site Near Jerusalem. *IEJ* 31: 1–36.
1990a Iron Age I and II Towers at Giloh and the Israelite Settlement. *IEJ* 40: 77–101.
1990b *Archaeology of the Land of the Bible. 10,000–586 B.C.E.* New York: Doubleday.
2005 The Debate over the Chronology of the Iron Age in the Southern Levant: Its history, the Current Situation, and a Suggested Resolution. Pp. 15–30 in *The Bible and Radiocarbon Dating*. Ed. T. E. Levy and T. Higham. London: Equinox.

Mazar, A., and E. Netzer
1986 On the Israelite Fortress at Arad. *BASOR* 263: 87–91.

McCarter, P. K.
1980 The Balaam Texts from Deir ʿAlla. The First Combination. *BASOR* 249: 49–60.
1991 The Dialect of the Deir ʿAlla Texts. Pp. 87–99 in *The Balaam Text from Deir ʿAlla Re-evaluated*. Ed. J. Hoftijzer, and G. van der Kooij. Leiden: Brill.

McCarthy, D. J.
1978 *Treaty and Covenant*. Rev. ed. Rome: Pontifical Biblical Institute.

McGovern, P. E.
1986 *The Late Bronze Age and Early Iron Ages of Central Transjordan: The Baqʿah Valley Project, 1977–1981*. Philadelphia: University Museum.
1987 Central Transjordan in the Late Bronze and Early Iron Ages: An Alternative Hypothesis of Socio-economic Transformation and Collapse. Pp. 267–73 in *SHAJ*, vol. 3. Ed. A. Hadidi. Amman: Department of Antiquities.

McKay, B.
1997 *Ethnicity and Israelite Religion: The Anthropology of Social Boundaries in Judges*. Ph.D. Dissertation. University of Toronto.

Mendenhall, G. E.
1955 *Law and Covenant in Israel and the Ancient Near East*. Pittsburgh: Biblical Colloquium.
1962 The Hebrew Conquest of Palestine. *BA* 25: 66–87.
1973 *The Tenth Generation: The Origins of the Biblical Tradition*. Baltimore: Johns Hopkins University Press.
1992 Amorites. Pp. 199–202 in vol. 1 of *ABD*. Ed. D. N. Freedman et al. New York: Doubleday.

Merling, D., and L. T. Geraty, eds.
1994 *Hesban after 25 Years*. Berrian Springs, MI: Institute of Archaeology, Siegfried H. Horn Museum, Andrews University.

Meyer, E.
1885 Der Krieg gegen Sîchon und die zugehörigen Abschnitte. *ZAW* 5: 36–52.

Milgrom, J.
1990 *Numbers*. Philadelphia: Jewish Publication Society.
1992 Numbers, Book of. Pp. 1146–55 in vol. 4 of *ABD*. Ed. D. N. Freedman et al. New York: Doubleday.

Millard, A.
   1992   Assyrian Involvement in Edom. Pp. 35–39 in *Early Edom and Moab: The Beginnings of the Iron Age in Southern Jordan.* Ed. P. Bienkowski. Sheffield: Collins and National Museums and Galleries on Merseyside.
   2011   The Ostracon from the Days of David found at Khirbet Qeiyafa. *TynBul* 61: 1–13.
Miller, C. L.
   2003   *The Representation of Speech in Biblical Hebrew Narrative: A Linguistic Analysis.* HSM 55. 2nd corrected printing. Winona Lake, IN: Eisenbrauns.
Miller, J. C.
   2008   Ethnicity and the Hebrew Bible: Problems and Prospects. *CBR* 6: 170–213.
Miller, J. M.
   1991   *Archaeological Survey of the Kerak Plateau.* Atlanta: Scholars Press.
Miller, P. D.
   1973   *The Divine Warrior in Ancient Israel.* Cambridge: Harvard University Press.
   2000a   *The Religion of Ancient Israel.* Louisville: Westminster/John Knox.
   2000b   *Israelite Religion and Biblical Theology.* JSOTSup 267. Sheffield: Sheffield Academic Press.
Miller, R. D., II
   2004   Identifying Earliest Israel. *BASOR* 333: 55–68.
   2005   *Chieftains of the Highland Clans: A History of Israel in the Twelfth and Eleventh Centuries B.C.* Grand Rapids, MI: Eerdmans.
Misgav, H., Y. Garfinkel, and S. Ganor
   2009   The Ostracon. Pp. 243–57 in *Khirbet Qeiyafa,* vol. 1: *Excavation Report 2007–2008.* Ed. Y. Garkinkel and S. Ganor. Jerusalem: Israel Exploration Society.
Monroe, L. A. S.
   2007   Israelite, Moabite and Sabaean War-ḥērem Traditions and the Forging of National Identity: Reconsidering the Sabaean Text RES 3945 in Light of Biblical and Moabite Evidence. *VT* 57: 318–41.
Moran, W. L.
   1963   The Ancient Near Eastern Background of the Love of God in Deuteronomy. *CBQ* 25: 77–87.
Morgan, C.
   2009   Ethnic Expressions on the Early Iron Age and Early Archaic Greek Mainland. Where Should We Be Looking? Pp. 11–36 in *Ethnic Constructs in Antiquity: The Role of Power and Tradition.* Ed. T. Derks and N. Roymans. Amsterdam: Amsterdam University Press.
Mullen, E. T.
   1997   *Ethnic Myths and Pentateuchal Foundations: A New Approach to the Formation of the Pentateuch.* Atlanta: Scholars Press.
Münger, S.
   2003   Egyptian Stamp-Seal Amulets and Their Implications for the Chronology of the Early Iron Age. *TA* 30: 66–84.
Nakhai, B. A.
   2001   *Archaeology and the Religions of Canaan and Israel.* Boston: American Schools of Oriental Research.

Nash, M.
1989 *The Cauldron of Ethnicity in the Modern World.* Chicago: University of Chicago Press.

Netzer, N.
1973 We Ploughed the Amalekites: Num 21:30. *Beth Mikra* 56: 101, 104.

Niditch, S.
1993 *War in the Hebrew Bible: A Study in the Ethics of Violence.* New York: Oxford University Press.
1996 *Oral World and Written Word: Ancient Israelite Literature.* Louisville: Westminster John Knox.

Noort, E.
1987 Transjordan in Joshua 13: Some Aspects. Pp. 125–30 in *SHAJ*, vol. 3. Ed. A. Hadidi. Amman: Department of Antiquities.

Noth, M.
1940 Num 21 als Glied der "Hexateuch"-Erzählung. *ZAW* 58: 161–89.
1944 Israelitische Stamme zwischen Ammon und Moab. *ZAW* 60: 11–57.
1960 *The History of Israel.* 2nd ed. New York: Harper & Row.
1968 *Numbers.* Trans. J. D. Martin. Philadelphia: Westminster.

O'Connor, M.
1997 *Hebrew Verse Structure.* Rev. ed. Winona Lake, IN: Eisenbrauns.

Ollenburger, B. C.
1991 Introduction: Gerhard von Rad's Theory of Holy War. Pp. 1–33 in *Holy War in Ancient Israel*, by Gerhard von Rad. Trans. M. J. Dawn. Grand Rapids, MI: Eerdmans.

Ottosson, M.
1969 *Gilead: Tradition and History.* Coniectanea Biblica: Old Testament 3. Lund: C. W. K. Gleerup.

Palumbo, G.
2001 The Early Bronze IV. Pp. 233–69 in *The Archaeology of Jordan*. Ed. B. MacDonald, R. Adams, and P. Bienkowski. Sheffield: Sheffield Academic Press.
1990 *The Early Bronze IV in the Southern Levant: Settlement Patterns, Economy, and Material Culture of a 'Dark Age.'* Rome: University of Rome Press.

Parker, S. B.
2002 Ammonite, Edomite, and Moabite. Pp. 43–60 in *Beyond Babel: A Handbook for Biblical Hebrew and Related Languages.* Ed. J. Kaltner and S. L. McKenzie. Atlanta: Society of Biblical Literature.

Parr, P.
1982 Contacts between North West Arabia and Jordan in the Late Bronze and Iron Ages. Pp. 127–33 in *SHAJ*, vol. 1. Ed. A. Hadidi. Amman: Department of Antiquities.
1988 Pottery in the Late Second Millennium B.C. from North West Arabia and Its Historical Implications. Pp. 73–90 in *Araby the Blest: Studies in Arabian Archaeology.* Ed. D. T. Potts. Copenhagen: Niebuhr Institute of Ancient Near Eastern Studies.

Peckham, B.
1993 *History and Prophecy: The Development of Late Judean Traditions.* New York: Doubleday.

Petter, T. D.

2005a Arad. Pp. 39–41 in *Dictionary of the Old Testament: Historical Books.* Ed. H. G. M. Williamson and B. T. Arnold. Downers Grove, IL: InterVarsity.

2005b *Diversity and Uniformity on the Frontier: Ethnic Identity in the Central Highlands of Jordan during the Iron I.* Ph.D. Dissertation. University of Toronto.

Polzin, R.

1976 *Late Biblical Hebrew: Toward a Historical Typology of Biblical Hebrew Prose.* Missoula, MT: Scholars Press.

Porter, D. H.

1981 *The Emergence of the Past.* Chicago: University of Chicago Press.

Postone, M., E. LiPuma, and C. Calhoun, eds.

1993 *Bourdieu: Critical Perspectives.* Cambridge: Polity.

Provan, I., V. P. Long, and T. Longman, III

2003 *A Biblical History of Israel.* Louisville: Westminster John Knox.

Puech, E.

2010 L'Osctracon de Khirbet Qeyafa et les débuts de la royauté en Israël. *RB* 117: 162–84.

Rad, G. von

1991 *Holy War in Ancient Israel.* Trans. M. J. Dawn. Grand Rapids, MI: Eerdmans.

Rainey, A. F.

2001 Israel in Merneptah's Inscription and Reliefs. *IEJ* 51: 57–75.

2007 Whence Came the Israelites and Their Language? *IEJ* 57: 41–64.

Rainey, A. F., and R. S. Notley

2005 *The Sacred Bridge: Carta's Atlas of the Biblical World.* Jerusalem: Carta.

Rast, W.

1978 *Taanach I: Studies in Iron Age Pottery.* Cambridge: American Schools of Oriental Research.

Ray, P., Jr.

2001 *Tell Hesban and Vicinity in the Iron Age.* Berrien Springs, MI: Andrews University Press.

Redford, D.

1982a Contacts between Egypt and Jordan in the New Kingdom: Some Comments on Sources. Pp. 115–19 in *SHAJ*, vol. 1. Ed. A. Hadidi. Amman: Department of Antiquities.

1982b A Bronze Age Itinerary in Transjordan. *JSSEA* 12: 55–74.

Revell, E. J.

1996a *The Designation of the Individual.* Kampen: Pharos.

1996b Gentilics and Geography. Pp. 113–23 in *Studies in Hebrew and Jewish Languages.* Ed. M. Ben-Asher. Jerusalem: Mossad Bialik.

Rice, P. M.

1987 *Pottery Analysis: A Sourcebook.* Chicago: University of Chicago Press.

Robertson, D. A.

1972 Linguistic Evidence in Dating Early Hebrew Poetry. SBLDS 3. Missoula, MT: Scholars Press.

Rollston, C.

2011 The Khirbet Qeiyafa Ostracon: Methodological Musings and Caveats. *TA* 38: 67–82.

Römer, T.
  2002   The Pentateuque toujours en question: Bilan et Perspectives après un quart de Siècle de Débat. Pp. 343–74 in *Congress Volume: Basel 2001*. Ed. A. Lemaire. Leiden: Brill.
Routledge, B.
  1994   Intermittent Agriculture and the Political Economy in Iron Age Moab. Ph.D. Dissertation. University of Toronto.
  1996   Learning to Love the King: Urbanism and the State in Iron Age Moab. Pp. 130–44 in *Urbanism in Antiquity: From Mesopotamia to Crete*. Ed. W. E. Aufrecht, N. A. Mirau, and S. W. Gauley. Sheffield: Sheffield Academic Press.
  2000a Seeing through Walls: Interpreting Iron Age I Architecture at Khirbat al-Mudayna al-ʿAliya. *BASOR* 319: 37–70.
  2000b The Politics of Mesha: Segmented Identities and State Formation in Iron Age Moab. *JESHO* 43: 221–56.
  2004   *Moab in the Iron Age*. Philadelphia: University of Pennsylvania Press.
Rowton, M. B.
  1974   Enclosed Nomadism. *JESHO* 17: 1–30.
Sáenz-Badillos, A.
  1993   *A History of the Hebrew Language*. Trans. J. Elwolde. Cambridge: Cambridge University Press.
Sakenfeld, K. D.
  2002   *The Meaning of* Hesed *in the Hebrew Bible*. Eugene, OR: Wipf & Stock.
Sauer, J. A.
  1986   Transjordan in the Bronze and Iron Ages: A Critique of Glueck's Synthesis. *BASOR* 263: 1–26.
Savage, S. H., and S. E. Falconer
  2003   Spatial and Statistical Inference of Late Bronze Age Polities in the Southern Levant. *BASOR* 330: 31–45.
Schermerhorn, R.
  1970   *Comparative Ethnic Relations*. New York: Random House.
Schloen, J. D.
  1993   Caravans, Kenites, and *Casus Belli*: Enmity and Alliance in the Song of Deborah. *CBQ* 55: 18–38.
  2001   *The House of the Father as Fact and Symbol: Patrimonialism in Ugarit and the Ancient Near East*. Studies in the Archaeology and History of the Levant 2. Winona Lake, IN: Eisenbrauns.
  2002   W. F. Albright and the Origins of Israel. *NEA* 65: 56–62.
Schmitz, P. C.
  1992   Canaan (Place). Pp. 828–30 in vol. 1 of *ABD*. Ed. D. N. Freedman et al. New York: Doubleday.
Schöpflin, K.
  2002   *Māšāl*: Ein eigentümlicher Begriff der hebräischen Literatur. *BZ* 46: 1–24.
Schorn, U.
  1997   *Ruben und das System der zwölf Stämme Israels: Redaktiongeschichte Untersuchungen zur Bedeutung des Erstgeborenen Jakobs*. BZAW 248. Berlin: de Guyter.
Schultz, R.
  1999   *The Search for Quotation: Verbal Parallels in the Prophets*. Sheffield: Sheffield Academic Press.

Seebass, H.
1999 Erwagungen zu Numeri 32:1–38. *JBL* 118: 33–48.
Seger, J. D., and H. D. Lance, eds.
1988 *Gezer V: The Field 1 Caves.* Jerusalem: Hebrew Union College / Nelson Glueck School of Biblical Archaeology.
Service, E. R.
1962 *Primitive Social Organization.* New York: Random House.
Shils, E. A.
1957 *Center and Periphery: Essays on Macrosociology. Selected Papers of Edward Shils.* Chicago: University of Chicago Press.
Shortland, A. J.
2005 The Challenges of Egyptian Calendrical Chronology. Pp. 43–54 in *The Bible and Radiocarbon Dating.* Ed. T. E. Levy and T. Higham. London: Equinox.
Shryock, A.
1997 *Nationalism and the Genealogical Imagination: Oral History and Textual Authority in Tribal Jordan.* Berkeley: University of California Press.
Sillitoe, P.
1978 Exchange in Melanesian Society. *Ethnos* 43: 7–29.
Singer-Avitz, L.
2002 Arad: The Iron Age Pottery Assemblages. *TA* 29: 110–214.
Smelik, K. A. D.
1992 *Converting the Past: Studies in Ancient Israelite and Moabite Historiography.* Leiden: Brill.
2000 The Inscription of King Mesha. Pp. 137–38 in *COS*, vol. 2: *Monumental Inscriptions from the Biblical World.* Ed. W. W. Hallo and K. L. Younger. Leiden: Brill.
Smend, R.
1970 *Yahweh War and Tribal Confederation: Reflections upon Israel's Earliest History.* Trans. M. G. Rogers. Nashville: Abingdon.
Smith, M. S.
1991 *The Origins And Development of the* Waw-Consecutive. Cambridge: Harvard University Press.
2002 *The Early History of God: Yahweh and Other Deities in Ancient Israel.* 2nd ed. Grand Rapids, MI: Eerdmans.
Soggin, J. A.
1981 *Judges.* Philadelphia: Westminster.
Soldt, W. H. van, ed.
2005 *Ethnicity in Ancient Mesopotamia: Papers Read at the 48th Rencontre Assyriologique Internationale Leiden, 1–4 July 2002.* Leiden: Nederlands Instituut voor het Nabije Oosten.
Sommer, B.
1999 Reflecting on Moses: The Redaction of Numbers 11. *JBL* 118: 601–24.
Sparks, K. L.
1998 *Ethnicity and Identity in Ancient Israel.* Winona Lake, IN: Eisenbrauns.
Spickard, P., and W. Burroughs, eds.
2000 *We Are a People: A Narrative and Multiplicity in Constructing Ethnic Identity.* Philadelphia: Temple University Press.
Stager, L. E.
1985a The Archaeology of the Family in Ancient Israel. *BASOR* 260: 1–35.

1985b Merneptah, Israel and Sea Peoples: New Light on an Old Relief. *ErIsr* 18 (Avigad Volume): 56*–64.*

1989   The Song of Deborah: Why Some Tribes Answered the Call and Others Did Not. *BAR* 15/1: 50–64.

1998   Forging an Identity: The Emergence of Ancient Israel. Pp. 123–75 in *The Oxford History of the Biblical World*. Ed. M. D. Coogan. New York: Oxford University Press.

2003   The Patrimonial Kingdom of Solomon. Pp. 63–74 in *Symbiosis, Symbolism, and the Power of the Past: Canaan, Ancient Israel, and Their Neighbors from the Late Bronze Age through Roman Palaestina*. Ed. W. G. Dever and S. Gitin. Winona Lake, IN: Eisenbrauns.

Stager, L. E., and P. J. King

2001   *Life in Biblical Israel*. Louisville: Westminster/John Knox.

Stark, M. T.

1998   Technical Choices and Social Boundaries in Material Culture Patterning: An Introduction. Pp. 1–11 in *The Archaeology of Social Boundaries*. Ed. M. T. Stark. Washington, DC: Smithsonian Institution Press.

Steen, E. J. van der

1996   The Central East Jordan Valley in the Late Bronze and Early Iron Ages. *BASOR* 302: 51–74.

1999   Survival and Adaptation: Life East of the Jordan in the Transition from the Late Bronze Age to the Early Iron Age. *PEQ* 131: 177–92.

2004   *Tribes and Territories in Transition*. Leuven: Peeters.

2006   Tribes and Power Structures in Palestine and the Transjordan. *NEA* 69: 27–36.

2010   Judah, Masos and Hayil: The Importance of Ethnohistory and Oral Traditions. Pp. 168–86 in *Historical Biblical Archaeology and the Future: The New Pragmatism*. Ed. Thomas E. Levy. London: Equinox.

Steen, E. J. van der, and K. A. D. Smelik

2007   King Mesha and the Tribe of Dibon. *JSOT* 32: 139–62.

Stern, P. D.

1991   *The Biblical HEREM: A Window on Israel's Religious Experience*. Atlanta: Scholars Press.

Stolz, F.

1972   *Jahwes und Israels Kriege: Kriegstheorien und Kriegserfahrungen im Glauben des alten Israel*. Zurich: Theologischer Verlag.

Strange, J.

2001   The Late Bronze Age. Pp. 291–321 in *The Archaeology of Jordan*. Ed. B. MacDonald, R. Adams, and P. Bienkowski. Sheffield: Sheffield Academic Press.

Stuart, D. K.

1976   *Studies in Early Hebrew Meter*. Missoula, MT: Scholars Press.

Swinnen, I. M.

2009   The Iron Age I Settlement and Its Residential Houses at al-Lahun in Moab, Jordan. *BASOR* 354: 29–53.

Taylor, J. G.

1993   *Yahweh and the Sun: Biblical and Archaeological Evidence for Sun Worship in Ancient Israel*. Sheffield: Sheffield Academic Press.

Terrell, J. E.
  2001 Ethnolinguistic Groups, Language Boundaries, and Culture History: A Socio-linguistic Model. Pp. 199–221 in *Archaeology, Language and History: Essays on Culture and Ethnicity*. Ed. J. E. Terrell. Wesport, CT: Bergin & Carvey.
Thomas, N.
  2010 *Islanders: The Pacific in the Age of Empire*. New Haven, CT: Yale University Press.
Tonkin, E.
  1992 *Narrating Our Pasts: The Social Construction of Oral History*. Cambridge: Cambridge University Press.
Tonkin, E., M. McDonald, and M. Chapman, eds.
  1989 *History and Ethnicity*. London: Routledge.
Toorn, K. van der
  1996 *Family Religion in Babylonia, Syria and Israel: Continuity and Change in the Forms of Religious Life*. Leiden: Brill.
Trimm, C.
  2012 Recent Research on Warfare in the Old Testament. *CBR* 10: 171–216.
Van Seters, J.
  1972 The Conquest of Sihon's Kingdom: A Literary Examination. *JBL* 91: 182–97.
  1980 Once Again: The Conquest of Sihon's Kingdom. *JBL* 99: 117–19.
  1994 *The Life of Moses*. Louisville: Westminster/John Knox.
  2013 *The Yahwist: A History of Israelite Origins*. Winona Lake, IN: Eisenbrauns.
Van Zyl, A. H.
  1960 *The Moabites*. Leiden: Brill.
Veen, P. van der, C. Theis, and M. Görg
  2010 Israel in Canaan (Long) before Pharaoh Merenptah? A Fresh Look at Berlin Statue Pedestal Relief 21687. *JAEI* 2: 15–25.
Vincent, M. A.
  2000 The Song of Deborah: A Structural and Literary Consideration. *JSOT* 91: 61–92.
Von Dassow, E.
  1999 Text and Artifact: A Comprehensive History of the Arameans. *NEA* 62: 247–51.
Vyhmeister, W. K.
  1989 The History of Heshbon from the Literary Sources. Pp. 3–23 in *Historical Foundations: Studies in the Literary References to Hesban and Vicinity*. Ed. L. T. Geraty et al. Hesban 3. Berrien Springs, MI: Andrews University Press.
Ward, W. A., and M. F. Martin
  1964 The Baluʿa Stele: A New Transcription with Palaeographic and Historical Notes. *ADAJ* 8–9: 5–29.
Watson, P. J.
  1999 Ethnographic Analogy and Ethnoarchaeology. Pp. 47–65 in *Archaeology, History and Culture in Palestine and the Near East: Essays in Memory of Albert E. Glock*. Ed. T. Kapitan. Atlanta: Scholars Press.
Webb, B. G.
  2012 *The Book of Judges*. The New International Commentary on the Old Testament. Grand Rapids, MI: Eerdmans.

Webb, J., T. Schirato, and G. Danaher
  2002 *Understanding Bourdieu.* London: Sage.
Weber, M.
  1978 *Economy and Society*, vols. 1–2. Ed. G. Roth and C. Wittick. Berkeley: University of California Press.
Weinstein, J. M.
  1986 The Scarabs and a Ring with a Cryptogram. Pp. 284–89 in *The Late Bronze and Early Iron Ages of Central Transjordan: The Baqʿah Valley Project, 1977–1981.* Ed. P. E. McGovern. Philadelphia: University Museum, University of Pennsylvania.
Weippert, M.
  1971 *The Settlement History of the Israelite Tribes in Palestine: A Critical Survey of Recent Scholarly Debate.* Trans. J. D. Martin. Studies in Biblical Theology 2. Naperville, IL: Allenson.
  1972 'Heiliger Krieg' in Israel und Assyrien. *ZAW* 84: 460–93.
  1979 The Israelite "Conquest" and the Evidence from Transjordan. Pp. 15–34 in *Symposia Celebrating the Seventy-Fifth Anniversary of the Founding of the American Schools of Oriental Research (1900–1975).* Ed. F. M. Cross. Cambridge, MA: American Schools of Oriental Research.
  1983 Remarks on the History of Settlement in Southern Jordan during the Early Iron Age. Pp. 153–62 in *SHAJ*, vol. 1. Ed. A. Hadidi. Amman: Department of Antiquities.
  1997 Israelites, Araméens et Assyriens dans la Transjordanie septentrionale. *ZDPV* 113: 19–38.
Welsch, R. L., and J. E. Terrell
  1998 Social Boundaries on the Sepik Coast of New Guinea. Pp. 50–77 in *The Archaeology of Social Boundaries.* Ed. M. T. Stark. Washington, DC: Smithsonian Institution Press.
Wellhausen, J.
  1957 *Prolegomena to the History of Ancient Israel.* Repr. Cleveland: World Press.
Wenham, G. J.
  1999 Pondering the Pentateuch: The Search for a New Paradigm. Pp. 116–44 in *The Face of Old Testament Studies.* Ed. D. W. Baker and B. T. Arnold. Leicester: Apollos / Grand Rapids, MI: Baker.
White, H.
  1980 The Value of Narrativity in the Representation of Reality. *Critical Inquiry* (special issue: *On Narrative*, ed. W. J. T. Mitchell) 7: 5–27.
Whiting, R. M.
  1995 Amorite Tribes and Nations of Second-Millennium Western Asia. Pp. 1231–41 in *Civilizations of the Ancient Near East.* Ed. J. M. Sasson. Peabody, MA: Hendrickson.
Whittaker, D.
  2009 Ethnic Discourses on the Frontiers of Roman Africa. Pp. 189–205 in *Ethnic Constructs in Antiquity: The Role of Power and Tradition.* Ed. T. Derks and N. Roymans. Amsterdam: Amsterdam University Press.
Whybray, R. N.
  1987 *The Making of the Pentateuch: A Methodological Study.* JSOTSup 53. Sheffield: JSOT Press.

Worschech, U. von
  1992   Collared-Rim Jars aus Moab Anmerkungen zur Entwicklung und Verbreiting der Krug mit "Halswulst." *ZDPV* 108: 148–55.
Yellin, J., and Gunneweg, J.
  1989   Instrumental Neutron Activation Analysis and the Origin of Iron I Collared Rim Jars and Pithoi from Tel Dan. Pp. 133–41 in *Recent Excavations in Israel: Studies in Iron Age Archaeology.* Ed. S. Gitin and W. Dever. Winona Lake, IN: Eisenbrauns for American Schools of Oriental Research.
Yelvington, K. A.
  1991   Ethnicity as Practice? A Comment on Bentley. *Comparative Studies in Society and History* 33: 158–68.
Young, I.
  1993   *Diversity in Pre-exilic Hebrew.* Tübingen: Mohr (Siebeck).
  1995   The "Northernisms" of the Israelite Narratives in Kings. *ZAH* 8: 63–70.
Young, I., and R. Rezetko
  2008   *Linguistic Dating of Biblical Texts,* vol. 1. London: Equinox.
Young, I., R. Rezetko, and M. Ehrensvärd
  2008   *Linguistic Dating of Biblical Texts,* vol. 2. Oakville, CT: Equinox.
Younger, K. L.
  1990   *Ancient Conquest Accounts: A Study in Ancient Near Eastern and Biblical History Writing.* Sheffield: Sheffield Academic Press.
Younker, R. W., L. T. Gerraty, Ø. LaBianca, L. G. Herr, and D. Clark
  1996   Preliminary Report of the 1994 Season of the Madaba Plains Project: Regional Survey, Tall al-ʿUmayri, and Tall Jalul Excavations. *AUSS* 34: 65–92.
Yurco, F. J.
  1997   Merneptah's Canaanite Campaign and Israel's Origins. Pp. 27–55 in *Exodus: The Egyptian Evidence.* Ed. E. S. Frerichs and L. H. Lesko. Winona Lake, IN: Eisenbrauns.
Zertal, A.
  1986–87   An Early Iron Age Cultic Site on Mount Ebal: Excavations Seasons 1982–1987. *TA*: 105–65.
Zevit, Z.
  2001   *The Religions of Ancient Israel: A Synthesis of Parallactic Approaches.* London: Continuum.
Zuure, B.
  1931   *L'Âme du Murundi.* Paris: Beauchesne.

Index of Authors

Ackerman, S.   63
Adams, R.   2, 3
Aharoni, M.   89, 95
Ahlström, G. W.   29
Albertz, R.   57, 62
Albright, W. F.   4, 5, 26, 27, 29, 35, 41,
    57
Alt, A.   5, 7, 9, 29
Alter, R.   45, 47, 67
Anderson, B. W.   36
Artzy, M.   26, 27, 118
Ashley, T. R.   44, 48, 54

Banks, M.   17
Barth, F.   18, 19, 24, 25
Bartlett, J. R.   43, 54
Beck, P.   118
Bentley, G.   18, 20, 21, 73
Bienkowski, P.   12, 13, 14
Biran, A.   26, 39
Blenkinsopp, J.   10
Bloch, Y.   50
Bloch-Smith, E.   26, 30, 32, 33, 56, 85,
    86, 94, 96
Block, D. I.   46, 61, 63, 70, 71
Boling, R. G.   48, 52, 68, 70, 78, 102
Bourdieu, P.   20, 21
Bramlett, K. V.   77, 79, 80, 83
Braudel, F.   4
Bright, J.   57
Bunimowitz, S.   4
Butler, T.   35, 41, 61, 62, 63, 65, 69, 70,
    71

Cassuto, U.   35
Clark, D. R.   xv, 11, 54, 77, 79, 80, 81,
    83, 97
Cohen, R.   28
Conroy, C.   35, 36

Cooley, R. E.   88, 97
Cornell, S.   57
Coughlin, R.   18
Cross, F. M.   xv, 9, 10, 11, 29, 32, 33,
    35, 36, 37, 39, 41, 43, 50, 53, 57,
    58, 65, 66, 68, 71, 72, 73, 74, 98

Dajani, R. W.   76, 77, 86, 87, 88
Daviau, P. M. M.   79, 88
David, N.   22
Daws, G.   103
Dearman, J. A.   39, 53, 76
Derks, T.   16, 23, 24
Dever, W.   3, 4, 5, 6, 7, 8, 16, 22, 24, 25,
    27, 29, 57, 74, 96, 97
Dion, P.-E.   23, 34
Dolan, A.   96
Dornemann, R. H.   94
Dresher, B. F.   51
Drews, R.   4
Driver, S. R.   65

Edelman, D.   12, 28, 29, 30, 93
Eggler, J.   94
Ehrensvärd, M.   24, 51
Eichrodt, W.   41, 57
Eller, J.   18
Emerton, J. A.   39
Epstein, A. L.   20
Esse, D.   8, 26, 27, 31, 32, 61

Falconer, S. E.   79
Fantalkin, A.   39
Faust, A.   4, 6, 16, 22, 24, 25, 26, 29, 31,
    96, 97
Finkelstein, I.   4, 5, 6, 24, 25, 26, 28, 29,
    30, 31, 37, 38, 39, 54, 58, 76, 78,
    88, 89, 90, 91, 97, 120, 121
Fischer, P. M.   87

148

Fishbane, M. A.   47
Foran, D.   77, 78, 83, 84, 86, 87, 92, 93
Freedman, D. N.   35, 39, 40, 41, 50, 51
Friedman, R. E.   37
Fritz, V.   26, 35

Gal, Z.   26
Ganor, S.   39
Garfinkel, Y.   39
Garr, R. W.   24
Geertz, C.   17, 18, 20
Geraty, L. T.   51, 54, 72, 103
Gibson, J. C. L.   39
Gilmour, G.   93, 94
Glazer, N.   20
Glueck, N.   9, 35, 41, 54, 75, 76, 78, 102
Gogel, S. L.   45, 51, 95
Gonen, R.   93, 94
Goody, J.   38
Görg, M.   59, 102
Gosselain, O. P.   22
Gottwald, N.   7, 29, 62
Gray, G. B. A.   41
Grenfell, M.   20
Gressman, H.   35
Grosby, S.   4

Hackett, J. A.   31, 32, 52, 65, 71
Halpern, B.   11, 43, 57, 63, 64
Hankey, V.   76
Hanson, P. D.   48, 51
Harding, G. L.   77, 84, 86, 87, 91, 92, 94
Harrison, T.   8, 11, 14, 26, 27, 35, 78,
     79, 83, 84
Hasel, M. G.   58, 61
Hawkins, R. K.   90, 95, 96, 119
Hennessy, J. B.   76
Herr, L.   xv, 5, 10, 11, 24, 33, 54, 72,
     76, 77, 79, 80, 81, 83, 87, 90, 91,
     92, 94, 97, 119
Herzog, Z.   89, 90, 95, 96
Hess, R. S.   56, 57, 65, 68, 69
Hesse, B.   26, 33
Higham, T.   37
Hodder, I.   22
Hoerth, A. J.   5
Hoffmeier, J. K.   5, 58, 60, 61, 102
Hoftijzer, J.   52

Holladay, J. S.   5, 25, 81, 93, 94, 95
Holl, A. F. C.   1, 4, 5, 6, 7, 24, 32, 54,
     102
Holmstedt, R. D.   51
Homan, M. M.   55, 102
Homès Fredericq, D.   xiv
Huehnergard, J.   68
Humbert, J. B.   27
Hutchinson, J.   17, 23

Ibach, R. D.   78
Ibrahim, M.   27, 76, 77, 92

Jenkins, R.   20
Jeto, S.   38
Ji, C. H.   11, 12, 25, 77, 102
Joffe, A.   22
Jones, S.   17, 18, 20, 21, 22, 33

Kafafi, Z.   87
Kamrada, D. G.   60, 61, 70, 71
Kang, S.-A.   59, 60, 61, 63
Kenyon, K. M.   52
Kessler, J.   47
Keyes, C. F.   20
Khoury, P.   12
Killebrew, A.   4, 5, 7, 16, 24, 25, 27, 31
King, P.   3, 37, 56
Kitchen, K. A.   5, 89, 94
Klassen, S.   77, 78, 83, 84, 86, 87, 92, 93
Kletter, R.   16
Knoppers, G. N.   72
Kochavi, M.   118
Kooij, G. van der   52
Kostiner, J.   12
Kramer, C.   16, 22, 24, 34

Laband, J.   103
LaBianca, Ø.   12, 13, 14, 29, 34, 78
Lance, H. D.   93
Lattimore, O.   1, 2, 3, 7
Lawlor, J. I.   81, 96
Lee, B. P. Y.   39
Lemaire, A.   55
Lemarchand, R.   19
Lemonnier, P.   22
Lentz, C.   17
Levine, B.   35, 42, 45, 46, 54

Levy, T.   xv, 1, 4, 5, 6, 7, 24, 32, 34, 37, 54, 102
London, G.   27
Longman, T., III   37, 39, 60
Long, V. P.   37, 39
Lord, A. B.   38
Low, R. D.   80, 81
Lyons, W. L.   59

MacDonald, B.   8, 37, 40, 42, 54, 58
MacEachern, S.   22
Macumber, P. G.   8
Malkin, I.   18
Mallowan, M. E. L.   16
Marfoe, L.   xv, 2, 3, 4, 7, 8
Martin, M. F.   94
Master, D.   3, 13, 31, 37, 89, 97
Mazar, A.   5, 6, 26, 28, 29, 52, 54, 58, 89, 95, 119
McCarter, P. K.   52
McCarthy, D. J.   58
McDonald, M.   10, 53, 68, 69, 100, 103
McGovern, P.   8, 9, 77, 78, 86, 87, 88, 91, 92, 97
McKay, B.   29, 56, 57, 63, 64
Mendenhall, G. E.   7, 29, 41, 51, 52, 58
Merling, D.   54, 103
Meyer, E.   53, 54
Milgrom, J.   39
Millard, A.   39
Miller, C. L.   45
Miller, J. C.   17, 24
Miller, J. M.   58
Miller, P. D.   36, 57, 58, 59, 61, 63
Miller, R. D.   12, 22, 26, 96, 97
Misgav, H.   39
Monroe, L. A. S.   59
Morgan, C.   20
Moynihan, D. P.   20
Mullen, E. T.   4, 29
Münger, S.   91

Najjar, M.   77
Nakhai, B. A.   30, 95, 96
Nash, M.   17
Naveh, J.   39
Netzer, E.   89
Netzer, N.   48

Niditch, S.   37, 41, 59, 60
Noort, E.   53, 68
Noth, M.   9, 39, 40, 54, 68
Notley, R. S.   4, 5, 11

O'Connor, M.   51
Ollenburger, B. C.   59
Ottosson, M.   42, 45, 63, 68, 69

Palumbo, G.   8
Parker, S. B.   23
Parr, P.   58
Peckham, B.   35, 36, 37, 41, 62, 102
Petter, T. D.   54, 55, 83
Piasetzky, E.   89
Postone, M.   20
Pratico, G. D.   88, 97
Provan, I.   37, 39
Puech, E.   39

Rad, G. von   59, 60, 67
Rainey, A. F.   4, 5, 6, 7, 8, 10, 11, 23, 24, 35, 102
Rast, W.   118, 119
Ray, P. J., Jr.   78
Redford, D.   94
Reid, D. G.   60
Revell, E. J.   66, 68
Rezetko, R.   24, 51
Robertson, D. A.   50
Rollston, C.   24, 39
Römer, T.   35
Root, R.   94
Rosenberg, A.   18
Routledge, B.   xiv, 3, 7, 8, 9, 13, 26, 31, 33, 39, 54, 56, 65, 69, 77, 78, 79, 94, 97
Rowton, M. B.   3
Roymans, N.   16, 23

Sáenz-Badillos, A.   35, 50, 51
Sakenfeld, K. D.   58
Sauer, J. A.   76, 78
Savage, S. H.   79
Schermerhorn, R.   28
Schloen, J. D.   3, 9, 26, 31, 32, 34, 56, 58, 64
Schöpflin, K.   46

Schultz, R.   47
Sebba, M.   23
Seebass, H.   35
Seger, J. D.   93
Service, E. R.   12
Shils, E. A.   17
Shortland, A. J.   88, 89
Shryock, A.   38, 41, 56, 102
Silberman, N. A.   4, 38
Sillitoe, P.   23
Singer-Avitz, L.   89, 95
Smelik, K. A. D.   12, 13, 39, 54, 73
Smend, R.   60
Smith, A. D.   17, 23
Smith, M. S.   48, 57
Soggin, J. A.   62
Soldt, W. H. van   16
Sparks, K.   29, 30, 58
Stager, L.   xv, 1, 3, 4, 5, 6, 7, 8, 10, 24,
    25, 26, 27, 30, 32, 37, 56, 58, 63,
    65, 89, 91
Stark, M. T.   22
Steen, E. van der   12, 13, 14, 38, 41, 42,
    54, 58, 73, 76, 77, 78, 89
Stein, B.   13
Stern, P. D.   39, 59
Stolz, F.   60
Strange, J.   xiv, 8, 76, 89, 93, 94
Stuart, D. K.   42, 45, 51
Swinnen, I. M.   xiv, 78

Taylor, J. G.   95
Terrell, J. E.   22, 23
Theis, C.   59, 102
Thomas, N.   102
Tonkin, E.   17, 18, 38
Toorn, K. van der   57, 74

Trimm, C.   59

Ussishkin, D.   89

Van Seters, J.   35, 36, 40, 41, 43, 45, 47,
    48
Van Zyl, A. H.   9
Veen, P. van der   59, 102
Vincent, M. A.   62
Von Dassow, E.   23
Vyhmeister, W. K.   35, 41, 43

Wapnish, P.   33
Ward, W. A.   94
Watson, P. J.   22
Webb, B. G.   69, 70
Webb, J.   20
Weber, M.   13, 19, 20, 58
Weinstein, J. M.   90, 91
Weippert, M.   7, 9, 35, 45, 49, 51, 57, 72
Wellhausen, J.   35, 36, 59
Welsch, R. L.   22
Wenham, G. J.   36
Whiting, R. M.   52, 53
Whittaker, D.   24
Wright, G. E.   4, 68

Yadin, Y.   4
Yelvington, K. A.   21
Young, I.   23, 24, 51, 52, 62, 64, 68
Younger, K. L.   40, 61, 102
Younker, R.   12, 13, 29, 34, 77, 78
Yurco, F. J.   25, 58

Zertal, A.   11, 26, 90, 91, 95, 119, 120
Zevit, Z.   34, 91, 95, 96, 97
Zuure, B.   19

Index of Scripture

Genesis
6:4   53
15:16   41
19   60, 65
19:30–38   101
31:21   69
32:28   102
37:29–30   71
49   50, 71, 99
49:3   9
49:11   50

Exodus
2:15–22   64
3:1   64
4   58
12:38   7, 62
14   36
14–15   43
15   36, 50
15:1   42, 47
15:4   48
15:5   42, 50
15:13   50
15:19   48
17:8–16   39
18   58
24:4   95
27:1   95

Leviticus
27:28   59

Numbers
1:1–10:10   39
10:11–20:13   39
11:4   62
13:19   55
20:14–36:13   39
21   9, 35, 36, 40, 41, 44,
   46, 47, 48, 50, 52,
   54, 70, 99, 101

Numbers (cont.)
21:1–2   41
21:1–3   40, 41
21:6   61
21:10   40
21:10–35   40
21:14–15   40, 41, 54
21:15   42, 51
21:17–18   40, 41, 54
21:19   42
21:21–25   43
21:24   70
21:26   70
21:27–30   39, 41, 42,
   43, 99
21:27–35   41
21:28   47
21:29   46, 48, 67
21:30   83
21:31   69
21:31–35   69
22   43
22:2–3   40
22:5   40
22:6   39
22:7   40
22:12   39
22–24   40
22:36   51
23:7   46
23:8   39
23:11   39
23:11–12   46
23:15   46
23:18   46
23:20   39
23:20–21   46
23–24   50, 52
24:3   46
24:9   40
24:10   39
24:17   47, 48

Numbers (cont.)
24:23   46
25   10
25:5   10
25:6–17   10
25:7   10
26:29   69
27:1–4   39
27:5–11   39
32   35, 40, 72
32:1–2   72
32:6   72
32:6–15   68, 71
32:25   72
32:29   72
32:31   72
32:33   46, 72
32:33–41   40
32:34   53
32:34–37   72
32:40   69
33:40   40
33:45–46   72
34:11   68
36:5–12   39

Deuteronomy
2   65
2–3   35
2:4   101
2:9   60
2:24   45, 46
2:24–37   41
2:26   45, 46
2:26–37   43
2:37   41
3:1–7   41
3:4   69
3:12   69, 72
3:12–13   69
3:12–17   41
3:13   69

Deuteronomy (cont.)
3:14   69
3:16   69
3:29   10
4:43   69
4:44–46   10
4:46   10
6:11   102
7   67
7:3–6   61
28   65
29:8   72
32–33   50
32:36   50
33:2   58
33:6   9, 71, 72
33:20   72
34:1   69
34:6   10

Joshua
1:12   72
2:3   64
2:9   65
2:12   64
2:13   65
2:14   64
6:12   64
6:17   59
6:18   64
6:21   64
6:22   65
6:23   65
7:1   61
9   62
12:2   46, 55
12:3–4   69
12:6   68
12–13   35
13:8–33   68
13:9   83
13:12   53
13:15–17   72
13:15–21   98
13:15–23   33
13:15–33   41
13:16   83
13:20   10

Joshua (cont.)
13:25   98
17:1   69
22   10, 68, 71
22:9   68, 69
22:10   72
22:10–34   40
22:11   68
22:12   68
22:13   68
22:15   68
22:21   68
22:25   68
22:30   68
22:31   68
22:32   68
24:2   53
24:14   59
24:17   59

Judges
1:16   64
1:17   59
2–3   74
3   65, 100
3:5–6   61, 95
3:6   100
3:13–14   70
3:15–25   64
4   64
4:4–5   65
4–5   43, 56, 63
4:9   64, 65
4:11   64
4:17   64
4:21   63
5   28, 30, 50, 56, 57, 62,
    64, 69, 94, 100
5:1   62
5:1–3   62
5:4–5   58, 62
5:5   50
5:6–11   62
5:7   50
5:10   62
5:12–18   62
5:14   71
5:15–16   71

Judges (cont.)
5:19–23   62
5:23   49
5:24–27   62
5:28–31   62
5:31   64
6:33   70
7:3   69
8:6   71
10   70, 100
10:3   68, 70
10:8   69, 70
10:17   69
11   35, 57, 100
11:1   69
11:8   70
11:11   70
11–12   69
11:13   70
11:19   46
11:19–26   43
11:24–26   70
11:25   40
11:28   70
11:30   70
11:33   103
11:34–40   71
11:39–40   71
11:40   70
12   42, 71
12:4   71
12:6   68, 71
13–16   32
20:1   69, 70, 72
20–21   42
21:11   59, 61

1 Samuel
4–8   32
11   9
13:7   72
13–14   32
13:19–22   33
17–18   32
17:26   33, 47
20:14–20   57
23   32
27:8   53

1 Samuel (cont.)
27:10   64
28–29   32
30:13   48
30:29   64
31   32

2 Samuel
1   50
5   32
5:7   54
8   32
11   67
11:3   67
21   32
22   50
22:5   50
23   32
23:37–39   67
24:5   9, 72, 73

1 Kings
12:16   102
17   52
17:1   68

2 Kings
3   14
3:4   13
3:37   71
10   52
10:33   69, 73
11:36   43, 48
15:29   73
16:25   100
16:27   100
20   51

Isaiah
3:1   49
15:2   83
42:14   53
46:9   53
63:16   53
63:19   53

Jeremiah
2:20   53

Jeremiah (cont.)
5:15   53
7:14   47
7:15   61
48   47
48:1–47   40
48:45   48
48:45–46   43

Ezekiel
16   46
16:3   46, 61
16:44   46
16:45   46, 47
26:20   53

Hosea
1:9   61

Habakkuk
3   50
3:3   10, 58, 101
3:7   58

Haggai
2:22   47

Psalms
18   50
25:6   53
68   50
93:2   53
103:17   53
119:52   53

Proverbs
8:23   53

Ruth
1:1   65, 66
1:2   66
1:4   65
1:6–8   66
1:11–13   66
1:14   66
1:15   67
1:16–17   66
1:22   66

Ruth (cont.)
2:1   66
2:2   66
2:3   66
2:4   66
2:6   66
2:8   66
2:10   66
2:11   66
2:11–12   67
2:12   67
2:18–19   66
2:20   66
2:21   66
2:22   66
3:1   66
3:2   66
3:6   66
3:9   66
3:11   66
3:12   66
3:16   66
3:16–17   66
3:18   66
4:3   66
4:5   66
4:6   66
4:8   66
4:10   66
4:13   67
4:14   66
4:15   66

1 Chronicles
5   73
5:1–3   72
5:9   100
11:42   73
12:37   73
19:7   83
26:32   73
27:16   73
29:10   53

2 Chronicles
5:26   73
20:23   61